# Delusions of Grandeur

### A Few Hundred Tales from the
### Emperor of St. Louis

## Chris Andoe

"The characters feel like people we know, yet they're archetypal. They're flawed and eccentric, but you want to keep following them, listening to what they say—and sometimes they make you laugh out loud. Chris Andoe is unflinching in his evocation of people and place, but always underpinning that is a deep respect for human dignity. No matter how gritty the anecdote (and there are plenty of gritty anecdotes here) it's never written in a salacious or exploitive spirit, but as a means to pursue those universal truths that literature has been concerned with for forever.

"Chris Andoe has already been crowned Emperor of St. Louis, but if there is any justice in the world, he'll also be coroneted as one of its finest, funniest writers."

Stefene Russell, *St. Louis Magazine*

"On the rare occasions when my family gets together, we gather around the dinner table telling great stories, laughing and gossiping. Sitting down to read Chris Andoe's "Delusions of Grandeur" each day has been like having dinner with my family: smart, delicious, scandalous and spit-out-your-food-funny!"

T. Scott King, *Bay Area Reporter*

"Good writing requires a good story. And Chris tells them, with style"

Joe Holleman, *The St. Louis Post-Dispatch*

"I love, love, love the book. Part satire, part murder mystery, part autobiography, part biography, part gossip column, and part brutal honesty -- as is looking into a clear mirror under fluorescent lights. The reader doesn't quite know where one part ends and the other begins -- and that is the delightfully delicious part!"

Joseph Paul Smith, Bishop of San Francisco


"The stories that fill *Delusions of Grandeur* are titillating, hilarious, heartfelt, and raw. Andoe does an impeccable job of shedding a light (a rainbow!) on my hometown of St. Louis and its cast of colorful characters."

Gina Sheridan, author of *I Work at a Public Library*


"Ben Franklin said that one should either write something worth reading or do something worth writing. *Delusions of Grandeur* shows that Chris Andoe has done both of those things."

Jon Green, AMERICAblog.com


"Wickedly delightful"

Jill Moon Whitworth, *The Telegraph*


"'Delusions of Grandeur' is all that and so much more! Chris Andoe slices and dices and reveals his life encounters across America in a very heartfelt, humorous, and engaging way."

Ken Busby, CEO, Route 66 Experience, Tulsa, OK

# Preface

When I first met Chris Andoe, he struck me as a writer who was overflowing with ideas and possessed of an extraordinary desire to share life's undiscovered stories, preserving a world of fabulousness before it could fade. I didn't know the half of it.

My first clue that there was more to Mr. Andoe than had initially met my eye came when I noticed that his Facebook feed was far from the average parade of re-shared memes and questionably-angled selfies.

Chris's writing - in particular his chronicles of the goings on in and around St. Louis - had the urgency of an embedded journalist in a war zone. He had clear enemies and fervent allies who agitated for their downfall. He opened doors to a world of people with multiple aliases and secret identities, sinister perpetrators of long cons, and drag personalities who embody every aspect of the word legendary.

*Delusions of Grandeur* is the cream of this crop - a distillation of Chris's exploits as an inciter of Bacchanalian revel and a muckraker of the seedy underbelly of the gay community. The maxim that truth is stranger than fiction may be worn out as an over-the-hill hooker, but there are times when the details in these stories are so deeply bizarre that truth is their only explanation. That said, it's worth noting they'd be worth reading as fiction, anyway.

St. Louis has offered the world a variety of artistic gifts, from the Oprah-inspiring poetry of Maya Angelou to the scintillating star power of Tina Turner. But in choosing it as a playground and battlefield for his epic exploits, Chris Andoe has ensured for the city a twisted new chapter in our shared cultural history.

No wonder they call him "The Emperor."


Paul Hagen
May, 2015
New York City

*Dedicated to Big David*

We all see the world through our own filters and from our own vantage points. While I stand by my stories, others may have viewed the same events differently or have been privy to information I was not.

I've changed many names of both people and places, and due to the short story format, some events don't line up in perfect chronological order.

# Contents

The Tawdry Tales of Rotten Crotches

The Twisted Tale of Ryan McCormic

# 1.  Welcome to Saint Louis

From my home in Northern California I emailed my St. Louis-based editor and mentor, William Collins, to tell him I was bringing my next Jet Set Event—where friends from all over the nation converge for a big party—to St. Louis, and this promised to be the biggest one yet.

Many planning to attend were relatively unfamiliar with the haunted old river city before reading my stories, and were now intrigued by this gritty, authentic place filled with lively characters, and some not so lively, like the late Midnight Annie, an old drag queen entombed in the brick wall of a historic bar.

My dapper San Francisco event planner, Thurston Marks, blocked two floors of the historic Chase Park Plaza Hotel, and the patio stage at Sensation, a prominent nightclub, had been secured for my show. I asked Collins if we could run a piece about the event in *Vital Voice*, the LGBT lifestyle magazine where I ran my *Tales from the Emperor* column.

Publisher Darin Slyman had always sent his paparazzi boys to cover my local events, and Collins had run stories about my soirées in other cities, but was not responding this time. Tim Beckman, the handsome and affable owner of Sensation, indicated Collins had wanted to throw a huge birthday bash for his best friend William Lowe, board president of the LGBT Community Center, on that same Saturday night, but had to settle for Friday because I was already booked. After several unreturned calls and messages I figured he was sore about it and decided to switch gears.

I would instead run a piece on *AMERICAblog.com*, where I was also on the roster. Unlike my column in Vital Voice, I could speak freely, without worry of upsetting local advertisers (i.e. bar owners). The piece served as a promotion for the event and as an introduction to the city and its LGBT community for a national audience.

To outsiders, the piece was interesting. To civic leaders, it was something to boast about—and was proudly tweeted by Mayor Francis Slay's chief of staff—but for many in the local LGBT community, where these things weren't openly discussed, it was a scandal.

## A Hot Gay Mess in St. Louis (AMERICAblog.com, 8/19/13)

I'm a collector of colorful characters. And I've summoned them all to St. Louis for Labor Day Weekend, a city that not only has character, but is a character in itself.

Following the local LGBT community over social media is like watching a soap opera—and I'm not talking about your run of the mill bar feuds or relationship drama. No, in St. Louis you have a queen successfully pretending to be an attorney for months, handling cases in the courtroom and collecting fees before getting caught.

You've got a bar owner rumored to have burned down one of his bars for the insurance money, then getting his mug shot in the paper for embezzling funds from a Hamburger Mary's—all while former employees, who publicly complain of bad checks, vent about him showering his beautiful young boyfriend with expensive gifts, including a car.

You've got another top bar owner charging a $30 cover for an emotional going out of business gala, only to open up for business as usual the following morning.

You've got a beloved local celebrity forced to resign from leading the LGBT Center for misuse of funds.

You've got a heavily armed Trans advocate who, having fallen out of favor with the establishment, bitterly calls out community pillars in epic tirades vowing revenge.

Then there's the former Pride President turned convicted sexual predator. And this is just scratching the surface. I live in the Bay Area, have traveled from New York to New Zealand, and I've never seen a show like this.

Drama aside, St. Louis's sizable LGBT community is vibrant, interesting, and uncommonly hospitable. The city is rich with gay neighborhoods where couples enjoy palatial historic homes with lush gardens, many circa 1880 to 1925, for prices that make coastal queens cringe. They make use of those homes too. I've never seen anyone who can entertain in the home/garden like my friends in St. Louis. And speaking of friends, I've lived there on two occasions and have no greater concentration of friends in the world. St. Louisans aren't only a good time, they're fiercely loyal.

The city has an impressive backstory, which I'll attempt to highlight in one breathless paragraph.

A few miles east of the Gateway Arch is the World Heritage Site Cahokia Mounds. The ancient city of Cahokia was the largest settlement north of present-day Mexico and was larger than London in AD 1250. The French flag and the Spanish flag flew over St. Louis before the Americans took over. Little more than a century ago, she was the fourth largest city in the nation, neck and neck with Chicago, and was the largest city west of the Mississippi. A city mighty enough to host the first Olympics in the United States and to launch the first solo nonstop transatlantic flight. As recently as 1960, St. Louis was larger than Boston and San Francisco, so the old, brick urban core is substantial.

Guests attending my "Jet Set: Gateway Glitterati Weekend" include my San Francisco happy hour crew, known as "The Castro Consorts," "The Mayor of Gay Oklahoma City" Lloyd Spartan and his entourage, a group of high-powered Kansas City attorneys, a straight auto mechanic from the great plains, a gal from Tulsa who explained sex to me when we were in the third grade, and a couple dozen others from around the country.

We're taking over two floors of the historic Chase Park Plaza, and our main public event is a show called "HOT MESS" at Sensation on August 31st. Local gossip columnist Penelope Wigstock sums it up this way:

"Former St. Louisan and Vital Voice/AMERICAblog writer Chris Andoe is bringing his twisted dog and pony show to the Lou on August 30th.

He's named the weekend "Gateway Glitterati," and if you're wondering what treats might be in store for those who participate, check out an old David Lynch film or watch one of Stefon's club reviews

4

on Saturday Night Live: narcoleptic drag queens, loud drunks with access to limitless booze, an entrepreneur with a glory hole franchise, and garden variety predators and sycophants...these are a few of my favorite things! The highlight (?) of the event- Hot Mess- takes place at Sensation on Saturday, August 31st. Mark your calendars and make it a point to see the Emperor and his merry troupe of misfits as they entertain and delight the curious and uninhibited."

My cast of characters will take to St. Louis like catfish to the Mississippi, and any kindred spirits or voracious voyeurs are welcome to join us for an epic weekend in this storied metropolis. Like Sunset Boulevard's Norma Desmond—once the biggest star the world had ever known—St. Louis is a regal old diva. With her world-class attractions, fine architecture, fascinating residents and one of the most recognizable skylines in the world, she's just as BIG as ever! (End)

After comparing St. Louis to the aging and all but forgotten Sunset Boulevard character, I ended with a clip from the 1950 classic. In the short scene, the young and attractive Joe Gillis finally recognizes aging star Norma Desmond.

Gillis: "Haven't I seen you before? I know your face.."

Desmond: "Get out! Or shall I call my servant?"

Gillis: "You're Norma Desmond! Used to be in silent pictures, used to be big."

Desmond: "I *am* big! It's the pictures that got small."

## 2.  Introductions

My life is defined by the numerous characters I encounter and the short stories I tell about them. I'll begin with introductions of three people brought up in the *AMERICAblog* piece, and then move on to a few of the Jet Setters.

Behold our brilliant sociopath Rustin Winchell, the most prolific conman in the history of St. Louis, and for many years, the most feared man in the LGBT community.

He was born Baptist in a small Missouri town but decided he was Jewish somewhere along the way. At his zenith he had high ranking state Republicans believing he was a major donor, and he picked them up for lunch in a rented limousine he never paid for. Those in LGBT circles believed he was a successful businessman, attorney, and a candidate for lieutenant governor who was hyper vigilant about his image. At the first whiff of bar gossip a Cease & Desist letter would be served to the offending party, threatening severe legal consequences.

A master at media manipulation, he was listed in magazines as one of the Most Eligible Bachelors, bogus press releases always floated around on social media about the tens of thousands of dollars he'd donated to various charities, and he was regularly mentioned in the business section of the paper, even after his felony conviction and prison sentence.

The larger than life Simone Shasta, a towering diva reminiscent of Mariah Carey, was the most beloved drag queen and community leader in St. Louis, and rose to become the executive director of the LGBT Center. In the annals of local LGBT History, her fall from grace after an embezzlement fiasco was eclipsed only by the Pride President turned convicted sex offender, but while he went into seclusion, Shasta still made appearances, hosting her "Canasta with Simone Shasta" game nights at a local bar.

Shasta's biggest detractor was Transsexual Advocate Rita Revlon. Equally imposing, with her impressive height and big trademark Alexis Carrington hats, Rita was an ill-tempered and heavily armed male to female Trans woman in her late fifties who envied and bitterly resented Shasta's stature and Teflon reputation.

Alone over cocktails, the spiteful Rita Revlon often sat on her suburban veranda plotting revenge on the entire community because of their unwavering support of Shasta.

Following are a few backstories of the Jet Setters who travelled to St. Louis for my events.

**Donald**

My best friend Donald was originally from Bartlesville, Oklahoma, about forty miles north of Tulsa, where I grew up.

In the early nineties underage guys were referred to as chickens, and we met at Tulsa's chicken park, at 21$^{st}$ & Riverside Drive. We had the same flop of hair we'd incessantly toss and the first thing he said to me was, "You have great hair!" to which I replied, "You do too!"

He tossed his head, blew smoke as he flipped his cigarette and replied, "Mine looks like shit today."

I was only sixteen and he was eighteen. I figured if he knew how young I was he wouldn't be my friend, so I told him I was seventeen. A lie I maintained for six months until someone ratted me out.

The two of us loved adventure and pranks and quickly moved on from Tulsa to the more action packed pastures of Oklahoma City, which had many more gay people at the time.

Our love of good times briefly landed us in jail.

"So I found a way we can get an ID," Donald began.

New Year's was rapidly approaching and we desperately wanted to get into the bar where all the action was.

"I talked to Harley last night and he's gonna send us a copy of his birth certificate. We can take it to a tag agency, say we lost our driver's license and need a replacement."

It was so easy. Donald went first and everything went according to plan, then a few days later I went, and again, smooth as silk. But within the week the police contacted Harley demanding answers.

On the 28th of December, Donald came home to a message demanding we both turn ourselves in on January 3rd. We were nervous and rattled, and over the next few days it was all we could talk about at the bar.

We found a gay attorney who'd handle our cases cheaply, and Donald's parents agreed to front the fee and let me pay them back so I didn't have to tell Mom.

We were walking around a junky outlet mall when Donald's dad called to discuss the potential consequences.

"Well, they might just let you off, seeing as you have no priors, or they might decide to make an example outta you," he said.

After rambling on for some time he became irritated that Donald wasn't more engaged in the conversation. "Well, what do *you* think Donald?" he demanded.

"Well, I think it's hit or miss," Donald replied.

"Yeah, yeah, I guess it is," his dad said, satisfied.

Donald actually wasn't paying attention, but at that very moment we happened to be walking past a ladies' discount store called Hit or Miss.

## Gloria Wholegroves

Gloria Wholegroves was one of several Jet Setters I'd known since I was a kid. She held a place of honor in the first and second grade because she possessed the finest sticker album, and after some intense lobbying she gave me a sticker.

I changed schools in third grade and we didn't reunite until high school, when we ran a shoe store together at the mall.

She stayed in Tulsa after we graduated but travelled for my events.

While I knew nothing of her sex life and assumed her to be quite straitlaced, I'd once made a joke

9

about her love of glory holes and the nickname "Glory Hole Groves" stuck, and she embraced it, adopting an online persona of one who frequented the XXX arcade at Downtown Tulsa's Midtown Adult Superstore.

At the Jet Set events she'd boast about how Tulsa had the most glory holes per capita while carrying a Siamese twin baby doll with one normal head and one of a demon child.

## Elaine

I befriended Elaine in elementary school while bonding over how dirty a mutual friend's house was. As teenagers, we'd sneak out every weekend to go to a gay* after-hours club. I'd try to get home before the sun came up, while Elaine would go to Denny's for breakfast with the fading and smudged drag queens, then while neighbors were watering their lawns, she'd roll up in a car full of guys, climb out looking a mess with her giant ratted hair, dark eye makeup and bright red lipstick, short skirt, fishnets, and heels. She'd proceed to nonchalantly walk to the side of the house, climb the chain link fence, and then climb into her bedroom window.

During our senior year she wasn't getting along with her parents, so she took up residence in my closet.

Our scheme relied on my mom's tight and predictable schedule. She left for work by 7:15am, returned home around 5:30, and went to bed at exactly 10:00. She knew Elaine was having problems at home and would be spending a lot of time with us, so her constant presence didn't arouse too much suspicion. At 9:45pm I would leave to take her home. We'd drive around for half an hour, then return together at 10:15.

Through the louvered doors of my closet we'd talk until we drifted off to sleep. In the morning I'd get ready first, then as soon as Mom pulled out of the drive, Elaine would jump up, shower, then on the way to school she'd put on her makeup.

We pulled this off for an entire month, but had gotten lazy and stopped putting her bedding away each day. Traipsing through the dark house one night my stomach sank when I heard Mom ask, "Chris, who's been sleeping in your closet?"

I've always been a heavy sleeper and as a teenager it was a challenge to wake up, yet Mom regularly opened the door first thing in the morning to tell me some major news. During the Rodney King riots, for example, she opened my door at 7 a.m. and said, "Chris, the blacks are burning down Los Angeles!"

She popped in and out as suddenly as a bird in a cuckoo clock.

Since Elaine was a light sleeper she really helped fill in the blanks when I'd finally come to. Once Mom opened the door and said, "Chris, your Aunt Martha died," then closed it. I laid there for five minutes or so, then whispered, "Elaine, did my mom say someone died?"

"Yeah," she whispered. "Your Aunt Martha."

## Feather & Francis

My first friend was Feather. I remember her staring at me though the chain link fence when we were both three.

"Hi! My name is Christopher," I said.

The first few times she just stood there, but when she did start speaking all she'd talk about was her baby brother Francis, who was too little to come out and play. Once he began coming outside I saw what the fuss was about and wanted him as my own little brother. I'd initiate games of hide and seek as a ruse to take him inside to play while she hopelessly looked for us.

Their family moved from Tulsa to Ottawa, Kansas when I was about twelve, but since their Grandma stayed behind I'd still see them once or twice a year, usually on holidays.

I helped Francis move to St. Louis when he was twenty one.

## Lenny

The straight mechanic from the Plains mentioned in the *AMERICAblog* piece was Lenny, the awkward, prematurely grey second husband of my first friend Feather. Born and raised in rural Kansas, he was criminally shy the first few times I was around him, so Feather spoke on his behalf.

Lenny enjoyed buying junk cars for a few hundred dollars and fixing them up. Once, just for kicks, he bought a beat up old minivan for five hundred dollars and drove it from Kansas to Washington D.C. just to see if it would make it.

He became a big fan of me and Donald, often being the first to like whatever we posted. After a few months he began sending friend requests to anyone we knew.

Preparing for his first time in a gay bar for an event we were hosting, he became obsessed with finding the perfect outfit, and texted a dozen times with the details of his ensemble. Finally, just to be ornery, I replied, "What's Feather going to wear?" To which he replied, "I don't know."

He had the most bizarre ideas about what to wear around a bunch of celebratory gays, the signature piece being a hat that looked like the bastard child of a ball cap and a Jiffy Pop bag. It looked like something a sassy retiree would wear to mall walk.

When Francis, his brother-in-law, saw his getup he exclaimed, "What are you going as? The queer engineer?"

## Lloyd Spartan: Mayor of Gay Oklahoma City

Lloyd was a large man who loved to drink, and many considered him the best storyteller in Oklahoma. He earned the moniker "Mayor of Gay Oklahoma City" because he knew everyone who'd ever sucked a dick in that town, and like a mother hen he kept track of their whereabouts.

"Hey Lloyd, whatever came of that crazy bitch everyone used to call Balcony Tossins? The queen who threw his lover over the ninth floor railing at the Tiffany House," I once asked randomly over way too many cocktails.

"Oh honey, she moved on down to Dallas back in '97 to try to get away from that damn nickname. Last I heard she's still alive and selling furniture," he said.

I met Lloyd when me and Donald threw our first party in my first apartment the summer after high school. He was with a date and later in the evening they decided to streak the apartment complex. Buck naked they ran with wild abandon, gleefully darting through the streets and dodging moving cars as they laughed, then all the way at the other end of the property something happened. They discovered modesty.

They carefully made their way back to the apartment ducking behind bushes, hiding behind cars, all the while covering their junk. Once they were back at the party, they were so pumped up on lust and adrenaline they made out at the brass and glass dinette set until they broke a chair.

A year later when me and Donald showed up at the dance club where he was working the door and presented our matching fake IDs, Lloyd cocked his head back in laughter and said, "Oh God, just steer clear of the owners."

To my knowledge Lloyd only had one enemy, a redhead we all called The Power Line Princess because he believed being raised beneath power lines gave him special powers. They only dated briefly, but the unremarkable break up resulted in a lifelong vendetta on the part of the princess.

Lloyd's handlers and financiers were a couple named Brae & Kevin, and if Lloyd travelled outside of Oklahoma City they accompanied and bankrolled him. Lloyd sometimes worked, mostly at call centers, but if they wouldn't let him take a day off when he wanted to he'd just quit.

A feature in Oklahoma City's Gay Pride Parade, Lloyd always marched wearing his trademark sun hat and rainbow flag wrapped as a dress. During my Hot Mess event he joined me on stage and delighted the audience with a few salty tales.

## The Castro Consorts

For a time I met my Castro Consorts once or twice a week for happy hour in San Francisco. Event planning guru Thurston Marks and his eccentric, slim and statuesque partner Lovey were Castro royalty, living high above the district in a glass box they called the Tree House, where they enjoyed a panoramic view of the city, the bay, and the East Bay all the way to Mount Diablo from their sweeping terrace.

Living in the center of it all they didn't need to drive often, but when they did they pulled out their large black BMW, which formerly belonged to the Japanese Embassy.

Most bars were largely standing room only, but even during the busiest happy hours, Thurston and Lovey held court at a table. One evening they were running late and I arrived to find half a dozen consorts huddled in a corner.

"I can't even picture Thurston & Lovey huddled in this corner," I said as I awaited their arrival.

Minutes later they arrived, smiling and greeting patrons not unlike the president when heading to the podium for the State of the Union address.

Thurston, wearing a sport coat with a big scarf, glanced over at us in our sorry circumstance, then turned to the occupants of an under-utilized table and greeted them enthusiastically.

"Hi! How have you been? Mind if we sit with you?" and voilà, the Consorts were seated.

For their St. Louis debut, Thurston and Lovey held court in one of the finest penthouse suites at the Chase, where they surveyed the city approvingly from their veranda high above the ornate marquee.

### That's Our Tatters!

Tatters was a cute, fun, big drinking, sexually promiscuous guy whose claim to fame was doing cocaine with Hollywood's most high profile bad girls when he worked in television.

Whenever he'd do something like disappear into the gangway to have sex, we'd just say, "That's our Tatters!"

To kick off his St. Louis debut, Tatters was photographed nude on an observation deck overlooking the skyline.

## Truman

I met the Consorts through Truman, a big guy with a '90s slacker vibe. I met Truman at a party in St. Louis and when I moved back to San Francisco, he graciously sent a virtual introduction to his San Francisco friends. A few years later I helped him land a job and an apartment in San Francisco.

We became close after his arrival in California, and went camping together.

## And the Rest

In addition to the Jet Set regulars there was a revolving cast of attendees. Notable examples include the former drug dealer turned tech executive from Austin who, via Facebook, saw his friends having fun the eve of my Hot Mess event and jumped on a plane that night to attend, and a guy from Cleveland whose claim to fame was having an extraordinarily large penis, making him the toast of the town.

### 3. The Confluence

St. Louis is a city people leave and return to time and again, and some say there's something magnetic about the very ground where it sits, at the confluence of the nation's two great rivers. Something that attracted the Mississippians, a tribe who built the largest and mightiest civilization in present day America on this site, where they used the rivers to explore great distances. Something that spurred French explorers to build here, and led the Americans to decide this was the jumping off point for westward expansion.

Now, I'll take you on an eighteen-year journey, via my short stories, back to 1996. You'll meet countless characters along the way, some who are with us for a short time, others for the duration, and many who turn up when you least expect it. Don't work too hard keeping track of them all, lest you go mad. I'll reintroduce you as we go along.

The journey takes us around the world, but always weaves in and out of this place, where I'd gather my most loyal friends, meet my greatest nemesis, discover my talents, and become an Emperor.

### 4. Change of Scenery

In 1996, Donald was my roommate in a drafty old house we'd dubbed Shenanigans Mansion in Oklahoma City, but he was in a new relationship, spending most of his time in tony Nichols Hills, the Beverly Hills of Oklahoma City, and I was getting restless and considering a change of scenery.

I wanted to move to a larger city but preferred to be within a day's drive of Tulsa so I could still see my family regularly. Cities that fit the bill included Dallas, Denver, and Kansas City.

I ruled out Dallas for several reasons, the main one being everyone moved there. That town was half Oklahomans, and they all acted like their two-hundred mile move was the equivalent of conquering Paris. God were they insufferable.

Denver was nice, but Colorado had just passed the anti-gay Amendment 2, which sent the signal gays weren't welcome.

Kansas City was lovely, but in style, scale and density, it reminded me of a larger Tulsa.

There was one city, however, that was nothing like the rest and sparked my imagination. It was eight hours to the northeast and was the last Eastern metropolis, filled with brick row houses, smokestacks, and history: St. Louis. And few had anything good to say about it.

"Oh it's awful," began a friend from Dallas. "I had to go there on business, and the best way I can describe it is it's like Gotham City. It's really old and crumbling. A lot of the buildings have soot stains. It was cold and overcast the whole time I was there, but it seems like it would be dark and dreary even if it was sunny out. Everyone downtown wears wool trench coats, and there's this subway they all ride."

A friend from Kansas City, known as "Swamp Ass" because of her complaints about her sweaty bottom, was drunk when I asked for her thoughts, and she didn't mince words. "Oh God, I *hate* people in St. Louis! They're all a bunch of assholes who think they're in New York—they're so freakin' rude!"

Everything negative I heard only piqued my interest. Generally speaking, cities west of St. Louis were fairly uniform. They were built on a simple grid designed for the automobile. The density was relatively low. Predictable patterns, predictable chain businesses. But St. Louis, this sinister busted up metropolis everyone despised—now that was my kind of adventure.

I sent off for chamber of commerce and tourist brochures, beginning my research for a possible move.

## 5. A Big Deal in St. Louis

The family was together in Tulsa for Christmas, and I accompanied my oldest brother Joe on a morning drive to forgotten places around town. including a long abandoned amusement park. Joe was nineteen years older and was a successful artist in New York City.

"I think I'm going to move to St. Louis," I announced.

"If you're going to move, why don't you just move to New York?" he asked, knowing that was always something I intended to do.

I told him for the moment I liked being within a day's drive of home, and the city had sparked my interest.

"I think you'll like it there. It's a cool, understated place," he began. "I'm kind of a big deal in St. Louis" he continued, explaining he'd had several recent shows there, had been shown in the St. Louis Art Museum, and his print publisher was there. "Let me know when you go check it out, and I'll put you in touch with some people."

I travelled to the city with a short-lived boyfriend named Ernest. When I arrived I called Joe's publisher, Archer Andronico, and he offered to give us a tour and take us to lunch. "Let's meet at my place," he said.

Archer lived in Ladue, one of the area's most blue-blooded enclaves. As we drove past the palatial old homes, many largely obscured by big trees, I thought about Joe describing the city as understated, and considered how showy things back home could be by comparison, remarking, "People in Oklahoma or Texas wouldn't bother having such big houses unless everyone could see them."

We arrived at his low-slung Frank Lloyd Wright-inspired home. Florence, the wiry housekeeper, escorted us down a grand staircase to the airy white living room with twenty-foot floor to ceiling windows overlooking lush gardens and the U-shaped pool that surrounded the centerpiece Trova sculpture.

Ernest whispered in amazement, "That's a Basquiat," pointing to a large piece on the wall with TAR! TAR! TAR! painted across it.

Archer, a tall and elegantly dressed man of about fifty, glided into the room followed by his business partner Miles, a handsome, fit and tan guy in his early thirties, and they greeted us like VIPs. Archer had our day planned out, which would conclude with a personal tour of apartments with a gay realtor.

"So do you smoke?" Archer asked Ernest, and we knew he didn't mean cigarettes.

"Yes, I do," Ernest said laughing.

21

As impressed as Ernest was by the Basquiat, I don't think anything could have prepared him for the big silver tray full of joints.

A little loose from the pot, we loaded into Archer's shiny black Land Rover and began our tour of St. Louis.

"Clayton is our other downtown," he said, pointing to a cluster of high rises, "Forest Park is one of the largest urban parks in the nation, roughly the size of Central Park."

He pulled into the fire zone near Café Balaban in the fashionable Central West End and proceeded to park.

"This is a fire zone!" I warned.

"Oh, I've got too many cops in my back pocket to worry about things like that," Archer replied.

Based on our low budget, he recommended we live in South St. Louis city and showed us several interesting neighborhoods, including Soulard, which was like St. Louis's French Quarter with a bar on every corner and the Budweiser plant at the south end.

"Soulard is the neighborhood for drunks," Miles said, explaining it was even legal to walk around with an open container in the district.

Historic brick homes built in the 1800s, some covered in ivy, opened right onto the brick sidewalk, and the front doors were decorated for Mardi Gras.

"Soulard had the second largest Mardi Gras in the country," Archer mentioned.

He then turned us over to a high-end Clayton real estate firm where a well-dressed broker named Alex personally greeted us curbside. Archer handed me a card and said, "If anyone has any questions have them give me a call."

We followed Alex to the leasing department where we were introduced to the lucky realtor who'd spend his afternoon showing four-hundred dollar apartments to two wide-eyed, broke, unemployed kids who'd just rolled in from Oklahoma.

## 6.  Real Estate Coup

Jay had been the realtor who showed us around, and he called two days later to let me know he'd no longer be assisting us directly. Alex, the head of the leasing department, had accepted a position with a rival brokerage and took the entire team with him. One night all of them just packed up and left.

He assured me the company who owned the apartment, Rothschild, would take care of us. The following day Nelly, the agent from Rothschild, called to let me know the owner went with another application.

"There were two applications and they went with the other guy, because, well, he had a job," she explained.

It wasn't all bad news, though. They'd still rent to me and offered me a comparable unit in Soulard.

Nelly was at a nearby bar when I pulled into town on a Saturday afternoon, and she took a break from her whisky to move me in.

## 7.   The Traveling Circus

The Crab was far and away my most pretentious and obnoxious friend. A few years older, he had blond hair, blue eyes, narrow shoulders, and a muffin-top waist he was in denial about.

"I'm a size thirty!" he'd boast as bulges of flesh spilled out from above his belt.

I hated the guy when we were first introduced, but eventually I grew to like him, even though he was often overwhelming.

He had a different car every six months. I'd known him to have a few BMW convertibles and a Camaro, but at the time I was moving he happened to have a truck and offered to move us. One catch was him bringing along the Power Line Princess, Gay Mayor Lloyd Spartan's bitter ex-boyfriend.

The Princess was an artist specializing in odd, sexual caricatures of famous people, like Garth Brooks in fishnet hose, or Roseanne Barr making out with Madonna while sticking something up her anus.

"Oh Chris's brother Joe is really famous and can help you get discovered!" the brash Crab promised.

"Princess, if you want to get discovered you need to go to New York. That's the way it works," I tried to explain.

"Well I guess I'll never get discovered, then, because I'm not leaving Oklahoma City," he said.

Despite the dashed hopes, the Princess remained upbeat and seemed to really like St. Louis. Sitting on the light rail train with his bright orange hair glistening in the light he kept repeating, "This is so cool!" but he did remark that the city needed more chain restaurants, and when he saw a story in the paper about how the region wasn't growing, he said, "Oklahoma City *is* growing so there's no need to move because someday it'll be the same size."

We needed to return to Oklahoma to tie up loose ends and were following them back when the Crab decided to stop at a convenience store in the suburb of Fenton to get a sandwich for the road, but after he heated it up he couldn't find the mayonnaise.

"Excuse me. I can't find any mayonnaise," he said to the cashier.

"I'm sorry, we're all out," the woman replied.

"Well I'm not buying this without mayonnaise!"

"You already opened it and heated it up. You *are* buying it!" the clerk barked.

"*You* try eating this without mayonnaise!" the Crab said as he flung the sandwich at her head.

"I'm calling the police!" yelled the enraged and splattered clerk.

The Crab was on his own. We pulled out of the lot as the cop pulled up, and the Crab greeted him with a big smile and wave, determined to talk his way out of the mess he created.

## 8. Crying Chorus

Ernest and I were settling into the brand new city, and other than Archer and Miles, we didn't know a soul. Our social network started to form once we began attending the predominately gay Metropolitan Community Church.

The first new friend to take an interest in us was a guy named Larry Benton who'd been a married florist in Paducah, Kentucky for many years but recently came out of the closet, moved to the big city to live with his sister, and went on disability for diabetes.

The first day we met he took me out to lunch and told me about his boyfriend.

"Manny lives with Ray David, his partner of seventeen years. They're not really together anymore, but they have a big beautiful brownstone on Compton Hill filled with antiques and crystal chandeliers. I'm not sure if there's much of a future for us," Larry said, trailing off.

"Well, it doesn't sound like Manny's going anywhere," I replied. "Seventeen years is a long time and it sounds like they're pretty settled."

"That's what it sounds like to me too," Larry began, "and when I first agreed to date him I told myself I'd give it six months. If he hasn't either left Ray or made significant progress towards moving out by then I'm not wasting any more time. It'll be over."

I was traveling to Chicago for the weekend and offered my Soulard apartment to Larry & Manny, figuring they'd appreciate a private love nest. When I returned, Manny asked me to come by to pick up the key.

26

"Oh, there's no rush. I can just get it from you at church next weekend," I replied.

"Well, I'd like you to meet Ray," he said.

Their tall, narrow brick house reminded me of something you'd find in the Northeast with its little ivy covered yard framed with an ornamental iron fence, marble steps, oversized front door and ornate cornice. Manny answered and led us down the long main hall past sets of tall French doors leading to the living and dining rooms, each with their respective glimmering chandeliers, to the kitchen in the back where I was introduced to Ray David. Ray was a tall, imposing man in his late forties with dark hair and clear blue eyes, while Manny was short and thin.

Manny & Ray immediately took me under their wing. Regardless of how broke I was, when Saturday night rolled around I didn't have a care in the world. Every single weekend the big wide door to Villa Compton opened up, the cocktails flowed, and multi-course meals were enjoyed in the dimly lit dining hall surrounded by sparking crystal. Many nights did devolve into *Who's Afraid of Virginia Woolf?*, but it didn't bother us. It was all part of the show.

If dinner wasn't served by nine it was a crap shoot as to whether it would be served at all. By that point in the night they'd lose interest and fight over who should finish it. Ray became more focused on his music, normally disco or Cher, which he'd turn up really loud as Manny shouted, "Turn that down! It's too loud!"

Then Ray would get frustrated with Manny about something and yell, "Dammit Mann-strosity!"—that was his angry nickname for Miss Manny.

27

Seasoned guests learned to watch the clock, and if it looked like they were behind schedule, around 8:30 everyone sprang into action to wrap it up.

On Manny & Larry's six-month anniversary—to the day—Larry sat Manny down.

"Well, when we first met I told myself I'd give it six months…" and with that Larry was finished and Manny was wrecked. Totally blindsided. Each Saturday night for months he'd pull me to the side and cry over Larry.

"He never told me anything about six months! He never said…I didn't know!" he'd repeat on a drunken, breathy loop.

His Post-Larry grief was trumped by the death of his grandmother a couple of months later. Each Saturday night for the following six months he'd pull me aside to look at her belongings and weep. It might sound depressing but it really wasn't. We were all drunk and having fun in our own way, even Ol' Mourning Manny.

One evening Manny was clearing dinner plates and preparing for dessert, when just as he was leaving the dining room I mentioned something about my grandma and caught myself.

Fortunately Manny was out of earshot, but I can still remember the pregnant pause in the room and Ray's startled face at the other end of the long table, past two candelabras and half a dozen frozen guests, where sitting in his regal upholstered chair he leaned forward and stressed, "Please, don't *anyone*, mention *anything*, about a grandma!" After taking a drag he flicked his cigarette and mumbled rolling his eyes, "We'll have a crying chorus in here!"

## 9. Mayor's Ball

My first gig in St. Louis was a commission-based job with an apartment referral service, and part of that job was giving corporate tours to people transferring in with the May Company department stores, which meant I had to learn they lay of the land quickly. An animated guy in the office who was always laughing about what a joke the company was did his best to give me a crash course.

Most of our business was in St. Louis County, which didn't include the City of St. Louis due to a city/county divorce in the 1800s. Though the county contained a byzantine assortment of ninety municipalities, it was thought of as four areas: Mid County, South County, North County, and West County.

On a paper map of the region, my coworker drew a long narrow rectangle like a belt crossing the county, beginning in the city's Central West End, continuing due west through Clayton, Ladue, Frontenac, and across Interstate 270 into Chesterfield and Wildwood.

"This is where people want to be" he explained. He then drew big fat circles around North St. Louis County and South St. Louis County where he scrawled "BANG FOR YOUR BUCK LAND."

Mid County, which included upscale Clayton, the county seat where Rustin Winchell practiced law, had the region's second major downtown area, complete with a cluster of high rise buildings. On the western border of the city of St. Louis, Clayton's minutes from downtown via highway or light rail train.

29

North County was home to the airport and Ferguson, and was the part of the region most impacted by white flight, with a large portion of its white residents flocking across the Missouri River to the vinyl McMansions of St. Charles County, home of Rita Revlon.

South County was considered stable and sedate. If South County were a car it would be a Chevrolet, and if it were a department store it would be Sears.

While my coworker was correct in his assessment of the company, my boss, a Black woman in her early thirties named Jennifer who drove a bright red Mercedes, was a socialite and took me to good parties. I'd only been in town a week when she asked if I wanted to attend the Mayor's Ball that evening. It seems someone had cancelled at the last minute.

My boyfriend Earnest was working the night shift and I arrived to drive him to work, intending to tell him the big news about the ball right away, but we began arguing about something the moment he got in and the argument continued for the duration of the twenty-five minute drive. When I dropped him off he leaned in the passenger window and barked, "Call me at eight so we can discuss this!"

I replied regally, "It'll have to wait because *I'm* going to the Mayor's Ball," and drove away while his incredulous look set in.

# 10. Andronico Finishing School

After my commission-only apartment hunter job flamed out I ended up working part time for a commuter airline, and part time for Archer's company, Andronico Fine Art Publishers, where I mostly ran errands. One of my first tasks was to stock the fridge with soda and other beverages.

I returned with everything on my list.

"No, no, no!" Archer began. "We don't stock plastic bottles. Very Big Gulp. Return these and buy only glass bottles and cans."

Miles was the poster boy for perfection, and I compared him to a Ken doll without any condescension or derision—he was so put together with his tight body, good skin, and the way he worked with such superhuman precision. I've seen him go outside on a humid summer day, dig a hole and plant a bush while wearing pressed khaki shorts and a crisp white shirt, all without getting dirty. I've never seen anything like it before or since.

On rare occasions he'd let his guard down, seeming to empathize with my newness to Andronico's standards, and talk to me about what it was like for him in the early days.

"Archer sat me down with a razor blade and had me cut straight edges on all the stamps. He thought it looked cleaner," Miles recalled.

Normally though, Miles was difficult for me to deal with, and it all came to a head one steamy afternoon when I was asked to pick up a stack of prints from the warehouse.

When he saw the stack he noticed one print had a bent corner.

"How did this one get bent?" he demanded, standing atop Archer's grand staircase, while I was at the foot.

"I'm not sure," I said nervously.

"There are two possibilities. Either you were careless and bent it, or you weren't paying attention, therefore you didn't notice it was bent!" He let out an exasperated sigh and walked off while exclaiming to himself, "FOOLS! All day I've had to deal with *fools.*"

Miles left, Archer was out, and I sat down at the desk and penned my resignation letter. I was twenty-two, passionate and impulsive, but somehow summoned the maturity not to burn the bridge, as I've been known to do at times. Archer had been so gracious in getting us set up, Joe had introduced us, and it could be embarrassing for all parties that it didn't work out. I attempted to thread the needle in the letter, which said I was resigning effective immediately because I wouldn't work for anyone who considered me a fool, but as far as anyone else would know I simply left in order to work for the airline full time.

This way was clean. Joe wouldn't be put in an awkward position. I wouldn't look defeated. Archer and Miles's professional relationship with him wouldn't be strained.

Several months had passed when Archer invited us to a cocktail party, and we attended.

## Story Box 1: The Gay Church

We got to know a lot of people very quickly through the predominately LGBT Metropolitan Community Church, including the legally blind choir director Blaine Festus, the star of the choir, Little David—one of only a handful younger than myself— and Miss Bags and his partner Andre, who led the Interracial Couples Group.

My favorite person to sit with was Gray Owens-Wilson because of his cutting wit and cattiness.

Gray would dish on queens in the communion line, and I remember one gaudy character coming down the aisle with slicked-back blond hair, orange spray tan, billowy red silk shirt largely open at the chest, and just dripping in gold jewelry.

Referencing an ancient diva from the soap *The Young & the Restless,* he quipped, "My God, he looks like a male Katherine Chancellor with a touch of formaldehyde."

Financially, Gray was doing quite well due to a recent watershed moment in his career—that being the moment he caught the married VP of his national retailer getting peed on at the bathhouse.

## 11. The Scene

The nightlife scene in St. Louis was more dynamic than what I was accustomed to. From my Soulard apartment I could walk to Clementine's, a neighborhood bar with the strongest drinks in town and the drag queen Midnight Annie entombed in the wall. If I wanted to stay out all night I could go to the massive east side clubs in Illinois, including Faces, which had three floors, including a debauchery filled basement. And there were numerous options in between.

I felt like the smallest tadpole in this big new pond, but I remember observing the titans of nightlife, many centered around the labyrinth Complex Nightclub, including Howard Meyer, the socialite owner who resided in an opulent West End mansion where he lavishly entertained, A-List party boys like handsome Black newscaster Linton Johnson, who was always dancing shirtless to show off his chiseled body. But none was so beloved, so well known, and none owned the spotlight like the Grande Dame of St. Louis, Miss Simone Shasta.

Simone was the larger than life mistress of ceremonies at the Complex and ruled the stage like nobody else. When many queens spoke or performed, the patrons listened with one ear and went about their business with the other, but Simone enraptured her audience—and God help anyone who attempted to heckle. She was quick-witted and could make you the laughing stock of the bar in seconds.

I watched the show anonymously from the shadows, unknown in this new place. Being anonymous did make it easier to pull pranks, though. Like the time I was at the Complex with Francis, my straight childhood neighbor who was in town visiting, and he dared me to drop a fake turd in someone's cocktail, *while* they were holding it.

I accepted the challenge, and it proved to be much more difficult than I had expected. People hold their cocktails close. After a couple of hours I found the perfect spot and the perfect victim. There was a heavily trafficked bottleneck between one bar and the dance floor, and a queen was squeezing against the rail as countless patrons walked behind him, and he was looking to the left while holding his drink to the right.

In passing I plopped the artificial feces in his drink, then stepped into the darkness like an arsonist watching his chaos. The laughing queen brought the drink towards his lips and then his face contorted in horror as he shouted, "What the fuck!"

## 12. Little David from Church

So I mentioned the debauchery filled basement at Faces in East St. Louis. One New Year's I was there with a big group including Ray David and Miss Manny. We were sitting in the basement bar when I saw who I believed to be Little David, a young choir singer from our gay church with a squeaky clean reputation, traipsing into the dark room.

I was no stranger to that dark room, but I was surprised to see Little David down there.

"Ray, I think Little David just went into the dark room!" I said.

His reaction was completely unexpected. With a dramatic flourish of his arm Ray let out an alarmed groan, and then the man, wearing a trench coat, standing 6'2", and weighing in at two hundred thirty pounds, charged into that dark room like a bull in a china chop in a desperate, drunken attempt to rescue Little David.

Glow sticks were all the rage, and throughout the room they were bobbing up and down as they illuminated Ray, standing in the middle of it all shouting, "DAAAAAAVID! LITTLE DAVID FROM CHUUUUURCH!"

I pulled his arm with all my might but he was as intractable as a tractor stuck in the mud. He leaned over and put his free hand on the shoulder of a young man with a mouthful of cock and asked, breathing heavily, "Are you...Little David...from church?"

The glow-stick wearing queen shook his head no. But I think it was.

## 13. Driving Miss Manny

We walked out of Faces around four in the morning to discover a blizzard had come through. I don't know why we had Miss Manny drive—she was probably drunker than all of us—but while crossing the frozen Poplar Street Bridge over the Mississippi her contact lens popped out and we began careening across the road. We all thought we were going to die and were screaming for our lives, except for Ray, who calmly smoked in the backseat.

A nervous quiet fell over us once Miss Manny regained control.

Ray took a puff of his cigarette and then mumbled, looking out the window, "I can't wait to get out of this crazy car."

## 14. Flying Low

As the hub of Trans World Airlines, Lambert-St. Louis International was one of the nation's busiest airports. Thousands of nearby mid-century homes were slated to be bulldozed to build a billion dollar additional runway when American Airlines acquired TWA, throwing the plans into question.

American assured the city that Lambert was critical to their mid-continent hub plans and insisted the additional runway was still necessary, but once the ink was dry on the deal they pulled out, adding to my pile of Dallas and Texas related grievances.

It was still during the airport's heyday in the late '90s that I worked for a commuter affiliate of TWA, which flew prop planes to exciting regional destinations like Cedar Rapids, Iowa and Terre Haute, Indiana.

Most of my time was spent on the tarmac, stowing bags and guiding planes on the ground with my glowing wands. It was about a hundred degrees on my first day, and a Ground Power Unit, which powered the planes while parked, was belching exhaust right in my face, which made me nauseous to the point I went behind a construction wall and threw up. During torrential rains there wasn't a dry spot on my body, and there were times it was so cold I had to hold my ink pen in a fist because I couldn't feel my fingers.

After serving time on the tarmac you were eligible to be promoted to a gate agent position, and while the climate was better, it was a lot more stressful because the flights were always getting cancelled and you had to deal with the irate passengers.

A perk was being able to fly for free on our airline, or for $50 on TWA. Since I only made $6.10 an hour, the TWA flights weren't that affordable, and besides, what would I do once I got to the destination? However, I would sometimes wake up on a Saturday and decide to hop a free regional flight to Memphis or Madison for the day, walk around town for a few hours and then fly home.

There was an odd couple that worked the service desk who I always found amusing. One was a devout Pentecostal woman named Cindra who didn't cut her hair and only wore dresses. The other was the biggest gay whore named Brent who everyone called "Ol' 7030" because he claimed to be a 70 percent bottom and 30 percent top. He was always talking about his most recent trick at the dirty bookstore he frequented on the east side. Interestingly, Cindra didn't seem to mind and actually looked somewhat amused as she'd just stand and smile.

"Girl, last night I met this guy who was *so* cute, well, he was bookstore cute, and we went in the booth and he just went to town on my booty and I am *so* sore today. Anyway after that I went to the baths but it was dead, aside from a few trolls, and I just ended up passing out by the pool."

I have no idea why he felt compelled to tell her all of this, but at the end of every story she'd just shake her head and say, "Brent you're a mess."

## 15. Wicked Little Town

Francis was at a dead end in Ottawa, Kansas. Twenty-one, living at home, and working at a factory. I'd been trying to convince him to move to St. Louis, because I thought that was the solution to everyone's problems, but his family was pressuring him to stay.

Then it looked like his fate might be sealed when a girl came up pregnant and said there was a fifty-fifty chance the baby was his.

"If the baby's mine of course I'll stay and raise it. But if it's not, I'm leaving town immediately," he vowed.

It wasn't his, and true to his word, with twenty dollars to his name, he packed up all his belongings in the back of a friend's hatchback and moved in with me.

He was looking really shaggy, so one afternoon I took him to get a haircut and told him, "I've got some people I want you to meet."

With his fresh, clean-cut look we walked into Andronico Fine Art and I casually introduced him to Miles. "Miles, this is Francis. I've known him since he was born, and he just moved to St. Louis. I'm out showing him around."

Incredibly, Miles responded, "Do you need a job?" and the rest is history. As of this writing, some fifteen years later, Francis still works for Andronico, handing art installations and overseeing the warehouse operations.

He's hung art in fine homes and galleries across the nation, and has vacationed in Archer's New York City and Miami Beach condos.

If I had to count on one hand what I'm most proud of, getting Francis out of Ottawa, Kansas would be on the list.

## 16. Wrong Side of the Tracks

Some backstory on my interest in gritty places.

Dad was from Tulsa's roughest neighborhood, in the shadow of downtown, and was born in the very house where *The Outsiders* was filmed. Grandma Andoe remained in the neighborhood, in a house she inherited from her mother, until I was grown.

My affinity for abandoned places and my love for storytelling began in that section of mostly black North Tulsa. I had the best time and felt the most at home at Grandma's, where she'd hold court in a metal rocking chair under the big oak tree and tell stories, some of which involved the railroad tracks bordering her yard and how during the Depression, men would ride the rails and my Granddad would befriend them and give them sandwiches.

I'd wander the tracks with my cousin Julia, discovering places you couldn't see from the road. There were rusting warehouses, crumbling brick buildings, and weedy salvage yards filled with cars from the 1940s, '50s, and '60s.

Decades later I'd recapture that feeling of adventure in East St. Louis, but on a much grander scale. There were towering factories collapsing on themselves, abandoned hospitals, and like North Tulsa, there were ruins you could only access via railroad tracks. I not only felt at home in East St. Louis because of the sense of familiarity, but that place, just across the Mississippi River—which is also the Missouri/Illinois state line—from downtown St. Louis, was long a capital of lawless good times.

A center of vice once ruled by the mafia, it's always been where one went for the things that weren't allowed in a respectable city like St. Louis: gambling, prostitution, and gay bars that didn't close until dawn, not to mention slaughterhouses and polluting industries. The latter two weren't a draw, of course, except they'd become crumbling, abandoned hulks—which were certainly a draw for me.

There's some folklore that East St. Louis was once a nice place, and while it was once a fully functioning municipality—unlike today, where the largely empty city was forced to sell City Hall to satisfy a judgment, and then rent it back—it was always an industrial suburb riddled with problems. I answer those "glory days" claims with a reminder of the 1913 mayoralty election where candidate John Chamberlin ran on the slogan, "Make East St. Louis a little more like home and a little less like Hell."

Joe moved to New York City in the early 1980s when it too had a lawless and sinister vibe. I was just a kid, but I remember when Times Square was nothing but porn theatres and drug dealers, and how cool I thought it was.

## 17. Dr. Laura

I got my first computer in the year 2000. I remember sitting at my rusty chrome table with the red formica top and trying to figure out what the big deal was.

I had a handful of friends who'd email me, and one message was a forward about a radio personality named "Dr. Laura," who was telling her eighteen million listeners that most gay men were pedophiles. Making matters worse was Paramount's plan to give her a television show. I went to the stopdrlaura.com website to see what was going on and checked in daily for the latest developments.

One day I saw that a protest was being planned in Chicago, and I sent a message of support.

"Many people my age seem to believe the gains your generation made are set in stone, and have no interest in fighting," I wrote, and went on to wish them luck with their protest. The national organizer based in Washington, D.C., John Aravosis, forwarded the message on to local organizers in Chicago, who in turn invited me to participate, offering room and board.

I didn't know if my old car could make the four-hundred mile journey. Tripp Hilton, a gray-haired gay man who was a fabulously wealthy client of Archer Andronico, expressed support for my plans to attend and offered me the use of one of his three vehicles.

In Chicago I was housed at the home of two hardcore veteran LGBT activists, an interracial couple named Bob and Ruffin. I arrived late Friday evening and we had a nice dinner, but Saturday morning was all business. They teamed me up with a buddy who was a few years older, and gave us a list of all the community meetings happening around town, which we were to crash. We were booked solid until the 2pm protest outside of CBS in downtown Chicago.

There were about a hundred and twenty five of us on the sidewalk picketing, and it was one of the most exhilarating moments of my life. Afterwards, I went to eat with a dozen or so community leaders, with special guest John Aravosis, the national organizer. I was sitting at the long table basking in the afterglow of a great experience when John turned to me and asked, "So what do you have planned for St. Louis?"

WhaWhaWhaaaat? It had never crossed my mind to organize a protest.

"Gay people in St. Louis don't really protest, so I'm not sure..." I replied.

Within three weeks I'd pulled together a major demonstration outside of a local station, which gained national attention with *Planet Out* noting, "The St. Louis demonstration was larger than recent demonstrations in Dallas and Atlanta combined."

Dr. Laura herself had a meltdown over it, calling us "The McCarthyists of the twenty-first century."

I'd earned my street cred as an activist and went on to lead and participate in other protests in the coming months and years.

# 18. The Young & The Restful

Tripp Hilton, the gentleman who loaned me the car
to travel to Chicago, was from old money. Aside
from managing his inherited fortune and amassing
an impressive art collection which included a
Warhol, he loved to surround himself with people
who partied hard.

He once offered me a job, but Francis, who was all
too familiar with him after seeing Andronico
entertain the aged party boy, and having delivering
artwork to his home on several occasions, advised
against it.

"I don't think you'd want to be around that all the
time."

And by "that," he meant the 24/7 lifestyle of drugs,
sex and seedy people that had Tripp looking and
feeling twenty years older than his fifty-five years.

He'd invited me to stay and swim when I returned
the vehicle. His South County mansion, which he
built after getting run out of his Central West End
high rise—the last straw being a six-foot inflatable
penis hung from the balcony—had the foreboding
feel of a mausoleum, with grey brick, dark-tinted,
single-pane windows, and a steeply pitched roof. It
sat at the end of a cul-de-sac surrounded by the
homes of Anheuser Busch executives.

He seemed to be home alone when I arrived,
although you could never be sure who was there
with the servants coming and going from the maid's
quarters downstairs. These weren't the polished
servants of Downton Abbey, but were white trash
and often seemed to be on drugs.

I swam alone for an hour or so, and when I entered the great room, with its twenty-foot ceilings and paneled walls, it felt like I'd walked into a Kubrick scene to find Tripp passed out in his green leather chair while a shirtless blond kid, maybe eighteen, stared intently at him.

"He has narcolepsy, so he might be out for a while," I told the kid from the other end of the long room. He briefly looked at me without saying a word and then turned back to Tripp.

I went up to the guest room where my clothes were, again witnessing the scene from the catwalk between the grand staircase and the guest quarters.

"I know he's undercover police. I know he was. They got this place surrounded," the kid said to the unconscious Tripp.

I was very uneasy and quickly dressed. I didn't want him to know I was leaving out of fear he'd follow me, so I crawled on my belly across the catwalk until I heard him climbing the stairs, and jumped up.

"What are you doing?" he demanded.

"Nothing, just coming back downstairs," I replied.

"Are you the police?" he asked.

"No, I'm just a friend of Tripp's."

"Come here," he said as he grabbed my hand and led me into Tripp's private suite, which was a part of the house I'd never seen.

Pointing to a crystal jar filled with cash, he said, "He pays us to shove things up his ass. Just gives us wads of money." He then took me to the master bath where he opened a drawer filled with sex toys, then closed it and locked eyes with me.

"I believe you. You're a good person, got a bright future ahead of you," he said, then peeked through the blinds at an empty parked car. "See that car right there? That's the police. They've got this place surrounded. I need to get out of here. Can you drive me?"

"Oh, I'm not leaving for a while," I replied.

We both went downstairs and he paced back and forth while discussing our exit and how we'd get past the police. My mind was racing, wondering how I could leave without being detected. I made several false starts, just to feel him out. I'd do things like pretend I was checking on something outside. Finally, after about an hour, he settled back onto the ottoman and resumed staring at Tripp, seemingly in a trance.

At that point I simply walked out. The lawns weren't fenced, and the neighbors were sitting in their garden visiting. They all turned and watched me as I got into my car and drove away.

I had been to some seedy places in my life, but I'd never felt as trashy as I did at that moment, leaving that million-dollar mansion.

## 19. Giving Satan the Shaft

Tripp was quite embarrassed about what had gone down during my visit and called to apologize. I inquired about the kid and was told he eventually opted to escape from the back, through the forest, while Tripp was still passed out.

He asked if he could take me out to dinner at Café Eau at the Chase Park Plaza. This was a huge treat, and I gladly accepted. Tripp delighted me with tales of the love of his life, Dino, who was currently and frequently incarcerated. He told me Dino was a demon sent by Satan to lure him to Hell, and spoke of being an unwitting participant in a ménage with Dino and a fallen angel.

"I was on my hands and knees while Dino was fucking me, but I had my glasses on and could see his reflection," Tripp began. "Then I saw him move aside and another, unfamiliar figure took over. He was a lot more muscular than Dino and was wearing a rope belt tied in a knot. I described this to a priest friend and he said it sounded like a monk's belt, and it must've been a fallen angel.

"When I die there's going to be a bridge that crosses into Hell, and it's Dino's job to take me across," he explained. "But he's not going to do it. He loves me too much, and when it comes time to lead me across the bridge he said he's not going to do it," Tripp said proudly.

## 20. Still With Mel

After my successful protest I started getting invited to political events, including a fundraiser for Governor Mel Carnahan, who was running for the U.S. Senate against Republican John Ashcroft. It was held at the West End mansion of Complex Nightclub owner Howard Meyer.

I arrived just as the governor was leaving for his doomed flight, which would go down thirty-five miles south of the city, killing all onboard.

With only weeks left to until the election, a new slogan was launched: "I'm Still With Mel," and entertainers with St. Louis ties, including Sheryl Crow, came to town and performed to raise money for the campaign.

By a two-percent margin, Missouri voters chose the deceased Mel Carnahan over John Ashcroft.

## 21. Metropolis

One of the things that excited me about St. Louis, in contrast to Oklahoma City or Tulsa, was the involvement of people my age in civic issues and the incredible access to people in power.

In the short time I was in town I'd attended the Mayor's Ball, had been to soirées in City Hall, and had lunched with politicians atop the city's tallest building, Metropolitan Square.

A big reason such access was possible was a group called Metropolis.

I learned of the organization while attending a nude play in a church basement. The plays were a lot of fun while they lasted, but then church elders took notice of what the liberal pastor was allowing and shut them down.

At a nude play I took a seat beside Harrison, an outgoing middle-aged guy with a shiny bald head who seemed much younger than his fifty years, and he struck up a conversation. When he heard my enthusiasm about St. Louis he asked, "Are you familiar with Metropolis?"

I told him I wasn't and he replied, "Oh, you need to get hooked up with those guys—they're a lot like you. It's a big group of kids in their twenties whose mission is to get young people to move to the inner city. The host a lot of events. Every Thursday they have a bar crawl event called The Walk where they go to numerous bars Downtown and if they pass one that's closed they'll leave a note telling the owner seventy-five or so people came by to support their business but they were closed."

During intermission he introduced me to two members and community activists, Emanuel & Reggie, who were plugged into countless things around town and invited me over to their home a few times.

I became a member, and wound up leading the LGBT outreach group called Out & Urban, and founded a wine club, which became the longest running group in Metropolis, actually outliving the organization, thanks to a brilliant hostess named Suzanne, who took it over.

Harrison was bisexual and had married a bisexual woman in the swinging seventies. They were monogamous and raised a beautiful family in a big house in the Illinois suburbs, but when the last child was grown his wife came home and announced, "I've decided to be a lesbian." Harrison was devastated, but decided that he, too, would reinvent himself.

He moved to a trendy and urbane Central West End apartment, bought a BMW sports car, updated his wardrobe and hit the town as a gay man. He had a youthful spirit and a lot of energy, and gravitated to people decades younger. With his magnetic, engaging personality he did well socially and was well known for connecting people.

I made many good friends and connections through Metropolis, and I credit the organization for kickstarting nightlife in downtown St. Louis with their events and advocacy, as well as for grooming many great leaders. Former members, now in their forties, are business owners, published authors, and elected officials.

Every organization has a lifespan, and new people came in over the years and propped up the name Metropolis like the *Weekend at Bernie's* corpse. Generally speaking, they were socially focused and had little, if any, interest in the founding principles, and would even host parties in affluent suburbs like Webster Groves, which was an anathema to the original members, who never had functions outside the city, for starters, and made it a point to patronize businesses in parts of town like north city, which was 95 percent black.

Hating what had become of the organization they founded, a group of founding members rejoined and ran for offices as a slate of candidates vowing to put the organization out of its misery.

50

The coup attempt failed, and Metropolis limped along for another decade or so until the wine club was all that was left, and the administrative responsibilities were dumped in Suzanne's lap. She decided to merge with another fledgling, but more effective organization, where she continued to run the wine club.

Only a year or two after I met Harrison, he died in a motorcycle accident. He was riding through Forest Park when he lost control and crashed into a curvy brick wall bordering the zoo. He'd been on his way to meet Emanuel & Reggie for dinner, and as he lay dying he kept asking the medics to call them and let them know he wouldn't be coming.

A few weeks earlier, one beautiful spring day, we were sitting at a sidewalk café when he mentioned all he missed out on, coming out so late.

"Oh no, Harrison, you've got the best of both worlds. You're really fortunate to have your kids, and now you get to experience all this too," I said.

"Yeah, that's true," he began. "I never bring that up with my gay friends but I do feel lucky having my family."

One daughter was in the Peace Corps, and he always talked about her adventures in Africa and kept her photos on his refrigerator.

His funeral service felt light and comfortable because his body wasn't present, only photos. Interestingly, the Harrison known around the city looked much younger and more dynamic than the guy in the photos, who was wearing a conservative suit and holding onto the little hair he had.

His wife and kids were warm and attractive people.

51

When offering condolences on my way out, I hugged his daughter and said, "Your dad was so proud of you."

She teared up and replied, "And we're proud of him."

## 22. Mistress Miltonia

Another good friend I met through Metropolis was a smart and ambitious woman named Miltonia. My first assessment was you couldn't get more vanilla. A native of Kansas and a graduate of the University of Kansas, she was often dressed in a sweatshirt, jeans and tennis shoes.

We hadn't known one another long when she hosted a "James Bondage Party" at Francis's Soulard loft—a theme based on both James Bond and S&M. None of us really got it, so we came in our street clothes, and if I remember correctly, Miltonia was dressed in her aforementioned style. Still, we were all in our twenties and were drinking, so we had fun.

As time went on she got deeper into the S&M scene, earning the nickname Mistress Miltonia, and she became a lot more fashionable as well. She acquired a foot slave, an attractive, physically fit guy who came over to obey orders, and if he did a good job, he got to massage her feet as his reward.

"I've never fucked him and don't think I ever would," she said. "He just cleans the house and stuff."

She spent a few months in New Orleans where she and her Russian dominatrix friend Karissa explored the scene and shared a slave from a Western Louisiana Air Force Base. The kid was at least a

52

decade younger and they rarely allowed him to speak freely because he was a Rush Limbaugh Republican. He was good at following orders, though.

One Sunday morning he needed to get back to the base so he left while everyone was still sleeping. Karissa woke up an hour or so later and called him.

"Where are you? I need cigarettes," Karissa demanded in her gravelly voice.

"Miss Karissa, I needed to get back to the base. Right now I'm all the way out in Baton Rouge," he said.

Karissa sat in complete silence.

"Um, do you need me to come back to bring you cigarettes?" he asked nervously.

"Yeah. I'm 'a need you to come back."

Miltonia was quite open about discussing her lifestyle with anyone. Once, while getting her hair done, she recalled a recent party.

"So Jake, Melissa's husband, was in this coffin with a baby monitor while she and Matt were having sex on top of it…"

But my favorite Early-Mistress Miltonia story takes place during Thanksgiving dinner back in Kansas.

"So what's new with you, Miltonia?" some hapless relative asked.

"Well, I've recently gotten into BDSM," she announced.

## 23. California

I was a leasing agent and was sitting in front of an apartment building in South St. Louis reading the paper while waiting for my appointment. In a full-page ad for Trans World Airlines I saw that a flight to Orange County, California, where my obnoxious friend the Crab lived, was on sale. I'd never been to the west coast and called to tell him I was coming out.

"That's great! But I don't really like Southern California, so we'll drive up to San Francisco."

The Crab was living in an upscale apartment community with his Chinese boyfriend I'd nicknamed Lucky Charms, because of his collection of good luck trinkets.

"It's a long story, but I promised Lucky Charms I wouldn't drink. He hates cranberry juice, so I pre-mix vodka and cranberry in this Ocean Spray bottle and he just thinks I *love* my juice!"

For the first couple of days we explored Los Angeles, San Diego and even went down to Tijuana, Mexico. I forgot the Crab wasn't supposed to drink.

"Want to stop for piña coladas?" I asked.

He must have figured Lucky Charms wouldn't mind, because he joined me for a round—but Lucky Charms was furious and just sat in silence with his arms crossed.

The silent treatment lasted through the night and well into the next day as we were traversing the central valley en route to San Francisco. As you can imagine, it was incredibly uncomfortable. We stopped for lunch and the Crab got up from the booth.

54

"I'm eating in the car," he announced before storming off.

"You must think I'm a bitch," Lucky Charms began, once the Crab was gone, "But the Crab promised me he'd never drink again. He's got major health issues and isn't supposed to be drinking, for starters, but he'll also get so drunk he'll wet the bed in the middle of the night and wake up freaking out, then I have to deal with changing the sheets and taking care of him."

Having Lucky Charms open up to me eased the tension, and once we reached the outskirts of the Bay Area, he was fully relaxed. We dropped him off at his parents' house in Oakland, then crossed the Bay Bridge on a gorgeous sunny afternoon. I could see the Golden Gate, hundreds of sailboats on the sparkling bay, and the city, chest puffed out at the water's edge.

"This is the most beautiful place I've ever seen," I said in awe.

He parked on a hill above the Castro and as I looked around, I said, "I'm going to live here one day. I don't care what it takes, or if I have to live with ten other people. I'm going to live here."

## 24. Meeting Damon at MCC

Metropolitan Community Church was located in an area known as Holy Corners, which was an accretion of five religious buildings and a Masonic temple within a two-block area of the Central West End, including a remarkable cluster of imposing Greek Revival buildings.

With several churches at the same intersection, sometimes people would wander into the wrong place.

When I first saw Damon, an attractive, conservatively dressed, fresh-faced Black man of twenty-three walking in like a young preacher with his excellent posture, serious expression and weathered old Bible, I thought to myself, "He's in the wrong church!"

There was a lot of talk about the upcoming Pride celebrations, so the service was even gayer than normal but he kept sitting there, so I figured he knew where he was. When service let out I hopped and elbowed my way up the isle to catch up with him.

"Hi, I'm Chris," I said as I shook his hand and invited him to stay for the potluck, but he politely declined. I assumed he wasn't interested, and didn't think anything more about it.

Three Sundays later I was working a booth for Metropolis during the Pride Festival when I saw him walking in the crowd. Although I'm horrible with names I remembered his.

"DAMON!" I shouted.

He walked over, dressed more casually than last time, but still very well put together, and we had one of those conversations where the butterflies drown out anything the other person is saying. He took off his mirrored sunglasses and asked if I'd like to go out sometime.

I learned he'd attended services for three Sundays looking for me, but I wasn't around.

Later that evening we went to dinner, then back to my place where we rolled around on the bed and made out. It was then he began sobbing and said, "Please don't leave me. Everyone leaves me."

He'd gone through back to back relationship horrors. The first being James, a guy he loved in college who wanted him to come out of the closet so they could be open about their relationship. When Damon refused, James went skiing over spring break and died in a car accident. A year or so after that he ended up in an emotionally and physically abusive relationship.

I'd gone on a few dates with a guy who would go on to become a local politician, and I wrote him to break if off, explaining I had met someone.

Damon needed me, and I felt the need to protect and take care of him.


## 25. The Bachelor Pad & the Master Plan


Damon arrived carrying a brown paper bag full of groceries with a big loaf of French bread protruding from the top. Planning a nice dinner, he turned on the oven.

"Oooh, you can't use the oven, mice live in there and they figured out how to pee on the pilot light," I said.

Inside he had to be reeling, being the Sultan of Sanitation I'd grow to know, but being on his best behavior, he simply replied, "Oh, okay. We'll work around that."

The big, drafty old Tower Grove flat where Francis and I lived was an acquired taste for most, but for me it was love at first sight with its incredible mahogany millwork—which included columns between the foyer and living room, between the living and dining room, stained glass windows, old chandeliers, etc.

The downsides were that it was infested by mice, that great old chandelier in the dining room would sometimes spark, there was a live wire touching the metal medicine cabinet, so mild electrocution was a daily occurrence, and we lived beneath the local drug dealer who'd often have parties that would go on for days.

Sometimes the cons turned into pros. For example, I'd hang my ferns in the basement window for the winter, and the leaking bathtub drain above perfectly watered them with no effort on my part. They actually grew more over the winter than on the front porch in the summer.

Damon didn't complain, although he was constantly making what he'd call "improvements." A few weeks in we were at Target and I suggested buying a washable cover for the bed since my dog Rox shed so much.

"We don't need that. Soon he won't be sleeping with us" he said.

"Wait a minute! You've got a whole master plan!" I exclaimed, more amused than concerned.

## 26. Advice on Monogamy

Nearly all of our gay role models seemed to be in agreement that gay relationships worked better when there's flexibility built in. This wasn't universal in the community at large, but it was within our group.

Fred & Jim, for example, had been together for fifty years, they were the co-patriarchs of our community of friends, mentors of Ray David and Miss Manny, and didn't believe two men should try to emulate heterosexual couples. They weren't only against gay marriage for that reason, they were against the whole idea of even "coming out."

"Why would you want to bring up that topic and put people in that awkward situation?" Fred remarked.

With Fred and Jim, it seemed to be Fred who had been most likely to cash in on the arrangement. In my relationship, I was Fred. From time to time, when we shared a computer I'd stumble upon a sexual email exchange Damon was engaging in, but we had a gentlemen's agreement and I'd let it be. We felt very civilized about it all and were even known to pontificate about the virtues of our arrangement at parties. The rules were no romance, no dating, and no high risk behavior.

The rules lent themselves to the way I was wired more so than Damon, who wasn't really built for a meaningless rendezvous. He enjoyed flirting, and would sometimes get crushes.

Two guys who were role models for more traditional relationships were the leaders of our Interracial Gay Couples Group at MCC, Andre and Miss Bags. They had a lovely home on Fairview, a heavily gay block in Tower Grove South. Andre was a wiry Black school teacher. Very upright, he carried himself with a masculine confidence. Miss Bags was tall, blond and slender with a whimsical artist's temperament.

Miss Bags's family was from New Orleans, but had lived around the world, from Paris to Curacao. He was quite worldly, as you might expect, and while kind and down to earth, he had the flippant nature of someone who never really had to worry about finances.

After about six months of knowing them, I was at church with Damon when Miss Bags approached and said, "I have the most incredible news. Andre and I are breaking up."

Apparently Andre had fallen for someone else.

We both thought that was a very odd way to preface such news.

## 27. Villa Georgia and the Caged Lions

We already planned to move to a nicer apartment in a four-family flat called The Georgia, which overlooked Tower Grove Park, when Miss Bags told us the news. Interestingly, the unit was vacant because the last tenant, an eccentric man with a public access television show, had a year-long feud with the downstairs neighbor which ended in a physical assault. Soon after, the downstairs neighbor decided to move as well.

"Live downstairs from us!" I excitedly suggested to Miss Bags.

The 1920s-era units were enormous and elegant. While only one bedroom, each had a spacious formal dining room, built-in china cabinets, thick crown moldings, pocket doors, sun room overlooking the park, office, and balconies on the back that conveniently overlooked the backyard across the side street—where for some reason a group of shirtless straight guys in their twenties would pace around and drink beer. It felt like we were looking at a zoo exhibit, so we referred to them as "The Caged Lions."

Miss Bags did move in and we had a great time living in the same building. Many late afternoons were spent together on our balcony talking about the workday and enjoying the scenery. More than once, though, we were in the throes of passion when we'd hear the downstairs door open and Miss Bags shout up, "Can you stand some company?"

## Story Box 2: Judy Garland

I was in a dive bar in San Francisco's gritty Tenderloin when I saw a woman who looked just like Judy Garland. I struck up a conversation with her and learned she was from St. Louis.

"I used to live in St. Louis!" I said excitedly.

"Wow! Where did you live?" she asked.

I began rattling off locations "Eleventh & Shenandoah, Christy Park, 1912 California, 4600 Arsenal..."

"4600 ARSENAL!" she exclaimed, and flipped around to grab a bleach blonde woman behind her. "This guy was your St. Louis neighbor!"

The blonde had been the girlfriend of the main caged lion—the cute guy who would pace around his backyard drinking beer. I told her about the nickname and how we enjoyed watching them from our balcony.

"Yeah, I don't know why he'd do that. He was stupid," she said.

### 28. Widow's Peak

Being a Southerner from New Orleans, Miss Bags was all about hospitality, and apparently down there it was rude to allow a guest to go home without objecting. He even applied this to tricks he met online. Such was the case with Ol' Widow's Peak.

Online he sounded hot, describing himself as a masculine, athletic, fit Black guy. His portrayal was only 25 percent accurate. Miss Bags opened the door to find a short, round, effeminate queen with his hair shaved in some peculiar Star Trek style where it made a V over his forehead, hence the nickname. I thought he was a disaster, but it was the heat of the summer and since Widow's Peak didn't have air conditioning, Miss Bags just insisted he stay, which he did for about three nights.

One of those evenings we all went out to dinner at Clementine's, Widow's Peak told us a story about breaking down in the country.

"My momma was so worried about us being out in the country with nothin' but rednecks around and I said, 'You don't worry about nothin', mamma. Just watch this!' and I got out of that car wearing my Daisy Dukes, opened that hood and just bent over. It wasn't more than *two minutes* (snapping from side to side) that a big ol' country boy stopped to help, and my momma didn't know WHAT to think!"

"Well, I'm surprised she didn't say, 'Here's your one chance, Fancy, don't let me down!'" I quipped.

Miss Bags shared a bed with Widow's Peak for three nights, so we figured they really hit it off.

When he finally went home, we went downstairs to debrief. After a pleasant conversation he stared contemplatively out the front window into Tower Grove Park and said, "You know, I don't find Widow's Peak to be erotic at all."


### 29. Big Faye & Her Men

I met pianist Big Faye through MCC choir director Blaine Festus. He weighed in at about three hundred fifty pounds, and was passionate about Cadillacs and Black men.

Good fortune seemed to shine on him because he always had a music gig, friends would just *give* him Cadillacs, and when it came to his Black gentlemen callers, it was an embarrassment of riches. Driving through North St. Louis men would see him coming and flag him down.

Blaine threw a grand soirée one evening and my group walked in just as he was holding court with tales of his old friend Georgia Leigh, who'd recently been acquitted of jewelry theft.

"...and sitting there on the witness stand was Georgia Leigh *WEARING* a big ol' diamond ring she'd stolen!" he said to uproarious laughter.

Off to the side was Big Faye with a stunningly gorgeous young boxer who'd made his way from North Carolina just to be with him. Although it was the first time he'd ever been in a room full of gay men, he sat on Big Faye's lap all evening and rarely looked away from his smiling round face. Truth be told, we were all a bit envious, but it really seemed to get under Ms. Bags skin in the wake of his breakup.

"I'm sorry, that's just tacky," he'd say about their displays of affection.

Afterwards, we took Miss Bags out to a predominately black gay bar in the hopes he'd have some fun. I was on one side of the booth, Damon on the other, and Miss Bags was in a chair between us with her back to the room.

"Nobody here's even talking to me, but that's okay," he bitterly remarked.

"Miss Bags *nobody* is going to bust into a party of three and start talking to you. You have you have to get up and mingle!" But he wouldn't budge.

I was drinking bottom shelf gin and growing more frustrated by Miss Bags's intractable position while the three other white guys in the club were working the room and mingling. They were like kids in the candy store and each time one would pass I'd try to urge Miss Bags to get up and wander.

Finally there was an unfortunate confluence of events. I began a sentence with the volume sufficient to be heard over the music, but right at that moment the music had stopped. My voice boomed through the bar.

## 30. First House

We all loved living at Villa Georgia and planned on being there for five years, but after only eleven months Miss Bags made an announcement.

"I really want to own my own home again."

We enjoyed living near one another, so we considered buying a two-family flat. One area that seemed ripe for appreciation was Fox Park, a blighted area sandwiched between the more affluent neighborhoods of Compton Heights, where Ray & Manny lived, and Soulard.

Walking around I saw that two townhomes my company used to manage were vacant and being prepared to put back on the rental market. They were great old Italianate attached row houses, circa 1890, with fourteen-foot ceilings and ornate cornices. A maintenance man told me they'd been rented to Section 8 tenants who tore them up, and both households had been evicted.

I left a message with the owner, who lived in Chicago.

"I noticed both of your townhouses on California Avenue are vacant. Would you be interested in selling?"

He then left me a message that began with "Yes!"

We agreed on fifty thousand each. I closed on ours, getting the mortgage in my name and adding Damon to the deed. But just before closing, Miss Bags got laid off from the Christian publishing house where he worked, and I wondered if it was because he'd been buying porn on his work computer.

Anyway, the seller agreed to let him rent until he got another job.

## 31. Francis Marries Well

Our home was looking great. We had it completely repainted in custom colors, rheostats were on all the lights, and we'd gotten a few pieces of new furniture.

With our revolving guest list, we thought of our living room as our talk show set, and we'd seat new guests in a big purple chair near the fireplace to be interviewed. One of the first to occupy the seat of honor was Francis's new girlfriend, Edie.

Francis had a few unusual girlfriends previously, including an older woman named Rosa, who he'd nicknamed Grocery Store Feet after he saw her unattractive toes in sandals. While Francis was pretty conventional sexually, Rosa tried to talk him into a three-way with another man, while the man was sitting right there, and over dinner told me all about how she prefers gay porn to straight.

"I like watching the power play with two guys. I'd totally love to have a dick, and if I did I'd really fuck some ass!" she excitedly said.

I thought Rosa was a riot, but she wasn't right for Francis. It felt like he was her boy toy.

Edie, by contrast, was his speed. She was young, cute, and fresh.

"We met at the Way Out Club, and when he told me he was from Ottawa I thought he was Canadian," she laughed.

Edie told us about a stalker who would watch her through her open window while she slept and whisper to her about how beautiful she was. She and her roommate found out where he lived and confronted him at his little shotgun home with foil-covered windows. He cracked the door and denied everything as he blinked incessantly.

She came from a good family in the upscale mid-county area of Brentwood. Her festive mother had a lucrative restaurant supply business and her father was in the riverboat barge industry. Over the coming years we'd get to know her parents, who were fun people and had us over for lively dinners.

After a few years Francis & Edie were married at the historic DeMenil Mansion and started a family.

## 32. The Crab's Bargain Angel

My obnoxious friend The Crab lost his job in California and was ready for a change. We were always encouraging people to move to St. Louis, and we offered him use of one of our spare rooms.

After drinking and sex, the Crab's favorite pastime was bargain shopping. He got the biggest rush off of buying cheap clearance rack or dollar store items and passing them off as expensive gifts. He'd sometimes put them in upscale boxes, and when the recipient opened them he'd say, "It's a limited edition from Tiffany's."

Once he dragged me to the dollar store and spotted porcelain angels. He picked one up and excitedly said, "My trick John collects angels so I'm going to buy this for him and he'll think I spent a lot of money for it!"

At the register he couldn't contain his enthusiasm and had to tell the broken down redneck gal all about his purchase.

"My friend John's a big sinner but he loves angels..."

### 33. Witnesses

I was talking to the Crab on the front steps one night when we saw a carjacking on the corner. A neighbor had just gotten out of her SUV when three armed men ran up and forced her back in, then drove away. I called 911.

"There's been a carjacking on California and Allen, and they've taken the driver."

The last piece of information was key, because St. Louis Police weren't allowed to chase a vehicle unless someone's life was in danger. The driver was released a few blocks away and back home within ten minutes, but the chase was already in progress and ended with a crash on Forest Park Parkway, under the Union Ave. overpass, which had the feel of a tunnel.

The police asked us to ride with them to identify the suspects. We sat in the back of the cruiser and knew the crash was serious when we saw the blockade half a mile away, at Forest Park and Euclid.

The cop driving us was a real manly guy, and I found myself trying to butch it up. We approached the entrance to the underpass, where ambulances, police cars, and reporters were set up, as well as spectators watching from above.

The Crab put his hand on his collar as if clutching pearls and said, "My God, it's Princess Diana revisited!"

## 34. The Crab's Last Hurrah

The Crab lived with us for two months and then in his own place for another six when he got an offer back in California. He was really high maintenance, with nonstop drama, so we were ready to see him go. He'd already run off Miss Bags with his abrasive comments, spurring his decision not to buy the row house next door and instead move to his parents' luxurious compound outside New Orleans.

He'd arranged his journey west around trick hot spots, so on the first day he was only going as far as Kansas City, which was too close for comfort for us. What if he changed his mind and came back? Or what if there was a Crab emergency? If he was in the state of Missouri and something went wrong, he'd call us.

On his last night in St. Louis he decided to get royally fucked up, and the following morning he showed up at U-Haul still a hot mess.
While urinating in the restroom he fainted, and was found sprawled across the floor in a pool of his own urine, confused and disoriented. He must've told the employee to call me, because I received a message letting me know some of what happened, and when I called back I got the full story. They said he was sent to St. Louis University Hospital.

We checked on him and he seemed fine, although still drunk, and they were keeping him to run tests. Later that evening we were at dinner and missed about a dozen calls from him.

"CHRIS! I was tired of waiting at the damn hospital so I left and I don't know where I'm at. I need you to FIND ME!"

Message two was similar. "I'm wandering through the streets of St. Louis. I don't know where I am. It looks like a bad neighborhood. I need you to come find me!"

Message three, "Dammit Chris FIND ME! FIIIIND ME!" And so on.

He departed a day late, and without incident.

## Story Box 3: One Night Only

I was in Tulsa visiting family and decided to get a group together for drinks at the Bamboo Lounge, which was the oldest gay bar in the state and sat in a desolate part of town near the airport and the dirty bookstores. Back when we were underage, Donald and I used to peep through the wooden fence trying to see the action.

The tired old bar rarely got new blood so my entourage caused quite a stir. A few of the well-worn regulars were jockeying for position, asking who we were and how long we'd be around. We kept stressing we'd only be there that evening and added to the intensity by playing "One Night Only" from the *Dreamgirls* soundtrack minutes before we busted out of there. As we left, phone numbers flew at us like confetti.

A crude and crass guy sitting near us at the bar reminded me of Moe from the Simpsons. I asked about the sex maze that was rumored to be out back.

"Oh, they had to take it out after the raid. The place was shut down for a while and has been slow since it reopened," he said.

His whole world appeared to be that bar, and he seemed to assume it was a major economic engine for the city. He got riled up taking about the raid, arrests, and shut down.

"And *now* the city's complaining about being broke! Well, they really shot themselves in the foot when they raided this place, I tell you! They lost *a lot* of money in sales taxes!" he ranted. "This town can fall in the lake for all I care!"

He asked where I lived and when I said St. Louis, he raised his eyebrows.

"Well, I bet *you* have some stories to tell!" then turned to the person next to him and exclaimed, "St. Louis! Why, he's probably seen more cock than you and me could even dream about!"

## 35. Sowing Discontent

My brother Joe was in town and I had just wrapped up a dazzling tour of the city culminating with the Cathedral Basilica, which has one of the largest collections of mosaics in the world.

"So what do you think?" I asked, fishing for compliments.

"About St. Louis? It's a nice place; I just didn't expect this to be the end of the line. I guess I thought you'd keep moving," he said disappointedly.

I would end up moving within a year of that conversation, and while there were several factors, I point to that interaction as the moment the seeds of discontent were sown.

Sowing seeds of discontent runs in my family, a skill passed down through the generations. Numerous friends have told me I said something that spurred a major geographical move, and Mom likes to tell the story of a family trip to Arkansas to see a friend of my grandfather's when she was seven.

It was 1943 and a coworker of my Granddad Oliver and his brother Leonard left Tulsa to move to a farm his wife inherited. In letters he painted a lovely picture of the good life and invited them out for a visit.

It was hot and dry as the family made the hundred-mile trip. The dust from the gravel roads coated the brush, and when they arrived to a chicken running out of the dilapidated home it appeared the reality wasn't nearly as charming as the rosy reports. Regardless, though, the friend and his wife were happy and proud.

The women and children stayed at the farm while the men went out drinking, and that's when Granddad and his brother began sowing.

"What are you doing out here? You've got chickens running around that Godforsaken wreck of a house!" they started.

As the whiskey poured Granddad put his arm around his buddy and said, "What you've got to do is forget about that dump and move back to Tulsa. *That's* where you need to be! The boss owes me a favor. I can get your old job back!" he promised.

Mom remembers the drunk men returning and the wife's smile turning to a scowl as she was told, "Pack up! We're going back to Tulsa!"

"Whaddya mean pack up?" she exclaimed, but the decision was made and everyone returned to Tulsa together.

## 36. Feather & Lenny

Feather was my first friend in the world and was like a sister. I didn't know what to make of her second husband Lenny's obsession with me and Donald, which was manifested over Facebook.

"Don't you think it's a little odd?" I asked Francis.

"Lenny's led a very sheltered life, and you and Donald are like the cool kids," Francis explained.

Lenny & Feather scheduled their next trip to St. Louis to coincide with Donald's visit. They were staying with Francis and Edie, and we all met for a very bizarre brunch in Soulard, where Lenny hid behind his phone, peeking over the top and giggling.

Donald and I were planning to explore abandoned buildings in East St. Louis afterwards and thought it would be nice to invite him along.

"Lenny, we're going to the East Side after this to explore some ruins. Would you like to come?" I asked.

Still hiding behind his phone, Lenny just giggled and peeked. Not knowing what to make of this, I turned to Edie and whispered softly, "So do you think he doesn't want to go?"

Smiling curiously, Edie analyzed Lenny's behavior and responded, "I'm not sure he knows what you're asking."

## 37. Curse of the Quiver

Miss Manny started seeing a very simple man named Robert who owned a cabin about an hour west of St. Louis on a stagnant, snake-ridden tributary of the Quiver River. They absolutely loved going there every weekend in the summer, despite the nonstop calamites.

Robert preferred to be nude, and he and Miss Manny would spend their weekends drinking excessively and running around naked while remodeling the cabin and doing various other projects.

Once, Robert was thrown from the back of a moving truck when it hit a dip in the dirt road, and another time he was standing on pipes in the back of his truck when he fell and damaged a vertebrae. He spent six months in a massive halo contraption that rested on his shoulders and screwed into his head, which looked like something right out of *Hellraiser*.

One Independence Day, drunk old Miss Manny decided what he needed to do was drive into town to get fireworks. Well, he pulled out onto a divided highway and got into a major accident, then proceeded to jump out of the wreckage and scream at the sober driver. He got a DUI and had to spend every weekend in jail for the next twelve months.

Not long after that, Miss Manny was riding on the tailgate when they hit the same dip in the road that tossed Robert out, and Manny hit his head and lost consciousness. That incident seemed to destroy his filter, because after that he said whatever popped into his mind, much like someone with Tourette's.

Despite all of this misfortune, they were just wild about that cabin. Though they were in the country, there were neighbors around and those folks weren't too wild about Robert being naked on the front porch. One day the police knocked on the door, and both Miss Manny and Robert figured it was because he'd been sitting out there earlier.

"They're going to search the house! We gotta get rid of the toys!" Robert said in a panic while running to the bedroom.

With the police still knocking, Robert threw on a robe, grabbed handfuls of dildos, flailed out the back door, and tossed the toys into the algae-covered waters, probably hitting a snake!

Surprisingly, he wasn't arrested. I still think about those submerged dildos and how people will find them on the riverbanks or standing in mud over the next couple hundred years.

## Story Box 4: Barging In

I once had a tenant named Robbie D who looked like someone wandering around after a nuclear war. About fifty-five, he was very tall and hunched over, with pasty white, pitted skin that looked like you could pull it off in chunks. He had no chin and only a few teeth, which were rotten. He was just hideous.

The old Tudor-style building on Christy Park had about thirty apartments and we were undertaking the big job of putting in central air units. This process took a couple of months from start to finish, and the contractors had to go in and out of the apartments on a regular basis.

Apparently, Robbie D had a fetish for being surprised. It seemed like an embarrassing mistake on the first occasion, when the contractor entered the unit after knocking to find him sprawled out on a recliner masturbating.

It was assumed Robbie D just didn't hear the door, but the scenario kept repeating. After a couple of times the men would bang angrily and yell, "Dammit Robbie, you better not be in there!" only to open up and see him in his recliner going to town on himself. He'd always gasp, clutch a blanket against his chest, and pretend they'd just barged in unannounced.

One of the workmen told me Robbie would sometimes be in the midst of inserting objects into his body when they'd "surprise" him, and that he had a row of teeth on his end table. I wasn't sure if that part was true, but my motto's always been, "Never question yourself out of a good story."

### 38. Post-Filter Party Fix

Ray built a big new house around the corner from his old home, and it featured soaring ceilings, several fireplaces, five bathrooms and as many chandeliers—including one that was Swarvoski crystal. He spared no expense, and a golden age of entertaining ensued at Villa Ray, but Miss Manny's lack of a filter was becoming problematic because he'd insult every single guest over the course of an evening.

I decided to make a party game out of it, and it made all the difference.

"Miss Manny doesn't have a filter anymore since the accident, and will probably insult you. Just keep a mental note of the insults, and we'll see who got the best one at the end of the night."

After that, guests enjoyed the insults. It was also better for Miss Manny because people were more understanding and didn't avoid him. If anything they chatted him up.

Towards the end of one event, Rita Revlon was putting on her coat.

"Oh, are you leaving?" Miss Manny kindly asked. When Rita said yes, Miss Manny curtly replied, "Good!" then shuffled off, grumbling to himself.

## 39. Going Into Exile

I was a volunteer on Al Gore's presidential campaign, and Damon and I were at the official Democratic Watch Party at the Chase Park Plaza. The camaraderie in the room was incredible. People who'd never met were sharing drinks. Florida went blue and everyone cheered. Then Florida began blinking. There was a problem. I wasn't worried, but Damon figured it would be a long night and went on home.

The party continued until the screens went blank, and then the huge caption read "PRESIDENT ELECT GEORGE W. BUSH." It was like a punch in the gut, and then the graphic showed all three branches of government in red.

Growing up in solidly Republican Oklahoma I knew this wasn't good, and would have a devastating impact on the lives of anyone who wasn't heterosexual and white. For example, I don't know anyone—gay or straight, young or old—who hasn't parked and either had sex or gotten close in a vehicle, but if you're gay in a red state, you're likely to be classified as a sex offender if caught. I know people who've had their lives ruined, lost jobs, or had their pictures in some Puritanical paper, all over something that's a rite of passage for every teenager.

I went home and woke Damon. Drunk, but dead serious I said, "We've lost everything. All three branches of government are in Republican control and we're moving to Vancouver."

Damon was up for it, and we began the process of applying for work visas. Since we didn't have a skill Canada was short of, neither of us spoke French, and we didn't have hundreds of thousands of dollars to invest, we had no pathway to emigrate.

I proposed we implement Plan B.

"I vowed I'd live in San Francisco one day, and if we're going to remain in the U.S. during the Bush years we might as well wait them out in the most progressive city."

Damon had some hesitation about moving close to the Crab but quickly got on board.

We put the house on the market and my whole life was consumed with applying for jobs. A company called Milpitas Management called me for an interview, and I borrowed six-hundred dollars from Mom to fly out.

The wind was at our back. I got the job, and the house sold for twenty-thousand more than we'd bought it for a year earlier. We were heading west.

## 40. Thoughts for the Road

Not long before we left St. Louis, we were at a big party for the re-opening of the Continental Building, an art deco skyscraper in Midtown that was mothballed for years but was renovated and made into luxury apartments. We were introduced to a friendly blonde woman who lived in Los Angeles, but was from St. Louis. She shared some thoughts about our move, and one line in particular stuck with me.

"It's a lot easier to make friends in California, but if you ever get a flat you'll want to call one of your St. Louis friends."

## 41. San Francisco

I wanted Damon to have the same first impression of San Francisco I'd had, so we crossed at the Bay Bridge and the city didn't disappoint.

Once we arrived in the Mission he was a bit shell-shocked by the density, San Francisco being the second most densely populated city in the U.S. after New York. I, on the other hand, was swept up in the uniqueness of the moment. I wasn't signing papers and getting keys to the new place for another hour, so we went to a crowded restaurant for lunch—the kind of place where you're inches away from your fellow diners.

"Isn't this an incredible snapshot in time?" I began. "We're in a brand new city, getting ready to start a whole new life, and we haven't even seen our apartment yet!"

I could tell from Damon's deer-in-the-headlights expression he wasn't sharing my excitement about the unknown.

## 42. Garden Court

The new job provided me with an apartment at the Garden Court Apartments, and we drove down Fifteenth Street looking for it. I pointed to the loveliest building on the block and said, "Oh I hope it's that one!" and much to my surprise it was.

Garden Court was a Mediterranean style building where all sixteen units overlooked a central courtyard filled with roses and an avocado tree. It was reminiscent of the building on the soap Melrose Place, but with elderly Latinos in lieu of the young and beautiful.

The building sat a mile south of downtown in the Mission District.

"For some reason the Mission always smells like pee," my friend Rob said the first time he drove me through the area en route to the tonier Castro District up the hill where he lived.
The blocks around our building were overrun with homeless people, prostitutes, and drug addicts. They'd shoot up, piss, shit, and sometimes fornicate just about anywhere. Sometimes they'd even set up shanty towns across the street.

Like all buildings in the Mission, Garden Court was a gated fortress. The contrast between the chaotic sidewalk and the tranquil courtyard immediately beyond the gate was stark.

One stepped on stage when entering the courtyard. Many of the elderly women had their kitchen tables right at their open windows, where they seemed to spend much of their time. Most had lived in this place for years, and when their time came, would die there as well.

A man I'd later befriend named Wes had previously lived in the manager's unit we were occupying, and before I met him I met one or two of his gentlemen callers looking for him.

In addition to my position managing two dozen small buildings around the city, I was the resident manager for Garden Court. I tinkered with the furnace in the basement in the middle of the night, kicked drug addicts off the roof, patrolled the back stairwells, dealt with the police and looked after the inhabitants—who didn't know what to make of a non-Spanish speaking interracial gay couple who just blew in from St. Louie.

### 43. Cast of Garden Court

The whiniest tenant in the building was a middle-aged Guatemalan woman named Elizabeth. I couldn't really blame her for her disposition. In some Central American cultures, one daughter is held back and groomed to be the caregiver of her parents, as was Elizabeth's case.

She lived with her elderly mother in a studio apartment, which unfortunately shared a wall with the noisiest possible tenant, Crazy Carol. Carol was a nocturnal schizophrenic who nicknamed herself "Crazy Carol" and would spend the nights screaming at people over the phone or out the window, or laughing hysterically.

In fits of frustration Elizabeth would pound on the wall and plead, "Carol, *please*, we're trying to sleep!"

In a mocking tone Carol would scream back, *"CAROOOL, PLEASE WE'RE TRYYING TO SLEEP!"* and then laugh maniacally.

So, she had a point about many of her complaints, but even if she was reporting a trivial issue she'd always end with "...and it's awful. Very, very awful".

Elizabeth would also feud with Juanito, a gay Mexican who lived above her. During her arguments with him she'd repeat, "And I'm Guatemalan!"

Nobody knows what that was about.

Juanito called one day in a panic. He was walking down the back stairs past Elizabeth's door and began to bleed from his ass. He was convinced that she and her mother were witches and had cast a spell on him. I assured him they were Catholic, and he seemed okay from then on out.

## 44. Six Month Sabbatical & the Rise of the Power Couple

With my good salary and the free apartment, we were living better on one income in San Francisco than we had on two in St. Louis, and Damon took six months off to regroup as he worked to transition from retail to something different.

One of our large closets had a window and he began raising orchids in there, setting up wire shelving and grow lights. He amassed an impressive collection.

Regardless of my assurances about our financial picture, he felt guilty for spending money while he wasn't working, so I began giving him a few hundred dollars cash on payday for whatever he or we needed.

I helped him get hired on at my company, Milpitas, as a Relief Manager, covering for managers who were on vacation. From there he was quickly promoted to an Assistant Manager, then to a Director position over a residential hotel for formerly homeless people.

We'd always been supportive of one another but at this point we were really in our groove. We'd bounce ideas off of one another, offer support and encouragement. We bought our first new car, which was black with black leather and a sunroof, we spent weekends either entertaining or taking road trips to places like Yosemite or the giant Redwoods in Humboldt County.

Our life together was part adventure, part strategy session. We were young gay men living large in San Francisco.

## 45. Garden Court Old Pervert

Back when San Francisco still had its soul it was very difficult to evict anyone, much less someone who was poor and old, regardless of their behavior.

The thorn in the side of every Garden Court tenant was a dirty old man named Don Marco. He was in his seventies but he seemed absolutely ancient—I would've pegged him at a hundred and ten. He was a short and slight man with a full head of silver hair that was slicked back. To be so frail, there was something so slimy, almost evil about him.

84

Before my tenure he used to stand in his bay window naked. While he stopped doing that, he didn't slow down much. From my kitchen table I could see right into his living room, and one evening glanced up from my dinner to see him getting a lap dance from a prostitute.

He had a strung out, deadbeat son named Pete, who was about thirty-five and rode a juvenile bike around the neighborhood. He'd often trade access to the building's common areas, allowing someone to turn a trick in the back stairwells or sleep on the roof in exchange for drugs.

Pete's girlfriend was a petite blonde crackhead we called Jitterbug because of her jittery motions.

For much of the four years I spent at Garden Court I was at war with Don Marco. His entourage compromised the security of the building and the elderly residents had lived in fear for too long. I told the tenants I was going to put an end to the situation, but they all said they'd heard that before, and that nothing would ever change.

### 46. Jitter Bug

Jitterbug was such a pain in the ass—yelling at the intercom at all hours and sneaking in prostitutes.

One afternoon we heard a commotion from the sidewalk and looked down from the bay window to see an enormous Black woman beating the shit out of Jitterbug, all the while shouting, "FUCK MY MAN AGAIN, BITCH!"

We called 911 as little Jitterbug was thrown around like a rag doll.

Such a scene was not unheard of, especially where Don Marco was concerned.

I didn't see her much in the following days, but when I did she didn't look well. Her coloring was off and she was slightly hunched over.

A friend was visiting from Dallas and we came back to Garden Court to find the coroners at the building. They were in Don Marco's unit.

I climbed the stairs, preparing to see him dead. His door was open and I looked into his filthy apartment to see him very much alive, standing by his bed in a tattered robe. For a moment I thought that meant nobody was dead. Then I looked down to see Pete kneeling on the floor, weeping over Jitterbug's body, her face was blue and she had a plastic object in her mouth that the paramedics left behind.

Jitterbug was, at most, my age. I stood on the roof with my friend, the beacon atop the Transamerica Pyramid shimmering in the night sky, and told him I was shaken by her death. I thought the fact that she was dead while Don Marco was still living was perverse, and I wondered if that occurred to him.

## 47. Life After Jitterbug

So Jitterbug was dead.

Wretched old Don Pedro and his worthless son Pete mourned her by having an entourage of prostitutes and drug dealers over at all hours. They'd stuff paper in the gate latch so street people could come and go with ease. The residents were vigilant about pulling out the paper, and the locked out party would stand at the gate and caterwaul, yelling up to the unit until Pete or some other shady character came down to let them in.

With the help of a few willing tenants who started to believe I'd get something done, I began to document everything. I took notes of all incidents and even photographed the prostitutes coming and going from my top floor window. The latter was more to make them uncomfortable than to obtain useful information.

I handed out whistles and tenants would sit in their darkened windows and blow them when people were coming and going from that unit. It had to be surreal for a high prostitute to walk into the courtyard with camera flashes and whistles from every angle.

If it sounds crazy, it was. And I was just getting started. I was responsible for these elderly people, and my hands were tied as far as evicting Don Marco anytime soon. My strategy was two pronged: build the strongest case possible to evict while making Garden Court as undesirable as possible for the prostitutes and drug dealers.

## 48. The Wonder Twins of Garden Court

Pete was not on the lease and repeatedly claimed he didn't live with his father at Garden Court, and there were times he wasn't around for a few weeks. It was as if Don Marco instinctively knew how far they could push things, how upset everyone could get, and then he'd shut it all down and play the frail and innocent old man for a while.

Others before me tried to evict him only to run up against social workers and tenant advocates who threatened bad press against Dolores Housing, the non-profit developer that owned Garden Court and relied on the city for funding.

We were in the immediate post-Jitterbug era and things were completely out of control at the building. Pete was propping open the back doors and drug addicts were crawling around the building like rats. After a long day at the office I'd get stopped by frantic tenants in the courtyard pleading with me to do something or scolding me for not doing enough.

Damon and I would meet at home for lunch, and our kitchen table overlooked the courtyard and west wing. I thought I saw someone walking on the roof, and the two of us ran up to investigate. A couple was sprawled and shooting up. I yelled at them while Damon called the police.

All of my rage about the overall situation was directed at this couple.

"Chill out man, what's your problem?" one addict said as they shuffled across the roof to the door. We followed them down to the alley, all the while Damon was telling the police where we were and imploring them to come.

Surprisingly, the police did meet us at the other end of the alley. Once detained, the male addict looked at us and asked, "Who are you guys anyway—The Wonder Twins?"

I looked over at Damon and we were dressed almost exactly alike but hadn't noticed.

### 49. The Big Promotion

Twice in a row Peter, the president of Milpitas, hired a property supervisor only to have them back out at the last minute. The open position was for the portfolio that included the Cadillac Hotel, which was owned by titans of the Tenderloin District, Leroy and Kathy Looper.

The Cadillac was their baby. A San Francisco landmark, the historic brick building was built right after the 1906 earthquake as a luxury hotel. The ballroom was once a gym and many notable boxers trained there, including Muhammad Ali.

The Loopers bought the property in 1977 and established the first non-profit "Single Room Occupancy" (SRO) hotel west of the Mississippi, housing about a hundred and sixty low income tenants. That SRO model now dominated the neighborhood, which was a great thing or a horrible thing, depending on who you asked. Because of the structural groundwork Leroy Looper laid, it was nearly impossible to gentrify the Tenderloin, which remained a centrally located island of realness and relative affordability, even as skyrocketing rents displaced longtime residents in the rest of the city.

The Loopers were known by everyone in the neighborhood, from politicians to homeless people on the street, and Leroy was referred to as "The Father of the Tenderloin."

Peter had really sold them on the first hire, and then he assured them he had another great candidate. Now, anxious to have someone in place, they were calling to get an update.

The position of Property Supervisor was a level above me. I'd hoped to get promoted one day—that day came sooner than expected when Peter decided he couldn't waste any more time. I was called to his spacious office upstairs where the dapper Swedish gentleman sat elegantly behind his big desk surrounded by his quirky décor, which included Catholic statues and Japanese pop art.

"Chris, I'd like to offer you the position of property supervisor," he began, going over the details.

I was smiling ear to ear as I listened, then he asked, "So, are you interested?"

"Yes, I am!" I said.

"Good, now here…" he said, handing me the phone as he was dialing. "You need to introduce yourself to Leroy and Kathy. They'll love you!"

### Story Box 5: Tenderloin Tip

If you see a drug addled person pushing a stroller through the Tenderloin, don't be alarmed. There are never babies in the strollers, only cats.

## 50. The Loopers

I'd seen Leroy around the office from time to time, a big and tall Black man in his seventies. We'd never been formally introduced, but he always greeted me with a smile. He and his wife Kathy, who was white and about twenty years younger, welcomed me warmly and soon became like my San Francisco parents.

Conversations with them were fascinating because they were so deeply rooted in that city. They personally knew all the players of the past fifty years including Harvey Milk, Diane Feinstein, every mayor, and even cult leader Jim Jones.

Leroy came up from the streets back East. In his younger days, the Black Panthers took one of his men, so Leroy shot up their headquarters.

## 51. Magali

The on-site Director of the Cadillac was a tough Cuban woman named Magali. She'd been there for about ten years, which was highly unusual for an SRO. Those positions were grueling, dealing with formerly homeless people who sometimes had severe mental health issues and occasionally turned out to be violent criminals.

I was once in court with her on an eviction, and the judge asked the defendant, a strapping man with a long rap sheet, why he didn't talk to Magali if he was having issues with his unit, as he claimed.

The man stuttered and fumbled, then said "Uh, your Honor, I be afraid of Miss Magali!"

Magali was my direct report, and despite her reputation as an aloof and intimidating figure, we got along great. Once or twice a month I'd take her to the Cliff House, a famous San Francisco restaurant overlooking the Pacific.

When a major incident happened at one of my buildings, the managers would call me on my cell, but Magali would just handle it and leave a message on my office line. I once returned to her voicemail from Christmas Eve. A tenant broke a bottle over another tenant's head, and in a dry tone, Magali began, "Well it's not turning out to be a Norman Rockwell Christmas at the Cadillac."

## 52. Chatters Introduction

When we moved to San Francisco we happened to fall in with a group of friends originally from St. Louis. It began when the Crab dated a towering, gorgeous man named Rob, who was originally from the St. Louis suburb of Edwardsville, Illinois.

I'd flown out for the job interview and Rob was with him when he picked me up from SFO. I couldn't figure out why in the world Rob chose the Crab, but I later learned he'd just come out of the closet when they met at Berkeley's only gay bar, The White Horse Inn. The Crab struck Rob as sophisticated and worldly, and easily dominated him with his assertive personality.

Their relationship was short lived as Rob became surer of himself and spread his wings, but much to the Crab's chagrin, Damon and I remained friends with him after the breakup, and watched him transform from a shy man to the hottest socialite in the Castro.

Two of Rob's childhood friends in the area were his roommate Molly, and a woman we called Chatters, who was a librarian and also worked at tech startups. I nicknamed her Chatters because she was always chattering in the backseat of the car on weekend trips, like a backup singer, lightly echoing what others were saying.

"Chatters was briefly married in Chicago, then came out here and finds the craziest, cheapest living situations because she doesn't like paying a lot for rent. She'll live in her car sometimes, rent a closet..." Rob began. "A few months ago she flew all the way to New Zealand and a drug dog smelled pot residue in her jeans, so they put her on the next flight back."

I ended up finding Chatters an incredible deal on a rent-controlled apartment around the corner from Garden Court, and she and her boyfriend Stormcloud—a nickname I gave him for his grumpy demeanor—spent nearly every Saturday evening with us, sometimes at beach bonfires but mostly at our apartment, where we'd drink, listen to music, tell stories and write drunken poetry.

One poem about Chatters began: "Chatters rhymes with ease, possibly because she's half Chinese."

## Story Box 6: Lilly Street

I managed a row of stately Victorians once owned by a non-profit called the Zen Center, and our company inherited the tenants, an eccentric collection of characters who'd lived there since the seventies.
Two had been feuding since 1982, and one wrote long letters about conspiracies her neighboring nemesis was supposedly involved in, clandestine activities designed to make her go crazy and move. She came in one morning demanding I resolve the issues.

"Ma'am, I've reviewed your file, and I was in the second grade when this all started."

The tenant I had the most difficulty with was a burned-out hippie named Silvia, who I suspect had done an enormous amount of LSD in her youth and smoked pot every day since.

She had a habit of leaving the doors open for stray cats, and of course, the rug was urine soaked. After the annual Section 8 inspection, we were required, once again, to replace the carpet.

The flooring guy called and said Silvia refused to let him lay the new carpet until the floors were sealed, insisting the problem hadn't been cat pee, but some water issue under the house causing moisture to seep up through the floor.

"The floor must be sealed or else we'll have to go through this all over again and it'll get blamed on the cats!" Silvia insisted.

I dropped what I was working on and went to the house, where she told me all of this in person. I calmly and slowly explained the law of gravity to her.

"Silvia, water drips downward. You have a big, deep basement here, so for water to seep through your floor, your entire basement would have to be submerged. There'd be so much water that it would be shooting out of the basement windows and flooding the streets. The wooden floors would be warped and rotten from all the water."

Not quite convinced, but overwhelmed with the amount of information I'd given her, she brushed back her long stringy hair, paused, and said, "Chris, what you're saying makes a lot of sense, and I don't know how to respond to it."

## 53. Garden Court: The Wall Shitter

We began to notice shit splatters running down walls in the neighborhood, and would sit with Chatters and Stormcloud and ponder who the wall shitter was. We'd become familiar with the homeless people camping all over the place, but none seemed like the culprit.

One day I was walking down Julian Street when a woman, wearing a long T-shirt as a dress with drugstore flip flops, was walking on the other side of the street carrying a large stack of T-shirts. She shouted, "HEY! Do you wanna buy some T-shirts?" Before I could reply she said, "OH! Hold on!" and squatted over the hood of a little sports car and showered it with diarrhea splatters.

The mystery was solved.

Another time we were walking to the 16th & Mission BART station and a homeless woman was sprawled out on the ground, right in the path of the escalator, masturbating with a look of sheer oblivious ecstasy on her sun-drenched face.

### 54. Garden Court: Bicycle Chick

A curly headed blonde chick on a bicycle started coming around. She seemed like Pete's new girlfriend, and was always yelling at the intercom and coming and going at all hours.

One afternoon she was causing a huge scene at the gate, yelling up to Don Marco's open bay window that she needed her jeans because they had her key in the pocket.

"PLEASE GIVE ME MY JEANS! I NEED THE KEY," she yelled repeatedly for a good half hour. Everyone was looking out their windows except for Don Marco and his worthless son.

My blood was boiling and I marched downstairs to the gate.

"I just need my—" she started to say before I interrupted.

"We all know why you're here. We've heard you for the past thirty minutes. We heard you last night at 2 a.m. That miserable old fossil obviously doesn't care about your plight. You should get some better friends. Meanwhile, you need to leave!"

Hanging her head, she mumbled in a sorrowful tone, "I just need my key..." and wandered off, pushing her bike in the street towards the busy 15th & Mission intersection, where she was narrowly missed by several honking motorists.

She seemed like a nice lady, and I actually felt sorry for her. The next time I encountered her at the gate I said, "You should be careful. People die in that unit!"

She wadded her face up with concern and replied "Oh...you mean Cathy (Jitterbug). Yeah, that old man's really mean. Once he hit me with a cane. Yeah, man, thanks for the tip."

## 55. Garden Court: Peek-A-Boo

As I mentioned earlier, I once looked out the window and saw Don Marco getting a lap dance in his living room. The viewings could and did work both ways. Not only was the courtyard narrow, but the French windows were usually swung open, so one didn't even have the slim privacy afforded by a window pane.

Mistress Miltonia came to visit with an obnoxious new boyfriend named Doug who was in the music business and had recently spent a few years in Los Angeles. He was very LA, and was always name dropping.

San Francisco and Los Angeles had very little in common, as San Franciscans were quick to point out. Anytime Mistress Miltonia would admire something about San Francisco, Doug would chime in with something like, "Oh, I know! I miss that so much about LA."

We were at work and they decided to get amorous on our futon, where they'd been sleeping. In the middle of the rendezvous, as Miltonia was straddling Doug, she looked over and saw the old widow across the courtyard watching her from her kitchen table. When their eyes met the old woman grimaced and quickly yanked the curtain, as if she were suddenly offended.

## 56. Iraq War Protests

We'd only been in San Francisco a couple of months when my old friend Elaine, who'd once lived in my closet, flew out for a visit. It was the eve of the Iraq War and protests were brewing over Bush's planned "Shock & Awe" campaign.

Stuck in downtown traffic on a rainy afternoon we noticed people running everywhere. I turned on the radio and learned the war had begun.
Elaine thought this kind of pandemonium must be occurring nationwide, not understanding the average American was sitting at an Applebee's enjoying chicken tenders.

For many days bands of protesters roamed the city day and night as police and news helicopters relentlessly hovered above. The constant chopper sound made us feel like we were under siege. We'd watch the entertaining motley groups of protesters, many on bicycles, from the bay windows of our apartment, which were like our own opera boxes to the city.

The news would show frustrated drivers stuck in traffic because the protesters had shut many streets down. "I'm being held hostage in San Francisco!" a red-eyed commuter told the reporter.

I, too, would be swept up in these protests, and there's nothing like being a part of a massive group, the beat of the drums, the costumes and signs.

Standing at my window one morning I saw two homeless guys passing one another on the street below, each with their respective carts. One said to the other, "Hey, are you going to the protest downtown?"

The other replied excitedly, "YEAH, I'm going! What's it about?"

We decided to get Elaine away from the chaos for the afternoon and took a drive down the coast. When we were almost home, sitting at the 15th & Mission light with the windows down, we saw the regular group of homeless people hanging out to our left, then in a deep tone one man said, "Oh........my.........God."

From our right came a parading Black transsexual in a beret with her collar pulled down below her exposed post op breasts. She was dancing in the crosswalk, performing for us and the elderly white couple in the neighboring Cadillac, who desperately tried to pretend she wasn't there.

Elaine was laughing hysterically as the performer leaned over the hoods of the cars while titillating her nipple with a folded dollar bill.

## 57. The Crab's Three Tiers

The Crab had three tiers of men in his life. At the top was Lucky Charms. The Crab lived in the city, and Lucky Charms lived with his family in Oakland, but they had a standing date every Sunday and their finances were entangled. The Crab always spoke of coming from great wealth and said he was coming into a large sum of money when he hit a certain age. I had no idea if this was true but suspected it was why Lucky Charms tolerated him.

The second tier were boyfriends who typically lasted one to three months, and were often Filipino. He always wanted us to meet them, which they'd take as a great indicator the relationship was going well. We felt sorry for them, especially one we called Imelda Marcos.

"I know he drinks way too much, and we may have to deal with serious health issues down the road," Imelda said to my surprise, revealing his long-term thinking.

The Crab loved to boast about his size 30 waist, but he was muffin topping big time. One evening we were waiting on the train when he started in about how trim he was and Imelda reached down and grabbed a big chunk of his side fat, as if to see if it was an illusion of his clothing. He was wrecked.

"Don't do that!" he barked.

On the bottom tier were the tricks he'd meet online. He loved to go on about his latest sexual conquest and I'd normally zone out because they all ran together, but one day in the middle of a story he said, "...and so I fucked him, and you know he's a eunuch, and then the other guy..."

"Wait a minute! You gloss over the only interesting part of this story?" I said.

It turns out the trick wasn't really a eunuch, but he did have a penis the size of a peanut.


## 58. Pete Sampras's Wedding

After too many cocktails, the Crab was infamous for his fantastical tall tales and fabrications. One of my favorites was the oft told story about him being the best man at tennis pro Pete Sampras's wedding.

He never remembered having told a story before, so I began having fun by inserting something random out of left field and acting like it had been part of the tale, then watching him work it in without skipping a beat.

Donald, his partner Evan, and friend Kim were visiting from Oklahoma City and we met the Crab for a drink in the Castro. He began to tell the Pete Sampras story and towards the end I said, "OH! Don't forget the part about the cake!"

There had never been anything said about a cake, but he flung his limp hand out and said with a big grin, "Oh, I'm getting to that!" and then continued, "So I thought Pete was trade (gay slang for bi and willing) and hit on him after the wedding. Well, I guess he wasn't because he made a *big* scene and kicked me out. But before I left I snagged the top of the wedding cake and ran out the door. It's still in my freezer!"

Later in the evening, Donald and I went to the South of Market bars and Evan got stuck Crab sitting. They split a taxi once the bars closed, and when the driver pulled over to drop off the Crab he turned to Evan, and slopping drunk, nonchalantly put his hand on Evan's leg and asked, "So, did you and Donald wanna have a three way?"

## 59. Mr. Furley

My company hired Jay, a middle-aged alcoholic, to manage Murray Senior Apartments, a small building for formerly homeless seniors in the Tenderloin. The position was hard to fill because it didn't pay much, was in a rough neighborhood, and only came with a small studio apartment. Jay was right at home in the area, though. His favorite gay bar where he tied one on every night was right around the corner.

The corporate office where I worked offered the illusion of privacy with partial walls, but everyone could hear everything. Jay was there reading orientation materials when his phone rang and he answered it.

Like many drunks, Jay was really loud. His voice had one volume setting which was "Loud Bar." His conversation, which I could hear clearly from my cubbyhole around the corner, was about a hustler-type character he brought home to his new company-provided apartment.

"Yeah, he did. Well, he's mostly straight so he just took his shirt off," he began.

At this point I started to get embarrassed as a fellow gay, then he continued, "Yeah, he wants to move in, and I'm like Hell no! If I can't fuck your butt!"

At that point I intervened, whispering, "Everyone can hear you."

His supervisor was planning to let him go when she decided to move to the East Coast and I was assigned his property. Overall he was doing a good job. The building looked great, the social workers and tenants had warmed up to him and he lovingly cared for all the plants on the back decks.
A few of the elderly tenants were a lot like teenagers, doing drugs and sneaking people in and out, and I had to coach him on keeping his cool with them. For instance, an elderly gay man would sneak in a meth addicted trick, then beg Jay to kick him out at three in the morning when he created a disturbance. Finally one night, Jay's head was pounding from his hangover and he exclaimed, "YOU CAN'T KEEP SNEAKING HIM IN HERE, YA OLD WHORE!"

Personally I found him wildly entertaining, and when Donald was in town I brought him by Jay's regular bar to meet him. Donald instantly nicknamed him "Mr. Furley" after the landlord on Three's Company because he thought they looked alike.

Of course, Mr. Furley was three sheets to the wind. After only about twenty minutes he put his hand on Donald's leg and asked, "So, are you horny?"

It took him awhile to warm up to his new nickname. A turning point was the night the non-profit owner of the building he managed held a big fundraiser. We attended it together and afterwards we went to a Polk Street bar where I turned his nametag around and wrote "Mr. Furley."

Two attractive guys stopped to ask why we were so dressed up.

"You've heard of Mr. Furley? Well, here he is, and I'm his assistant!" I boasted.
They were starstruck, apparently unaware that Mr. Furley was a character played by Don Knotts, who was long dead. Not to mention Jay would be thirty years younger than Knotts.
Settling in at the bar, I sensed he was thinking about those boys, then sure enough he got up and said, "I'm gonna go find those guys who think I'm Mr. Furley."

### 60. Rainforest Café

"Lucky Charms wants to treat you guys to dinner at Rainforest Café tonight," the Crab said.

This was strange because we weren't close with Lucky Charms and hadn't even seen him in nine months. We weren't excited about traipsing down to Fisherman's Wharf to eat at the theme restaurant, but we thought it was really nice to be invited, so we went.

At dinner, Lucky Charms was polite, but not overly friendly. He paid the bill and we all headed out. The following weekend over drinks I asked, "What spurred Lucky Charms to invite us to dinner?"

The Crab laughed mischievously. "Oh, he didn't really invite you, he didn't even know you were coming until a few minutes before. I just said that."

## 61. The Northern Hemisphere

One thing I loved about my job was representing the organization at splashy charity functions. These events were old hat to my seasoned coworkers, but I found rubbing elbows with the glitterati and local dignitaries like Mayor Gavin Newsom really glamourous.

Oftentimes the events included an auction, and one item up for bid intrigued Damon: "A New Zealand Getaway." Neither of us had been, and Mom, who'd never travelled abroad, had mentioned she'd like to go there someday.
The drinks were flowing and we got so swept up in the excitement we inadvertently bid against one another, not considering that the auctioneer had no idea the guys in the back were bidding as a couple.

The moment I won, it hit me that airfare was not included. The owner of the cottage came to shake my hand and I must've looked like a deer in the headlights as I wondered what I'd just done.

The next morning, my voice hoarse from the auction shouting, I called Mom. "Well, I hope you still want to go to New Zealand 'cause I rented a house there."

We pushed the trip out eleven months to give us time to pay for the flight, and off we went, along with Mom and her best friend Jane. On the twelve-hour flight, Mom and Jane were blocked in by a middle-aged Australian woman who downed wine until she passed out—and remained out for hours.

Mom had to climb over her a few times to get to the restroom, accidentally kicking and tripping over her sprawled legs. At one point, Mom got sick and some of her vomit leaked out of the bag onto the Aussie. When this gal finally roused herself she didn't seem to notice her bruised legs or moist pant leg. Or maybe she did.

"More wine" she said to the attendant.

The trip went well. This was during the Bush versus Kerry election and signs were in windows reading, "Tell an American to vote."
Damon fell in love with New Zealand and was depressed about leaving. On the flight home as we were crossing the equator, I presented him with an elaborate drawing on a cocktail napkin. I'd drawn a compass with a circling airplane, and in fancy script the message read "Welcome to the Northern Hemisphere."

He took a cursory glance, then turned away and mumbled, "I don't like the Northern Hemisphere."

## Story Box 7: East Coast Dancer

Lead abatement work was being done to our apartment so we were put up at the aging Travelodge motor inn around the corner. It was dated and crummy, but being situated at Market & Valencia, was walking distance to the Mission, the Castro, and Downtown.

We were drifting off to sleep when our neighbors behind the adjoining door returned from a big night out at the clubs pumped full of adrenaline.

"I'm from the *East* Coast and I dance with my whole body!" one of the disembodied voices boasted. "All night people kept coming up to me like, 'Whoa! You're so cool!'"

The other disembodied voice seemed much more level headed.

"Wait a minute. I was with you all night and didn't hear anyone come up and say, 'Whoa you are so cool,'" but the East Coast Dancer was unfazed and kept boasting.

We could hear every word, and when they decided to grab something to eat, I jumped out of bed and penned a note to place on their front door while they were out.
"I just wanted to let you know that I watched you dance all night and thought to myself 'WHOA! You are SO COOL!' but I didn't say anything because I'm sure everyone tells you that. xoxo"

Less than five minutes later the pair returned and there was a moment of silence as the note was read and digested.

"No number? What the fuck am I supposed to do with this when there's no number?!" exclaimed the East Coast Dancer.

"Dude, someone's fucking with you," the level-headed voice replied.

"No, somebody followed us home. And I'm not comfortable with that."

## 62. Garden Court: Bonding with Carol

Carol, the nocturnal schizophrenic, was desperate for human contact and whether you ran across her in person or she got you on the phone, she'd talk a mile a minute without pausing, because she knew when she paused the person she was speaking to would take that opportunity to end the conversation.

She'd call me at the office once or twice a week, and I decided to just let her rip. I put her on speaker and turned the volume down low, much like listening to the radio. I thought it was healthy for her to get it all out, so I wouldn't chime in until I needed to make another call or leave for an appointment. I wouldn't interrupt her if I simply needed to get some coffee from the kitchen, or run to the restroom. I'd just let her keep talking.

One day she was in the middle of her rapid thought stream when she suddenly skidded to a stop.

"So, um, well, what do you think about all that?" she asked.

Of course I had no idea what she'd been saying, so I replied, "Well, Carol I just don't know what to think!"

107

"Oh, I know!" she said, and proceeded to talk at full speed.

She'd grown to trust I wasn't going to cut her off, which was a breakthrough. Schizophrenia has no bearing on one's intellect, and Carol was very knowledgeable about history and many other topics. We grew to genuinely like one another, and when she was no longer my tenant, we exchanged Christmas and birthday cards for many years.

There was a homophobic tenant at Garden Court who was really friendly to me but would say hateful things about me to other tenants. Carol let that slip one day, and when I asked her to elaborate, she seemed like she regretted mentioning it, and wanted to spare my feelings.

"Oh, Chris don't worry about her. It's just her mental health issues."

## 63. Big Changes at Garden Court

Garden Court was a bad fit for Carol for many reasons. Since it was a wood structure with hollow walls, her noisy way of living disturbed neighbors, and since she had a prosthetic leg, the stairs getting to the courtyard and then up to her unit were laborious, and the doorways were too narrow for the wheelchair she thought she'd soon require. I thought of her when an opening came up in a solid masonry building that was once occupied by the telephone company and built to survive an atomic bomb. There was a ramp, an elevator, and the apartment was a corner unit above the office, with common hallways on two sides. It was by far the most soundproof unit in our entire portfolio.

She preferred it because her unit at Garden Court was a studio, and this was a one bedroom. Plus the new place was in a safer part of the Mission.

For years I'd listened to Elizabeth complain about how horrible it was to live on the other side of the wall from Carol, how for a dozen years she'd hardly slept, about the anxiety it had caused her and her mother, how it was awful, "very, very awful," so I was excited to personally deliver the news that Carol was moving.

"Elizabeth, I have great news. Carol is moving to another building!"

A surprised look flashed over her face, followed by a brief, blank stare, and then, "I'm glad you're here. My toilet has been running for days and it's awful. It's very, very awful."

### 64. Pete's Meltdown

I finally gathered enough evidence against Don Marco for our attorney to file for eviction. Pete made it clear he was planning to fight us, but I felt ready.
In the meantime, I kept up my patrols of the building, which included walking the roof and checking all access doors. One Saturday, Pete was home alone getting high, and the sound of walking on the roof made him so paranoid he called the police. When they arrived I followed them to Don Marco's unit where Pete was pacing and babbling.

"Someone's trying to get in this place. I just need to nail the windows shut, that's what I need to do, just nail the windows shut," he said.

The police, who had been unhelpful until now, actually took him in for an evaluation, and after that Don Marco's daughter decided to go ahead and move him instead of fighting.

The long Don Marco nightmare was over.

## 65. Dolores Housing

Our parent company, Dolores Housing, developed and owned properties, and the subsidiary I worked for, Milpitas Management, managed them along with the properties of other clients including the Loopers.

When I first set foot in the offices of our parent company, it was culture shock. I had just moved from St. Louis, where meetings happened on time, people were dressed in suits, etc. After wading past small children playing I arrived in the conference room where we all waited fifteen minutes for the extraordinarily sexy executive director, Enrique Lopez, who finally arrived dressed in an open collar shirt—partially revealing his hairy, muscular chest —jeans, and sandals, and then proceeded to begin the meeting while eating a huge, messy burrito he was dipping in salsa.
Development was highly political in San Francisco, and Dolores Housing was the darling of city government at that time and was very much on the inside track for development deals.

In turn, if City Supervisor Weekly was opposed to a development project in town, the tenant coordinators at Dolores, who were funded to provide or connect people with services, would rally tenants to protest.

Gail, a social worker from an outside agency, was at such a protest where dozens of formerly homeless tenants were raising hell.

"One tenant was particularly animated and passionate, yelling, pounding on the walls, and then he approached a tenant coordinator and asked in a very childlike way, 'Am I done now?' and I was like, whoa! This man has no clue what he's even protesting about!"

The board of directors, many of whom had founded the organization decades earlier, were increasingly uncomfortable with these political activities and worried about staff endangering their non-profit status. They began to clamp down, which angered Extraordinarily Sexy executive director Lopez, who was adamantly opposed to limiting political activities. At an impasse, the board terminated him, which put them on a collision course with the City and the majority of their own employees.

As an employee of their subsidiary, I wasn't in the chaos initially. Our president, Peter, was masterful at shielding us from the ups and downs of the parent company, which was always more volatile than smooth sailing Milpitas.

## 66. Coup d'état

A plan was hatched by City insiders and Dolores staff to replace the board. In advance of the next open board meeting, tenant coordinators falsely told people in Dolores properties that the board wanted to turn their affordable units into condos, and they needed to pack the meeting to register their opposition.

Board members arrived to an auditorium packed with outraged people shouting, crying, and gesticulating, and they were caught completely off guard.

In a theatrical production, a young activist with a bullhorn took over the meeting while people assisting him placed a chair behind each board member as he announced their replacement to cheers and chants from the rowdy audience.

Apparently, they expected the board would resign on the spot, and then they'd take control. But these weathered older folks were tough, and many had come out of Nicaragua where's they'd cut their teeth on political unrest. They weren't surrendering the empire they'd built from nothing over the past thirty years just because of a raucous meeting. So, the coup plotters went to Plan B.

## 67. Plan B

The new plan was to tar the board as anti-union, force Dolores Housing to collapse, and then the powers that be, led by City Supervisor Weekly, would usher their enormous assets to a waiting non-profit where the old gang would regroup and resume their old ways of doing business.

On company time, employees called governmental entities, funders, development partners, donors, and anyone they could think of to tell them not to cooperate with Dolores Housing until the anti-union board resigned. Several pending development deals fell apart within months, with Chinatown rival Red Dragon Development reaping the rewards.

The board brought back a former director, Jorge Wheeler, and he attended the Milpitas holiday party at John's Grill in Union Square. It was great for Wheeler to see friendly faces at the party, since day and in and day out he was surrounded by a hostile staff, with a couple of exceptions, including his executive assistant, Maria Shamos.

Damon had been upset about the way his tenants were being manipulated by Dolores staff, and I suggested he visit with Wheeler at the party. The two of them ended up talking for over an hour, and the following week Damon was hired as director of resident services for Dolores, a major leap in his career. The tough assignment was to revamp the department and to fire anybody who refused to get on board.

Of course, like Wheeler, Damon was loathed by the staff and immediately the union filed grievances on him. Meanwhile, staff expanded from targeting the company as a whole and began targeting individuals. The first shot across the bow came when one called the husband of Maria Shamos and said she was having an affair with Wheeler, which may or may not have been true.

Then they came after our apartment.

## 68. Palace of Perks

Per San Francisco code, any building with fifteen or more units had to have an on-site manager, which is why Garden Court always had a manager's unit.

The coup plotters launched a website called Save Dolores Housing, where they made their claims about the organization becoming anti-union, anti-worker, and anti-tenant. They also ran an exposé about our apartment, claiming we were displacing a low-income family as the result of a shady backroom deal.

At first we kind of got a kick out of the whole thing, nicknaming our apartment the Palace of Perks, but then the situation made me feel fatigued. Being targeted at home was disconcerting.

With our whole life consumed with Mission District drama, we'd sometimes make a left at the front gate and follow 15th Street all the way to the top of Buena Vista Hill. From that vantage point we could put it all into perspective. We could see where the Mission began near the Armory, where it ended at Bernal Hill, we could see San Francisco Bay and the giant ships, and on a clear day we could see all the way to Mount Diablo in the East Bay.

## 69. Forked Tongue

We'd been studying the way City Supervisor Weekly operated at public hearings. In particular, I noticed his strategy when losing an argument with a constituent.

"The citizen has one or two minutes to speak, and the timer is visible to all parties," I began during a war-room strategy session, "and when the person is winning the debate Weekly will keep them talking past their allotted time, and the second he gains the upper hand and trips them up he says, 'Time's up' and cuts their mic. We all need to be aware of the time and not fall into that trap."

When friends of Dolores Housing packed a meeting at city hall, all the preparation served us well. Damon said his piece at the mic, and with fifteen seconds to spare Weekly tried to lure him into a trap.

"Supervisor, you can put that forked tongue back in your mouth," Damon said to cheers from the gallery and protests from other supervisors.

The following issue of San Francisco's alternative newspaper had a piece about Weekly's war on our organization that was favorable to us, with the headline Doublespeak with Forked Tongue.


## 70. A Turnkey Operation

In the midst of the turmoil and uncertainty in San Francisco, my old college landlord, who I'd nicknamed Caligula, contacted me with an incredible opportunity. His Norman, Oklahoma-based company just doubled in size with the acquisition of an Oklahoma City portfolio that he didn't even want, but was too good of a deal to pass up. He wanted to bring me in to run it, and in a couple of years I could buy him out.

With all the drama at Dolores Housing, and our apartment being tied to my job, it seemed like exploring the opportunity was the grown-up thing to do. Caligula had given me my first real estate listing when I was only nineteen, and the idea of coming full circle struck me as romantic.

We flew to Oklahoma City where I laid eyes on Caligula for the first time in ten years. He looked exactly the same; he was in great shape and was happy to see me. The first night we were invited to his palatial compound where we were wined and dined, and the next day we were swept up in house fever as he showed us lovely properties which seemed free compared to San Francisco, where despite our substantial income, we couldn't even hope to buy anything.

I rode with Caligula, who'd driven to Oklahoma City from Norman, while Damon rode with Donald. Being a gardener, Damon was really excited about having a yard and would always bypass the house and survey the grounds first while the rest of us took the more conventional tour. He was still in the yard of one house when I found Donald and Caligula in the living room and felt like I was interrupting something. I could tell Caligula was attracted to Donald, for starters, but it seemed something more was going on. When Caligula drove me to the next property I got the impression Donald was really grilling him about his plans for me.

"Your friend Donald's protective of you," he remarked.

We returned to San Francisco and Damon was getting great responses from the resumes he'd sent out. He flew back to Oklahoma City for an interview where they said, "We look forward to making you an offer."

116

We felt confident pulling the trigger on a stately Dutch Colonial that once belonged to a player in the infamous savings and loan crisis of the 1980s. The two-story home had great curb appeal with its wide, formal sidewalk, substantial entryway, and side entrance complete with a portico. The cherub statues on each side of the front steps were a bit much, but so was I.

We began tying up loose ends in California.

## 71. Leaving San Francisco

As we were packing up our Garden Court apartment, I felt in my gut that moving to Oklahoma might be a mistake. California had been really good to us, we were both making great money, we had a coveted place in the city, and despite everything, we were comfortable. But I'd always been averse to not following through on commitments. The wheels were in motion and we were going.

One of the great things about being a San Franciscan was the camaraderie. It's thought that most people are where they are as the result of inertia, but San Franciscans travelled thousands of miles over deserts and mountains, or across half a world of oceans to live in this magical city perched on the edge of Western civilization, nestled in the clouds. San Franciscans were San Franciscans by choice, not accident.

In discussing the parallels between San Francisco and the lost city of Atlantis, Mrs. Madrigal, the eccentric landlady from Armistead Maupin's Tales of the City, repeats the folklore that San Franciscans are reincarnated Atlanteans. We migrate to the city because we instinctively know we must return to the sea together.

The harshest reality of this magical city that welcomed and celebrated us was that the camaraderie's withdrawn once you decide to leave. Perhaps if we were going to Portland to settle down or New York to ramp up, but leaving for Oklahoma? Nobody could figure that out.

This hit me the hardest at a party hosted by our friends Ted and Alexandra a day or two before our departure. They'd recently purchased a condo in an Art-Deco high rise and had hosted several fun parties, but I attended this last one alone and it was a completely different experience.

The hosts were wonderful but everyone else was as cold as ice. People I had lively conversations with in the past would simply say, "So I hear you're moving," and then they were done. The biggest cold shoulder came from a woman who was raised in Dallas, which was ironic since that city had long been the bane of my existence.

I awkwardly stood alone near the food, downed a few strong drinks, and then discreetly left to pay a final visit to my favorite haunts in the Tenderloin. It was early evening and the sky still had some light. I looked up at the fire escapes, the clouds, and the neon signs. I wanted to feel the city before it was too late. I felt so lonely.

## 72. Chatters in the Rearview

Chatters and Stormcloud came to see us off as we loaded the last of our things. Our garage had always had graffiti on the walls, and in those last few minutes I added a tribute to the four of us. I drove away from Garden Court watching Chatters wave in the rearview mirror.

Our next stop was Oklahoma City.

## 73. Caligula Realty Intro

In a darkened room littered with beer and liquor bottles, Caligula woke up around 3 a.m. to the sounds of sex. He'd been partying with several employees of his real estate investment company and college kids from the local university, where his partner Mills was a high-ranking official.

As everything came into focus he saw his young handsome maintenance guy, Danny, ramming himself into his plump wife as he pinned her against the wall. Danny's father was also an employee, and Caligula had known Danny since he was a boy. It was an open secret that Caligula coveted the young man and would do anything for him. When he finally noticed Caligula watching, Danny turned said softly, "Just jack off."

In an unlikely Great Plains college town the employees of Caligula Realty lead lives that were insular, intertwined, and decadent. A wealthy alcoholic sex-addict, Caligula created a life for himself on his own terms. Behind the walls of his company, he demanded blind obedience, and behind the walls of his residential compound, he required absolute discretion.

## 74. Caligula Realty: Rough Landing

Between the time I accepted the job and the time I arrived there'd been a seismic shift at Caligula Realty. Brassy, Caligula's bosomy assistant who was in the midst of a tumultuous divorce, had begun sleeping with his business partner Stan. This had elevated her standing considerably.

When Caligula first went through the roster with me, he simply referred to Brassy as "one of the office ladies," and now she was calling the shots. Being in charge of payroll, she was aware I made more than her, which didn't help matters.

My first day they had me report to their Norman office, which was in a prefabricated metal structure behind a car wash, and put me to work at the reception desk taking rent payments from the walk-ins and filling out forms.

I looked around the cramped space and thought about how one month earlier I was cracking jokes with San Francisco Mayor Gavin Newsom at a lavish fundraiser, and now I was processing $300 rent checks behind the token dispenser.

Caligula was preoccupied in a way I hadn't seen, but loosened up a bit en route to lunch. Once seated, however, it was clear he had some bad news. The color drained from his face, his eyes were wide and he began,

"I need to tell you I'm a real asshole to work for."

Well shit.

He looked to be in a cold sweat as he continued to explain how even some of his closest friends couldn't handle working for him, seeming to hope he could inoculate me from their fate. Of course, I thought he should've told me this before we left our lives in San Francisco, but there was no looking back now. I said I thought we'd work together fine.

Meanwhile, back at the ranch, Damon's leads dried up and blew away like Dust Bowl crops. The agency he'd flown out to interview with, the one who shook his hand and said "We look forward to making you an offer," changed its mind, and he had to call them to find that out.

We did love our big old house, though, and were committed to making things work. Little would grow in the red Oklahoma clay so we had rich black soil hauled in to create boulder-lined raised beds where Damon planted all kinds of shrubs and wildflowers. Jane, an older lesbian next door, looked at what we'd created, nodded with approval and said, "That's some gay guy stuff right there!"

### 75. Habana Inn

The cornerstone of Oklahoma City's 39th & Penn LGBT district was the Habana Inn, which began as a sprawling, state-of-the-art Holiday Inn-type hotel in the '60s, but quickly became obsolete and went into decline.

It was around the block from a string of gay bars, so in the '80s it was increasingly frequented by gay patrons, which was causing issues with the fledgling mainstream clientele. The straight owners had to make a decision—discourage LGBT patrons or go all in and make it a LGBT hotel. They chose the latter, and the rest is history.

After numerous raids and other problems, the owners of several neighborhood bars took the Oklahoma City Police Department to court and proved harassment. The judgment was one dollar, and a new policy that the police couldn't enter the establishments without probable cause.

In the hostile, anti-gay climate of the '80s and early '90s, this policy created an oasis in the heart of one of the nation's most conservative cities.

For a moment I'd like to take you back to the Habana Donald and I first discovered in our teens.

### 76. Habana Regulars

At its zenith in the early nineties, the Gay Times Square of the Plains was the Habana Inn, and guys from Amarillo to Wichita to Tulsa to Little Rock, and even some slumming it from Dallas would succumb to its siren song every weekend.

Unlike the stagnant bars with unmarked doors in most towns within a few hundred miles, the Habana, with its nearly two hundred rooms, two bars, two pools, restaurant and gift shop, was a sprawling hive of activity filled with excitement, colorful characters, and endless possibilities.

Upon our arrival the first vehicle we'd take note of was a blue 1974 Lincoln Continental with the vanity plate WIG WAGR. The car belonged to our friend Shad's mom who was a wig stylist, and since he always drove it, Wig Wagger became his nickname.

"Wig Wagger's here," one of us would say as we began taking inventory.

There was a residential wing where our friends
Philip and Monte lived. I dubbed their room The
Fly Girl Suite, which I carved into the door. We'd
check to see if their light was on and make a note to
stop by.

Another noteworthy car was a lemon yellow 1982
Cadillac Eldorado that sounded like it was about to
throw a rod. The driver was morbidly obese and
looked like he'd been poured into the vehicle. As
much time as he spent circling the hotel, or
"cruising the shame" as they called it, we never once
saw him sans the car, and because of his size and
the loud unsteady nature of his ride, our friend Sam
Hobbs nicknamed him Earthquake.

We'd tailgate on the side of the hotel all evening
since we were too young to go to the bars, and each
and every time this guy rolled up—we're talking
dozens of times a night—Sam, who wasn't a petite
guy himself, would flail into the street, arms
outstretched, swinging wildly back and forth while
shouting, "EARTHQUAAAAAKE!"

Donald's friend Kyle from Bartlesville, a hundred
and forty miles north, was always finding some
boyfriend down in Oklahoma City and would spend
summer weekends tanning at the Habana pools. He
despised another group of regulars, three
androgynous Native American brothers who,
because of their lumpy acne-scarred faces, he'd
nicknamed The Cottage Cheese Sisters.

Sprawled out on a lounge chair with his skinny body
as oiled up and golden as a Cornish game hen, he'd
catch a glimpse of these queens, sit up, tilt down his
sunglasses, and yell at the top of his lungs,
"WHOOOO, HONEY BETTER GETCH YOUR
FACE OUTTA THE SUN BEFORE IT SPOILS!
Cottage Cheese Face!"

There were no dead ends at the Habana, only twists and turns where more excitement might await. It's where the action was. The loitering chickens, the cruisey trolls walking past the windows, the guys looking out their windows with doors ajar and the window masturbators, the people and cars circling "the shame," the tailgaters, the queens going back and forth between bars, the eternally bitter Power Line Princess leafleting cars with rumors about Lloyd Spartan, the house phone in the lobby where you could dial any room, the fine diners under the gaudy brass chandelier overlooking the shenanigans at the pool though floor-to-ceiling windows, and then there was the nightly drama. There's nothing like seeing a drag queen get the bass in her voice, throw off the wig and heels, and fight like a man.

One drag queen who could really throw down was Fantasy, a big Black guy with his four front teeth missing. One night a smart talking punk mouthed off to her and she picked him up like a twig and tossed him into the chain link fence, mowing it over and knocking him out. A crowd formed but was quickly parted by a portly white guy who shouted, "Stand back boys! I'm a nurse!"

Something was always happening in the main lobby, like the time, late one night, when Lloyd Spartan was detained by security, who allowed him to call his dad.

"Tell him he's got twenty minutes to pick you up or you're going to detox!" they threatened.

His dad sprang into action, making it to the hotel from the hardscrabble south side in record time. Storming into the lobby red faced and disheveled, the rough and tumble man thundered,

"I'M LLOYD SPARTAN SENIOR AND I
DON'T GIVE A GOD DAMN ABOUT YOUR
GAY HOTEL! I'LL BURN THIS SON OF A
BITCH TO THE GROUND!"

Wig Wagger did something to get banned for
several months, with the ban set to end
Thanksgiving Day. During his forced exile he stood
opposite the chain link fence, longingly watching
the hotel and talking to everyone who walked by.
Each and every night when he saw the security
guard he'd ask,
"I can come back on Thanksgiving, right? My ban's
over on Thanksgiving!"

Donald and I would joke, "You know he's taking
his Thanksgiving dinner to go and eating it on the
shame!"

The first time we visited the Habana it must have
really warped our young minds. We returned to
Tulsa that Sunday afternoon and found ourselves at
Utica Square, a high-end retail district where
shoppers were strolling by storefronts checking out
window displays. Noticing the similarities between
those looking through windows at the Habana and
Utica Square, Donald said, "I feel like all these
people are cruising."

## 77. Opening Night

It was my first weekend back in Oklahoma City
after nearly ten years of living in St. Louis & San
Francisco, and Donald wanted to hit the strip to
celebrate. Damon preferred to hang out at the
house, but sent us off with one simple instruction:
"Have fun, just don't get in trouble."

While the Habana was still fun, it was a shadow of its former self. The internet had taken much of the oxygen out of gay bars, gays were more mobile, and like myself, many had moved to more tolerant parts of the country. Feeder cities like Amarillo, Wichita, Tulsa, and Little Rock weren't quite as oppressive as they once were, and the hotel owners didn't allow a lot of the old shenanigans like circling the shame all night and getting rowdy.

We ran back and forth between Lloyd Spartan's favorite haunt, Tramps, which had the strongest drinks in town, and the hotel.

Donald gave the Habana's notoriously angry lesbian security guard some kind of look she didn't like, and the next thing I knew I saw him sitting outside the entrance in plastic handcuffs.

"What's going on?" I asked.

"He's going to jail!" she angrily exclaimed.

Donald turned to her and said, "You look just like my maid. Just like her…"

"Shut up Donald! Let me do the talking!" I said, then turned to the angry guard, "Listen, we're all family here. I'm sorry he offended you, just let me take him home."

"That family crap ended when he said I looked like his maid," she furiously replied.

The officer who arrived was not happy with the guard for bothering him with such a trivial matter and was annoyed with Donald for his drunken talkativeness. The police officer barked to Donald, "YOU HAVE TWO CHOICES. DETOX OR JAIL."

126

Donald paused and thought for a minute, then with all sincerity asked, "What were those choices again?"

He was placed in the cruiser and driven away, but it turns out the cop was really nice and just took him home.

Damon was really irritated by all this.

"I don't know why he's so mad!" Donald said.

"Well, he gave us one instruction and that was not to get in trouble- and you got hauled off in a cop car!"

The following morning Donald called his friend Blue to tell him about how the whole ordeal.

"Oh, I'm so furious!" Donald began. "They can't get away with shit like this. I didn't do anything wrong and was detained in handcuffs for thirty minutes while every drunk in town walked by! That bitch needs to be fired!"

Blue replied, "Yup. So what time are ya headin' out there tonight?"


## 78. Managing Madness

I had one direct report at Caligula Realty, a maintenance slash leasing guy named Jimmy Little Moon.

Jimmy was a folksy, heavy set, middle-aged Native American guy who had a mental block against finishing tasks, and he largely got away with it because he was such a likeable bullshitter.

He'd rent someone a house that wasn't ready and tell them, "Oh yeah, no problem, we'll have it all ready for you," then switch gears and work on something else. On move-in day he'd return first thing in the morning and put on a big show when the tenants arrived.

"Well, folks we ran a little behind but we're just about finished up!"

Any frustration people had about work not being done was blunted by the warm, red carpet greeting they were given upon arrival. He could really give the old razzle dazzle and they'd figure, "Well, he's about finished." The show had to continue, though, because he still wouldn't finish. Basic make ready issues could linger for months.

The mountain of incomplete, unbillable work was just one reason the Oklahoma City operation was a complete mess.

The clients had been part of a bubble-era California-based investment club and bought properties sight unseen on the promise of healthy returns based on grossly exaggerated rent projections. The previous management company made a fortune selling to the club, so they couldn't really go back and say the rents needed to be dropped by thirty percent, which is why they sold the contracts to Caligula. Now that he was in charge he was mostly letting Little Moon run the show because his Norman based staff was averse to making the seventeen-mile trek to Oklahoma City.

He had a seasoned crew covering about fifteen square miles, meanwhile it was just me and Little Moon running a thousand square mile territory covering four counties. (No exaggeration. Oklahoma City alone is 621). We were drowning and when I said I needed more help he shrugged, "None of my people want to come to Oklahoma City."

So, it was just me and Little Moon. I told him I needed to meet each morning for twenty minutes to go over open tickets, but he wanted no part of that. He'd say he was too busy, or he just wouldn't show. When I'd call and ask why he wasn't there he'd reply,
"Look, I've got way too much going to sit around at meetings."

Since Little Moon preferred to act like an independent contractor rather than an employee I was able to modify our arrangement as such, paying him by the job versus a salary. That enabled me to hire a maintenance guy named Carl, and Damon came on board to assist me, which wasn't his dream job but it made ends meet.

The biggest item on our agenda was administering doses of reality to the California clients. For starters, we had an entire neighborhood of vacant, brand new duplexes nobody was going to rent at the asking price of $995. The market would bear $750. All units were identical, so we told each client if they wanted to hold out for anything more than $750 they'd have to wait until all of the lower-priced units rented before they could even hope to rent theirs. They'd be looking at months of vacancy.

"Unlike California, there's nothing but land here. There's no ocean or mountains making it scarce, so if things get expensive people just keep moving farther out. Space is abundant and people expect it to be cheap. Keep in mind, these renters are people whose ancestors showed up for free land!"

Prices were adjusted accordingly, and units were rented at a steady clip.

When clients expressed dissatisfaction with the way their property was performing, Damon would ask, "Have you considered selling?" then I'd swoop in and sign them up. The money we made from sales was pure gravy and usually went into projects on our house.

Jimmy Little Moon was alright as a contractor, and really pulled through for me during after-hours emergencies.

"Jimmy, I hate to ask this of you on Christmas Eve, but…" and I don't think he once turned me down.

"Well, Chris, I'll tell ya I spent twenty years out on the oil fields and work calls when work calls," he'd say.

Caligula wasn't so bad during those first few weeks. In fact, he was so relieved I was there that several times he just handed me a wad of cash.

## 79. Behind the Iron Door Knocker

There was a saying in the energy industry that America was the Saudi Arabia of natural gas, and Oklahoma City was its Riyadh. It was definitely a boomtown and there were some fun things associated with that. Living large was part of the culture, with an emphasis on having an impressive home. Since the main reason we moved there was to play house, we fit right in.

Our handsome Dutch Colonial was everything to us, we were so proud of it, and we entertained constantly.

Bill brought Mom and the kids to town for a visit and we were having lunch in Damon's beautiful garden when Bill asked, "So do you think you'll be here for a while?"

I had moved around a great deal, but we now had a long-term plan. We both loved our house, and in a few years I was going to buy the Oklahoma City operation from Caligula.

"Yes, we're not planning on going anywhere."

He then presented me with a black iron door knocker Dad had made in high school. It was heavy, substantial and impressive, and he affixed it to the center of our wide front door. It symbolized permanence, and I was honored to have the family heirloom.

Ray David gave us his long antique dining table, which had been handed down to him by Fred & Jim decades earlier. This was the table from his Compton Hill dining room where I'd first sat during those grand dinners, watching Ray hold court past the candelabras. We paid Francis to haul it down, and I broke into a cold sweat when I bought a period chandelier to hang over it, having never spent so much on a light fixture.

Damon was an excellent cook and it was a regular occurrence for us to host a brunch for fifteen.

Joe was coming for a visit and we planned a reception for him, inviting friends and gallery owners. In advance of his arrival he sent us a stunning wall-sized red buffalo. These were selling for thirty thousand dollars, making it by far the most valuable possession we owned. It presided over the living room from the east wall, with open space before it for viewing.

Damon's boulder-lined wildflower garden was lush and impressive, and his orchid collection was unsurpassed. We befriended some great neighbors, including an Air Force captain named Trish and an elderly retired professor and woodworker named William. William had an entire woodworking shop in his garage, and together we built a massive bar for my garage that lit up with colored lights around the base.

My famed city tours were more modest than in San Francisco or St. Louis, but our home was a destination within itself, and after a cursory tour of Oklahoma City and a dinner or two out, we'd simply entertain our out of town guests there.

## 80. Caligula Realty: Dual Personalities of Caligula

Caligula had two distinct personalities: The sober/daytime Caligula and the drunk/nighttime Caligula. The latter was a fun-loving guy who liked to drink at the local bar, at the football game, at his sex cauldron parties, and while traveling around the world with his Great Plains entourage, who could sit in the shadow of the Eiffel Tower and still talk of nothing but the local team or one another, most likely while wearing sweatshirts emblazoned with the university logo. Nighttime Caligula was loose, fun, and affectionate.

The sober Caligula was an irritable son of a bitch. Fortunately, I rarely reported to the cramped main office where he and Stan worked alongside his loyal assistant Brassy, a part-time girl named Shawnee, and the poor Cinderella of the group, a receptionist named Lolita.

The few times I did work in that office the same surreal scene would play out again and again. Caligula would angrily announce that some document or file was missing, and on cue everyone would halt whatever they were doing and run around shuffling through stacks and rummaging through drawers. This dance wasn't really about finding the missing item. It was a submission display designed to appease his anger. I never participated in this nonsense.

Nobody could create tension and uncomfortable silences like sober Caligula, for he was the King of the Pregnant Pause. The tension was always so thick, and the way Lolita coped was to run outside as often as possible to smoke. A down home middle-aged country gal with three-inch hot pink nails, Lolita was as skittish as an abused puppy. Caligula and Brassy had eroded any self-confidence she had with their daily tidal waves of abuse.

For example, Lolita had worked there two or three years when they hired a new girl to work evenings. Brassy was taking the new girl around to meet everyone, and when she came to Lolita, she said dismissively, "Oh, this is Lolita, but don't ask her anything, she doesn't know what she's doing."

I got to know Caligula's two personalities as if they were two separate people, and it seemed the other employees did the same. Even Brassy, who spent most nights drinking with him and Stan, was always trying to stay out of trouble at work and had mastered the art of throwing others under the bus to cover her mistakes.

I do have a story Caligula told me about Stan and his former wife. First of all let me say that Caligula really blurred the line between gay and straight.

Anyway, as Caligula tells it, they were at one of their notorious drunken parties when Stan approached Caligula and said, "My wife really wants you to fuck her. Will you do it?"

This request was a bit much, even for him. Plus he wasn't the least bit attracted to this woman, but Stan talked him into it and he was a sport.

The next morning this ol' gal approached Daytime
Caligula hoping for seconds. The answer was a
resounding no. She had to learn about the two
Caligulas.

## 81. Caligula Realty: The Elephant in the Room

Caligula's partner Mills gently spread white paint all
over a naked, muscular athlete. He savored every
moment of the process and then had the strapping
guy press his body against a large black canvas.

The painting adorned the walls of Mills's boudoir,
and he relished the telling of its origin. Of course
the model was from the university, and apparently
there were several fine specimens to choose from
for this project. Mills explained that the model
needed to be well endowed in order to hang
correctly for the piece. Otherwise the crotch area
would be kind of a messy blob of paint instead of a
clear representation of male virility.

Aside from his questionable judgment in
fraternizing with cute male students and interns,
Mills was proper and professional. Unlike Caligula,
he was an elegant master of etiquette, always
polished and right at home hosting dignitaries or
meeting with parents as he worked to recruit the
best and brightest scholars and athletes.

Mills adored Caligula from the first moment he laid
eyes on him two decades earlier but was always
frustrated with Caligula's nonstop party lifestyle.

They built an enormous guest house that, as far as size and style, was basically a mirror image of the main house for the sole purpose of keeping the constant party contained. Between the main house and guest house was a pool, and Mills regularly woke up to pre-twilight parties and would look out to see Caligula chasing naked guys around the courtyard.

As hard as Mills tried, you really can't contain or control a mess like drunken Caligula. Case in point: Mills inflicted Caligula on an exclusive event hosted by the president of the university. Caligula got slopping drunk, approached the president's stuffy wife, and licked her face.

## 82. Ol' Crankles

Caligula owned a rental house a few doors down from Tramps, the bar with the strongest drinks in town, and it was a pain because it was a dump that looked really good on paper, which meant daily, fruitless showings.

I'd set my appointments there for the end of the day so I could stop by the bar afterwards, but sometimes I'd arrive early and decide to stop in for one drink before the showing. Then I'd lose interest and call Damon.

"Damon, I'm at Tramps and don't feel like showing Flynn. Would you mind showing it?"

Sometimes he'd get mad, but other times he'd show it and meet me out. After one or two of those drinks we'd start talking about moving to New York, which was something I always intended to do, and we'd call Donald and ask him to join us.

39th & Penn had more than its share of unemployed deadbeats just lingering around looking for someone to buy drinks or be their meal ticket, especially at Tramps. Damon left to go to the store, and when Donald and I were leaving, a guy appeared out of nowhere and asked if he could ride around with us. Donald let him sit in the back and then asked, "So are you on crank?"

"No!" the guy responded.

We just circled around the hotel and neighborhood talking to people, and every few minutes Donald would ask, "How's it going back there, Crankles?"

In a classic Chris & Donald lapse of judgment we took him home. While he'd been deferential in the car, once we got to the house he became contrary and rude.

Damon pulled up and I met him at the portico.

"There's some meth head in the dining room arguing with Donald, and we're having trouble getting him to leave."

Damon got a serious, determined look on his face and said, "I'll put an end to this monkey business," and he did.

We didn't realize it until the next day, but he had stolen Donald's wallet. Before daybreak he was having himself a shopping spree at a Dallas Walmart.

## 83. Did I Mention Brassy Was A Bitch?

Begging Brassy for my paychecks was getting really old. I had to prostrate myself to her, sending gentle reminders that I needed the check, and I would get curt replies about how she was really busy and would get to it when she could.

From the few times I worked down there I knew she wasn't that busy, and she found plenty of time to talk to her daughters and fight with her estranged husband.

Lolita and I were always bonding over our stepchild status, and I sent her the following email:

"Hi Stepsister. Would you let me know when my commission check is ready? I don't want to ask Brassy again because she seems to resent the commissions I'm earning."

I didn't realize the busy Brassy regularly read Lolita's email. As bold as could be, and without any embarrassment for reading someone else's email in the first place, she sent me a furious response beginning, "FOR YOUR INFORMATION I DO NOT RESENT..."

## 84. Caligula Realty: Holiday History

When Brassy was still married there was speculation that she and Danny, the cute maintenance guy, might hook up. Danny was married too, but the marriage to his frumpy wife was a result of her teenage pregnancy ten years ago, and everyone could see there was strong chemistry between him and Brassy.

A decade older than Danny, she'd kept herself up, had a nice figure and large breasts.

Several people relayed a mental snapshot from a holiday party the year prior to my arrival. Danny was looking down Brassy's shirt while Caligula grabbed Danny's crotch.

With a Christmas tree in the background that could've made the perfect photo for the Caligula Realty holiday cards.

## 85. Caligula Realty: Family Values

Danny's wife gave Caligula a nude photo of Danny as a gift.

Although the inner circle knew about Caligula's lust for him, I have to assume that Danny's father, who was also an employee, had no idea how intense his obsession was, although he seemed to know there was a crush because he'd joked about it.

At one of the parties that had devolved into a sex cauldron, Caligula performed oral sex on Danny in the presence of his wife. That was the only time he had a sexual encounter with Danny that I know about, other than voyeurism. The next morning Danny pretended to have no recollection of the event.

I wasn't at this or any sex cauldron party personally. My only direct brush with the debauchery was at the company Christmas Party. The event started at a local restaurant where I was playfully flirting with Stan's female cousin, who was a plain woman in her early forties. Her husband was getting really irritated until she told him I was gay.

Well, later in the evening the party moved to the guest house and I was primed to see anything after all the stories I'd heard. Danny and his wife were there, Brassy was lit and festive, Caligula was drunk and happy, but everyone was more or less appropriate.

Then I was giving someone a tour of the enormous guest house when I opened a bedroom door and there was Stan's cousin buck naked on all fours with her husband just going to town behind her. The door wasn't even locked.
Did they forget, or did they want to get caught?
Had they been inspired at the Caligula Compound before, or was his jealousy the inspiration?

I didn't think that was the right time to ask.

## 86. Three Meal Lucille

Donald and I would go to the Habana's flagship restaurant, Gusher's, after the bars closed. He liked variety when he was drunk, so he got in the habit of ordering three entrees. The waiter would take our order and Donald would say,

"I'll have the chicken fingers…the pancakes…and a patty melt."

The first two items would change, but he'd always order that damn patty melt. Always fit and trim, he wouldn't eat much at all so I never bothered ordering and would simply eat from his buffet.

"No need to order with Three Meal Lucille over here," I'd say.

140

One night he made the biggest mess on his side of the table. Lettuce, gravy, crackers, and wrappers littered his whole area. He drunkenly looked at the mess, gave the restaurant a dismissive cursory glance and mumbled, "This place is a shit hole."

## 87. Caligula Realty: "I still like her tits"

Caligula was dogged in the pursuit of what he wanted, and at our sensational anniversary party in the garden he decided he wanted to titty fuck my married friend Suzanne, who was in from Kansas City.

Friends had come from all over for our event, even a few from San Francisco, including Magali, the director of the Cadillac Hotel, who had a front row seat for Caligula's advances.

The party was in the late stages, and I'd gone to bed, along with Suzanne's husband. Caligula was extremely drunk and had zeroed in on her generous bosom. At our garage bar he proceeded to tell her, in the most vulgar way, what he wanted to do with her breasts.

For whatever reason she didn't disengage. She wasn't interested, but her intellectual curiosity had been piqued. After all, as far as she knew he was gay. An attorney by trade, Suzanne fired questions while his eyes were locked on the target of his desire.

Suzanne: "So you're gay?"

Caligula: "Yeah, but I still want to fuck your tits."

Suzanne: "And you have a partner you live with, right?"

141

Caligula: "Yeah, but I just want to titty fuck you. You've got really great tits."

Suzanne: "So you're gay and have a partner but just want to use my breasts to get off?"

Caligula: "Yes! I want to fuck your tits."

In the middle of this exchange another female guest, who was single and elated that *someone* at this big gay party might be game, approached and said playfully,

"Oh! You like tits?" as she shook hers.

Caligula gave her goods a passing glance, and then focused again on the prize, saying in his trademark monotone voice, "Well, I still like Suzanne's tits."

Eventually Suzanne was through and completely read him in front of at least two dozen people. Among the damning laundry list, she told him he was a sleazy lowlife and stormed off, retiring for the night.

Now, any other human being, drunk or not, would have been completely humiliated. Not Caligula.

In a dead silence everyone watched as he stood in the wake of this scene. He seemed to contemplate what she had said, and then mumbled, "Well...I still like her tits."

## 88. Caligula Realty: Who Let The Dogs Out?

When Suzanne stormed off she took the dogs to bed with her, but Damon didn't realize it and was alarmed when he couldn't find them.

Our big lesbian neighbor Jane put her house on the market and moved back with her ex, but allowed us use of it for the weekend for house guests. Our friend Patrick, a cool Black guy from St. Louis who fixed up old cars, was in one of the upstairs rooms.

Damon and a few others checked our house, scoured the neighborhood, and then went to Jane's. He opened one of the doors and found Patrick reclining while a local banker, known as a subdued, white bread kind of guy, was going down on him.

Damon was on a mission and asked forcefully, "Have you seen my dogs?"

Patrick said he hadn't, and the local came up for air and shook his head no. Damon was shutting the door when Patrick, still lying back, said in his bass voice, "Hey, Damon. Leave it open for ventilation."

## 89. The Mayor versus the Motorcar

The Mayor of Gay Oklahoma City, Lloyd Spartan, was celebrating New Year's Eve, holding court from bar to bar in the gay district. It was as if NW 39th was his personal runway, the way he owned that block, especially during Pride when he sauntered though the parade in his iconic rainbow flag dress, greeting the adoring masses.

That New Year's evening he was crossing NW 39th Street when a drunk driver whipped around a corner and careened into him.

The following minutes were pure chaos as the young woman who hit him screamed in horror, people poured out of the bars, and bystanders rushed to his aid and yelled for help as the community's mother hen moaned in agony on the street until the ambulance arrived.

His leg was broken in twenty-four places and there was some doubt it could be saved. The following morning the surgeon said he thought he could save it if they did the surgery that day, but there was a caveat.

"We have a problem," the surgeon began. "You have cocaine in your nose, and I'm afraid to put you under since you weigh over three hundred pounds. Are you willing to stay awake during surgery?"

Seeing as there wasn't a choice, Spartan agreed. The surgeon then asked if medical students could watch.

"Sure, why not?" Spartan said.

Deadened from the waist down, ten students watched as he was put back together.

The Mayor was able to be repaired, but the Mazda that hit him was totaled.

## 90. Caligula Realty: Collision Course

We rarely left town because Caligula made it so miserable, but it was 4th of July weekend and we were audacious enough to visit family and friends in St. Louis, where we were constantly interrupted via phone and email. In addition to Caligula's grouchy questions, he would tell me to work. One email was sent at 4:40p.m, instructing me to call a demanding client right away.

My Caligula leash was being jerked continuously. I'd always felt at home in St. Louis, but this time was different. I was on the outside looking in, not really a part of it. I was property of Caligula and the Great Plains. I felt like Sophia in *The Color Purple*, when she couldn't enjoy Christmas with her family because she had to attend to her neurotic employer Miss Millie.

After a night out with friends I checked my email and found Joe had gotten mad at one of our brothers and angrily accused us all of "cashing in" on his success, among other things.

I was working harder and was under more stress than ever before, and was enraged at the notion I was riding his coattails. I fired back saying I hadn't asked him for anything in ten years, I made my own living, and I told him he was sick and delusional to think otherwise. A huge email fight ensued.

Between Caligula and Joe the non-vacation was ruined, and we cut it short, abruptly throwing everything into the car and returning to our insatiable master a few days early.

I felt the Great Plains wanted to break me. I had stepped out of line, and the coming months would show Caligula & Mills wanted me to submit to Brassy, which meant playing along with her conflicting directives and accepting the blame when she made mistakes. I would have none of it, and these trains were on a collision course.

As we drove through the forested hills outside of St. Louis I wanted nothing more than to find a way out of this horrible mess. I needed to get away from Caligula and the Great Plains. I feared the price of freedom would be high, but had no idea it would cost me everything.

## 91. Caligula Realty: Independence Day

We were back from our truncated 4th of July trip and the email fight with Joe was escalating, with him zeroing in on my drinking.

"Look how fucked up your life is. You're drunk and fat..." he began.

I was medicating with booze, and he with prescriptions. He continued, "If I haven't done anything for you, then you shouldn't mind donating the red buffalo the OU [The University of Oklahoma]."

A consistent theme in my life is a willingness to part with anything and everything in exchange for my freedom and dignity. I took Joe's words as a dare, and I didn't hesitate about parting with the painting. In fact it was strangely liberating.

I contacted the university and asked them to retrieve the piece. They asked what I wanted on the plaque and for twenty four hours I deliberated whether to have it read, "A gift from Francine Fishpaw," my favorite drunk in the John Waters cult classic Polyester. In the end I decided against that idea out of respect for the family.

Two art handlers arrived to retrieve the piece.

"Was Joe actually in this house?" one wide-eyed handler asked as he examined the room.

While Damon was miserable working for Caligula, he wanted to try to make things work. Our San Francisco fortune and all of our earnings since arriving in Oklahoma were tied up in that house, which we loved.

I, on the other hand, was overwhelmed with a fight or flight instinct, and wanted to leave sooner than later. It was a terrible mistake to come to Oklahoma. Damon was destined for so much more out of a career, and it would never happen there.

We argued about what to do, but agreed to work on sticking it out. There was still the possibility of the pot of gold at the end of the rainbow. If we could just learn Caligua's archaic way of doing things, we could fly into the eye of the storm and come out stronger and more prosperous.

We both did our best. I had a heart to heart with Caligula, and Damon went out of his way to be sugary sweet to Brassy, even using smiley emoticons in his emails with her—which was so not him.

## 92. Caligula Realty: Brassy's Internal Investigation

When someone moved out of one of our rental units, the Caligula Realty procedure was to charge the tenant for carpet and unit cleaning, regardless of how clean they'd left the unit. The reason was Caligula would sue a past tenant for as little as fifty dollars, and if they claimed the unit was dirty when they moved in, he wanted the receipts from the prior tenant to show otherwise.

I never liked nor believed in this procedure, but I lived with it. Once, however, I disregarded it because the military tenant had left the unit in move-in condition and the building was under contract to be sold in a few days. The new owners thought the unit looked great, and we wouldn't be handling the property once it sold, so the underlying premise for the policy wasn't relevant.

For days Caligula harped on how we must follow the procedure. I explained my rationale, but he was a broken record. Droning on he would say, "We have these procedures and I just don't know why you're not following them..."

After that, we rigidly followed the procedures regardless of circumstance. And now with everything so uncertain, we were trying not to make waves.

A tenant who'd left her unit in meticulous condition was upset about these charges, and after getting the company line from us, called the main office and spoke to Brassy. The two of them bonded over the Oklahoma Sooners, and the next thing I knew Brassy cleared her schedule to conduct an internal investigation about why we cleaned the unit if it didn't need to be cleaned. She interviewed the janitor and the carpet cleaners, and sent us an email demanding answers and photos.

I sent Caligula a message telling him Brassy was investigating us for following company procedure, and that I felt like I was in the twilight zone.

His reply left me speechless: "Well, Chris, you need to use common sense," he began as he explained there's no reason to have a clean carpet cleaned. He went on to say he's tired of our unfounded complaints about Brassy, and we needed to have a meeting to set things straight.

This was when I realized that I was at the Mad Hatter's tea party. There was no archaic method we could learn. Every established policy and procedure was subject to change without notice if Brassy declared it so. Our hope was replaced with a hopeless awareness that we'd been chasing illusions.

I knew one thing, though. I would hitchhike to Hell before I would kneel before Brassy.

It was time to turn in my notice.

## 93. Getting out of Dodge

We put our house on the market with high hopes because it looked so much better than when we bought it, and we paid cash for all of the upgrades, so we were confident we weren't upside down. An artisan painter had done a beautiful three-color paint job, and of course the landscaping was lovely.

Since Oklahoma City was a relatively new place, buyers weren't that familiar with older properties, which made them more difficult to sell. They liked the *idea* of an old house, but not the inspection report confirming the house is old.

We'd been in contract with a lady who backed out after getting a report which cited no major issues and wouldn't have raised red flags in an older city. Her realtor argued she should get her earnest money back and I said, "Hey, I don't begrudge anyone for not wanting to take on old house issues, but she shouldn't be shopping for an old house." However, I caved and refunded her money anyway.

Making matters worse was the market crash, and Jane's house next door was still for sale, which was the same price and had vinyl siding, which Oklahoma buyers preferred to our fancy San Francisco paint job.

Based on all of the feedback, we were going to be lucky to sell the house without bringing money to closing. In the meantime we'd have to leave without the house being sold, which was a big complication.

The good news was that my old employer in St. Louis, Marquette Realty, offered me my old job back, and agreed to put us up until we'd tied up loose ends in Oklahoma.

Caligula took the news well, he might have even been relieved. I told him our friendship existed before the business, and would still be intact after.

"I just want you to be happy," he said initially, but the tensions built in the final weeks as he planned to take over the operation, a task which made him moody.

After seeming to let us go without so much as a goodbye, at the very last minute he decided to have a going away lunch for us in Norman. Everyone was pleasant, but Caligula refused to have a drink, which in Caligula's culture was a major slight.

## 94. The Collapse of Chris Andoe

Marquette Realty agreed to put us up rent free in a modest little house in St. Louis until we wrapped up the sale of our home in Oklahoma City. We nicknamed our future residence Cashflow Cottage and kept ourselves upbeat about downsizing. Still, when it was time to leave our home it was very sad.

Eighteen months earlier, professional movers loaded up our belongings in San Francisco and delivered them to that proud Dutch Colonial. We'd poured everything into the house, hosted holiday dinners with family and friends, created lush gardens, built a bar in the garage, and my brother Bill installed an iron door knocker my Dad had made. Now on a sweltering day we were cramming what we hadn't liquidated into the back of a U-Haul. The dream was dead.

As I was closing up the truck I noticed Damon's hundred or so orchids were still sitting on a table in the backyard. This was his collection from San Francisco that he'd nurtured and kept going despite the challenging Oklahoma environment.

"There's no room. I'm not taking them," he said. I tried to argue but his mind was made up.

Our entire fortune had shriveled up on the sunbaked plains, and the orchids would be no exception.

Damon drove the car and I the truck, so he arrived in St. Louis over an hour earlier. As I entered the tired little house on a rough, inner city block I immediately saw it wasn't ready—someone at Marquette had really dropped the ball. The carpet was dirty, the walls weren't painted, but even if it had been ready the place wasn't merely modest, it was a dump.

Damon's biggest fear was being poor, and the hour alone in that hovel caused him to have a mental breakdown. His eyes were glassy, he had a blank yet slightly pained expression, and he wandered aimlessly while mumbling about the house's problems. Tapping on a window he said in a sedate, quiet tone, "This isn't even glass. It's some kind of plastic..."

"Damon, we're not going to live here. I'm going to get this straightened out right away," I attempted to assure.

When I hugged him he just collapsed in my arms and wept.

"I kept thinking I just want to go home, but we have no home to go to," he sobbed.

151

I walked him to the car and told him to relax while I straightened things out, then I sat on the front steps and placed several calls until finally reaching my boss. Keeping my composure I tried to sound friendly and relaxed when I told him the place wasn't ready and wouldn't work for us. He set me up with Tim, my former and future coworker, who showed me several other places while Damon waited with the U-Haul.

Within two hours I'd secured a nice house in Clifton Heights, a safe and desirable neighborhood of historic homes surrounding a park with a lake.

Like the house we'd just left, it was a two-story Dutch Colonial, and it sat confidently on a hill with a friendly front porch, fireplace, and a fenced yard. It wasn't free like the other place, but with the house I'd "fixed" the situation. That very night Damon would be able to rest his head in a house he wasn't ashamed of.

I grossly underestimated the amount of damage that had been done, and in retrospect my "fix" amounted to putting a Band-Aid on a bullet wound.

Before Oklahoma City, Damon was in awe of my ability to manage our finances and navigate our lives. I'd bought our first house and sold it for a good profit. I'd moved us to California and he didn't even need to work for six months. I'd helped him get hired with my company and pushed him to network, which landed him a director-level position with the parent company, and I bought an impressive house in Oklahoma City and earned a good living.

But Oklahoma City falling apart and the botched return to St. Louis changed our dynamic forever. He couldn't trust me to run things, he decided. In order for him to feel safe he needed control of the finances. Others, one man in particular, would sniff out this wound and settle into it like an opportunist infection, exploiting it to their advantage.

We would endure. We'd laugh again, make love again, but I'd never regain his respect or admiration, and I longed for it the way a flailing fish on dry land longs for water. The thought of what was lost made me feel emasculated, humiliated and defeated.

I would spend years pulling rabbits out of hats, landing good jobs, getting big promotions, making things happen, but the part of him that once looked at me with awe died during that breakdown at Cashflow Cottage, and it would take me seven years to come to terms with that.

## 95. Birth of a Tortured Writer

While I'd always been a storyteller, I didn't really begin writing until we'd returned to St. Louis after the Oklahoma City debacle. Initially the difference between telling and writing a story was like the difference between running down a hill and running through a swimming pool. It was a laborious exercise, but I was fueled by the need to share what we'd gone through.

My free time was consumed with crafting and posting the tales of Caligula Realty, and I was surprised by how much people enjoyed them. My list of friends grew while Damon became increasingly bitter about the time I spent writing after work, which he thought was a waste of time.

153

"Shouldn't you be out there selling houses?" he'd ask.

## 96. Rise of the Anti-Chris

I had an appointment downtown and planned to meet Damon for lunch.

"Mind if my co-worker Benny joins us?" he asked.

Benny Babbish was an executive in the office, and as the only other gay guy, he took an interest in Damon and became his mentor.

Benny was in his fifties and looked like a slightly younger Dick Cheney, but with reddish brown hair and a bigger belly, almost like a basketball shoved under his shirt. Over lunch he casually admitted to thoroughly researching us on the internet, which was unsettling, but certainly foreshadowed his noxious, invasive nature.

"I don't think you look anything like your Facebook photos," he said.

Despite his research, he still wasn't aware of what I did for a living. When I explained my work history he exclaimed, "You ought to be working with us!"

The lure was tossed and we took the bait, dedicating the next few years to doing a dance for Benny, for the benefit of Damon's trajectory and the career he wanted for me. Benny, as the story goes, was really pulling strings on our behalf, trying to get me hired on, and get Damon promoted, therefore we were obligated to attend each and every one of his dreadful suburban, alcohol-free parties.

For my part, I was expected to be the great entertainer for his stuffy guests, and to carefully consider Benny's critiques, which were relayed though Damon and included things like,

"Nothing about Chris's Facebook persona says he's looking for a serious career. He should post more things about real estate and management," "Chris isn't nearly as outgoing in person," and "I think Chris is only fun when he's drinking."

Each critique would cause Damon angst, and would be something he'd expect me to work on.

A big shot in Rainbow Steps, a local twelve-step group, he was always showing off a handsome new member just drying out—and that poor soul was usually the friendliest one at his party. It was remarkable how dull and antisocial many of the guests were. He threw the kind of party where you walked in and nobody even turned around.

Despite traveling the world, Benny was terribly bored with life. About the only things that amused him were sex and power. The pinnacle was paying straight, married men, who were hard up for cash, to bend over and get fucked. The fact they didn't want it, and were in fact humiliated by it, was what got him off. It was an elusive high, though, because few would actually go through with it.

"I ask them before they come over if they're willing to get fucked and they say no problem, then they try to worm their way out of it when they get here," he bitterly remarked at his cocktail-less party.

Cult leaders are known for their charisma, but I would come to know Benny as the most successful uncharismatic cult leader in the history of the world. Somehow people felt compelled to be in his orbit and to please him, even when he'd ruined their lives.

He was famous for breaking couples up. For those in the twelve-step program, he'd convince them they couldn't really be in recovery until they were single. For those not fighting addiction, he'd convince his target they were co-dependent or their partner was no good.

He wanted to be the alpha male, and would work against the alpha in the relationship by building trust with the more submissive partner, learning where the insecurities and weak spots were and relentlessly exploiting them.

For some reason, though, the couples he was trying to break up, and both parties to a relationship he dissolved, would still attend his events. One friend of his was dying of AIDS, yet Benny was still trying to get him to leave his partner, who sitting beside me at Benny's garden party, said, "Oh, Benny hates me! Everyone knows that!" while the dying partner grimaced, as if to say, "Yeah, but what can you do?"

Despite this pattern, Benny was a champion of ours, and we needed to stay in his good graces, which was challenging for me. I found him so repugnant, but Damon was fond of him, so I'd do my best to fall in line.

I think there are few greater sins than inhospitality to a guest, so I was particularly repulsed when a man who had gotten the short end of the stick in a Benny-induced break up, yet still attended his party, was lounging by the pool and Benny whispered to our group, "His ex dumped him because he has genital warts."

## 97. The Deed

After losing our shirts in Oklahoma City, selling the house for less than we owed, we were in no position to buy a home, but when I learned my company planned to invest millions in new properties I asked the owners if they'd help us buy a house and they agreed.

We could select what we wanted, they'd buy it, and we'd do a lease-purchase for up to three years until we could buy it outright. I called Damon with the good news, telling him after all we'd been through I wanted him to get what he really wanted.

Because he loved to garden he chose a house with the largest yard in Tower Grove South, the gayest neighborhood in the city. I thought it was a bit small, and suggested we consider a two-unit property, but in the end we went with his first choice and I was happy with it. He transformed the yard with rose bushes and perennials, and the house and yard were great for entertaining.

When it came time to buy the property from my employer, we needed to shop for a mortgage and I suggested we keep our money in the "family" and use Simone Shasta, the city's most famous drag queen mortgage broker. She was very efficient and everything proceeded in a timely manner. I was so impressed that when she arrived for closing I presented her with a bottle of champagne as a token of our appreciation.

I'd bought our first two houses and listed Damon on the deed, but this time we'd planned to do the reverse since I took the hit from Oklahoma. When Simone came over for the closing, there was nothing for me to sign.

"Isn't there a deed I need to sign?" I asked.

After a pregnant pause with no eye contact she simply said "No," kind of glossing over the question while gently shuffling papers.

I waited until she left, then asked Damon why my name wasn't on the deed.

"It was supposed to be, I'm not sure what happened," he said nonchalantly.

It was the first of many flimsy excuses I'd get in the coming years. I knew how simple the process was, and the issue became an oft visited topic during our frequent arguments, which were more radioactive and mean-spirited than they'd ever been in the past.

In the previous seven years we'd argue but then try to find common ground and make up, but now Damon didn't budge an inch, as if I were an enemy that needed to be crushed. When I'd express despair over his behavior or when I told him he'd hurt my feelings he'd accuse me of trying to manipulate him. Sometimes, though, after a bad fight he'd do an about face and break down.

"I'm sorry. I've been getting bad advice," he'd say tearfully, but who was giving it to him? He wouldn't tell me—but I felt it was Benny fueling his rage and also suspected that Benny advised him not to put my name on the house.

In a heated moment he threw out names of two guys who'd been talking to me online, which revealed he'd been going through my computer. I had a universal password for everything and didn't hide that, but I never suspected him of going through my email. After that I went through his computer and found an entire archive he'd been keeping on me. Invading one another's privacy became a new normal, and it was devastating to read the things he'd say about me to friends and strangers.

He found things to be upset about retroactively, like the money I'd given him to shop for us during his six-month sabbatical in San Francisco. We'd both looked back fondly on those times, but during a fight he sneered, "Oh, like when you used to give me a cash *allowance* like some child!"

During one of the worst fights I grabbed a crystal framed photo of us together and threw it at his chest. He slid out of the way and it almost hit our dog Sophie.

"NOW YOU'RE TRYING TO ABUSE THE DOGS!" he disingenuously accused.

"HOW DARE YOU SAY THAT?! YOU KNOW THAT'S NOT TRUE!" I yelled before shoving him and shouting, "GOD DAMN YOU!"

He immediately shoved me back, shouting, "NO, GOD DAMN YOU!"

He then said calmly and confidently, "You know what? I do want to you to leave."

I went in the bedroom to pack and be followed me, hovering around. "GIVE ME SPACE!" I demanded, but he'd leave for a minute and then come back, chest puffed out, and watch me pack. "I'm taking the dogs, at least part time," I said.

With a laugh he replied, "Oh, yeah. Where are you going to take them?"

"I'M NOT SOME BROKE BITCH! I CAN AFFORD A PLACE! I know you feel like *my* money is yours because I never see it, but I work and can make my own way. I've worked 100 percent of the time we've been together."

I put my suitcase in the backseat and had just opened the driver's side door when he let the dogs out. They darted towards me barking.

"It's not going to be that easy," he said.

The whiplash from being kicked out and pulled right back broke my spirit. I should have just loaded up the dogs and left, but I was so disoriented I didn't know what else to do in the moment.

Thoroughly defeated and emasculated, I carried my bag back into his house, locked the bedroom door, then fell to the floor and wept, wondering what I had become.

## 98. Saturday Night Reprieve

As bad as the fights could be, we weren't normally fighting. We had our routine and often enjoyed one another, although there was always a sense of disapproval from him, not unlike what a child might expect from a hard to please teacher. I was too messy. I didn't clean well enough. I didn't earn enough. I didn't negotiate a good enough deal, etc.

I couldn't fully relax around Damon anymore, but every Saturday night I could go out and cut loose. Out on the town, people liked, respected, and were happy to see me, and I came to live for those nights.

The evenings would begin at Villa Ray, where the rum flowed and we'd often laugh until we cried. Our first stop was generally Clementine's, the neighborhood bar in Soulard where we knew everyone.

Between eleven and midnight we'd head to JJ's Clubhouse, a massive industrial-looking bar that sat below an elevated section of the interstate in Midtown and catered to more masculine men than the young, polished queens of the Grove.

I started getting into shape after leaving Oklahoma and would dance shirtless on the riser with my friend JeCorey, a younger half-black guy who was often compared to Young & the Restless star Shemar Moore, and was easily one of the most sensual men I'd ever known. On the riser he'd belly dance, which is thought of as feminine, but somehow he pulled it off with a masculine sensuality.

I made many friends at JJ's, including a guy who'd become my main urban exploring partner, Kenneth. A heavy-set Black guy with his ball cap pulled far down, shadowing his face, he stood alone in the corner and looked like a fearsome man. Of course, I went right up to him and introduced myself, and the rest is history.

Off of the long dark hallway connecting the two halves of the club, with its black walls and red lights, was my "office," a closet-sized boiler room which was normally unlocked. On three occasions I'd taken a gentleman there for a moment alone.

Few knew about my secret spot, but Kenneth must have told his best friend Nikki because one night she got tired of me teasing her about something and said, "Listen, Boiler Room Billy…"

## 99. Tales from the East Side

Ray taught me much of what I knew about entertaining, and we loved to throw parties together. We held an East St. Louis storytelling event at his villa and invited all who wanted to share a colorful tale.

There were many stories about Faces, the massive after-hours bar with the infamous "men only" basement. In keeping with the East Side theme we recreated that feel in the basement of Villa Ray, complete with red lights, '70s porn on the big television, and a dark room—which drew a crowd.

We didn't know if any debauchery would actually take place down there, but it attracted a group of about eight guys and felt like something might go down, but our friend Paul, a quick-witted Black queen, stood in the middle of the dark room with his arms crossed talking about how he was too classy to be in a dark room, which killed the mood. He later admitted he was intentionally cock blocking someone who was about to hook up with a man he wanted.

The mafia long controlled East St. Louis and discovered they could run profitable homosexual bars since they and their patrons didn't have to worry about the constant police raids that were once common in places gays gathered. As far back as the 1940s there were such establishments on the east side, and our friends Fred & Jim, in their seventies at the time of our party, remembered them.

"The Olde English Inn was the Faces of its day. It didn't get popular until the bars closed in St. Louis. The restrooms were wild. If you didn't pick up a trick in St. Louis, you went over there as your last stop," Fred recalled.

One VIP in attendance was William Collins, editor for *Vital Voice Magazine*. As an LGBT history buff who also happened to live on the Illinois side, Collins was really interested in the event and wrote a feature about it in the next issue, quoting me:

"I always thought the whole idea of East St. Louis was fascinating. Most cities don't have this sinister alter-ego on the other side of a big river. It's kind of the equivalent of international waters. It's not quite reality and it's kind of dreamlike. You're not in your right mind when you get there, and whatever happens over there stays over there."

## 100.  The Mechanic at Brunch

I befriended a local decorator named Robert Hayden and met him for brunch in Benton Park. Exactly one week later I saw that Feather, Lenny, and the kids were in town, and were having brunch with the same man at the same place.

For a couple of years Lenny had been adding all of my friends, Donald's friends, and many of Lloyd Spartan's friends, but this took his odd behavior to a whole new level. I couldn't imagine what a straight mechanic from rural Kansas had in common with Robert Hayden, and the next time I saw Hayden, I asked him about the brunch.

"It was really strange. He added me on Facebook and then asked me to brunch, but just played on his phone the whole time. Feather did her best to keep the conversation going, mostly talking about her kids," he recalled.


## 101.  Ghostly Rendezvous

I was meeting with an older woman with burgundy hair named Pat, a new property management client who lived in San Mateo, California but was buying investment property in St. Louis. In addition to the buildings I was taking over for her, she mentioned buying an old mansion on a blighted block of North St. Louis, which really piqued my interest.

"I grew up in St. Louis but moved to San Francisco in the '60s. My late husband owned the strip clubs in North Beach, and when he passed I decided to invest in real estate here. My kids think I'm nuts! I was driving around when I saw an open house at a big old mansion. One of the neighbors came up to talk to me and asked, 'You're not planning to open a group home are you? We've had too many of those,' and I said 'No, I'm just looking around,' but I just fell in love with the place and bought it. Since then I've sunk about two-hundred thousand into it."

"I'd love to see it sometime!" I said.

"Sure! When would you like to come by?" she asked.
I arrived at the cavernous home that very evening. It was double the width of the typical city house and had twin parlors and dining rooms.

"The ladies and the gentlemen were often separated at parties, so each had their own parlors," she explained.

It was clear the house had an institutional past. There were illuminated exit signs, fire sprinklers, commercial-grade tile on the upper floors and a group restroom with three stalls, three sinks and three showers. It was sobering to see how much work was still needed even after hundreds of thousands were spent.

Pat only lived in the house sporadically, coming in for a few weeks once a season, and asked if I'd look after it. A few months later I asked if I could host a ghost storytelling party there. "Oh, that sounds like fun!" she said.

I named the event "Ghostly Rendezvous" and invited my friend Elaine, who lived in my closet back in high school and was my roommate in college, to come up from Tulsa for a few days and stay with me in the house.

The preceding weeks were a lot of fun as me and Elaine researched the history of the home, beginning with the prominent politician who built the residence and collapsed of a heart attack in the foyer after being betrayed by city hall colleagues over a piece of legislation.

We uncovered details about its group home incarnations, one as a home for unwed mothers, one as a hospice, and the last one as a halfway house for felons. We discovered articles about two convicts who'd escaped from the house and murdered a few people.

Elaine's life had become one of monotony and financial struggle, being a single mother working low-paying jobs, but this event made her the star of her office—where the women waited to hear about our latest findings and even helped with the research.

It felt like we were roommates again staying there together, and we'd skeptically explore every bump in the night. We had a good turnout for the big event, with about thirty people crowding around the extra-long table in the dimly lit dining room as guests took turns telling ghost stories, and then we held a séance on the third floor.

One person who couldn't make the party was my friend Stephen, who we all called Stephanie. Stephanie had a near death experience during a car accident a year earlier.

"I was in the tunnel, which was like smoked glass," Stephanie began. "This androgynous figure was escorting me and through the glass there were people trying to get my attention. 'Don't look at them, just keep moving this way,' the figure told me. But I did look, and then I was in the hospital bed. Since then I've been sensitive to spirits."

The following night, which was a Saturday, I took Elaine to meet Stephanie. After shutting down the bar we invited Stephanie to stay the night at the mansion with us. We pulled up to the back gate, which slowly opened for us, and then pulled up the long drive to the blocky three-story brick house.

Stephanie walked through the kitchen, and when he hit the dining room slowed down and said, "Uh-uh," then made it almost to the foyer and shaking his head said, "Uh-uh. Un-uh" and bolted out the back door, white as a sheet.

Smoking a cigarette while shaking, he explained that he started to feel a strong energy when he hit the dining room, but by the time he was near the foyer, spirits began pouring down the staircase and were mobbing him.

"It was like they were beggars, all trying to get my attention. They were confused, they didn't know why they were stuck there and they wanted help," he said.

There was no way he was going back inside, so we got in the car to take him to his downtown loft overlooking the ballpark. As we were backing up he pointed to an upper window. "There's an elderly Black man watching us leave," he said.

One thing about Ol' Stephanie is he didn't like anyone sleeping over at his place, but in light of the circumstance I didn't think he'd mind.

"Is it ok if we sleep here?" I asked.

"Oh, go back, you'll be fine. They won't bother you!" he assured.

One of the main objectives for the weekend was for something spooky to happen, so we should've crawled in bed together while everything was stirred up and enjoyed the show, but in that moment we were too scared, and went back to my house instead, where Elaine slept on a sofa.

The next day we went back to pack up.

"It really did feel like we were roommates again," I said.

"Yeah, it did, and I'm kind of sad to go," Elaine replied. As she was descending the front staircase she said, "It's the oddest thing, but I feel a presence next to me. I've kind of felt it the whole time, like a young woman, but it's stronger now and it feels like she's trying to get me to stay."

## 102. Big Faye's Mirror

Big Faye, the pianist who had a way with gorgeous Black men, was living in the first-floor flat of blind musician Blaine Festus's two family on South Grand, and invited me and Damon over for a southern-style dinner.

The topic turned to the bar and restaurant business, and how they never announce in advance they're going to close, when Big Faye told us about the last night a popular gay piano bar called Blake's was open.

"The owner had moved down to Florida and turned it over to his young cokehead boyfriend, who'd just run it into the ground. I was playing the piano one night when the owner called the boyfriend and said, 'Don't say anything to anyone, but tonight will be the last night we're open,' and gave him instructions on how to close up. Well, he must've told someone because in five minutes everyone knew and people just started grabbing shit and running out! I'd never seen anything like it!" he said, shaking his head.

"Wow, what a mess!" I replied.

"It sure was," he began, then regally flipped his open hand over his shoulder, "And that's where I got that mirror."

## Story Box 8: Erotic Villa

Pat's mansion was on the Old North House Tour, and me and Damon volunteered to help. When our shift was done we went on the tour ourselves, and while approaching a house that sat right on St. Louis Avenue, a Black woman in a big pink church hat walked out, took one look at us, and shuffled down the sidewalk, giggling.

When we went inside it made sense. We were in the world's most homoerotic home.

The owner was big in leather circles, and while the historic house was largely unchanged on the outside, the interior had been gutted and rebuilt in a loft style with photos of the owner donning his leather gear on the walls, an enormous bed on an altar with an adjoining viewing gallery, and a master bath featuring a glass block wall, urinals, and a group shower that could accommodate half a dozen.

169

The house was for sale and the owner's parents, like the giggling church lady, thought it was perfect for us.

"Do you like the house?" they asked with enormous grins. "It's for sale!"

## 103. Big Faye and the Not Quite Gay

Big Faye wasn't big anymore, after losing hundreds of pounds. He had a sexy gentleman caller from the Caribbean named Malik who lived with him part time, and worked at Dick's, the gay strip club on the east side. This guy was so fit and his core was so strong he could dance on his hands just as well as on his feet.

My activist friend Roberta was a proud bisexual, but I'd never seen her admire a woman the way she'd admire the male dancers at Dick's, particularly Malik. She was standing with our group watching him when he approached, bent her over, and proceeded to grind against her for a good ten minutes. Looking up at us with her brown hair falling in her face she asked, "Ok guys, how much did you tip him to do this?"

"Nothing! Honest!" we replied.

It turned out he was also bisexual and was very attracted to her.
They began dating, but he was vague about his living situation. She drove him to Big Faye's to pick up some clothes and knew something wasn't right.

"I know of Faye, but have never met him. We pulled up and he's just sitting there on the porch with an angry look on his face," she recalled.

170

Roberta was the type who hated to leave things like this unresolved, and knowing of my connection, asked if perhaps a meet and greet could be arranged that might result in all parties feeling good about the complicated arrangement.

I wasn't up for broaching that topic with Faye. When I'd bump into him did enjoy discussing our shared appreciation for Cadillacs, but I couldn't figure out how I'd even segue to the topic of ride sharing.

## 104. A Call from Slyman

I missed a call from an unfamiliar number and called my voicemail to see who it was.

"Hi, Chris. This is Darin Slyman at *Vital Voice*. Please give me a call when you can."

With no idea what he wanted, I called him back. I couldn't really follow what he was saying initially, then he said, "William Collins is a huge fan of yours, he's just wild about your writing. We'd love to have you write for us if you're interested."

I was blown away. My work had gotten a lot of attention on Facebook, but to have someone tell me they want my stories in print was a real boost to my self-esteem. Rather than merely a guy who spent too much time on Facebook, I was now a magazine writer.

## 105.  The Prince of Publishing

Fashionable and petite, publisher Darin Slyman was a celebrity stylist who'd lived everywhere from Los Angeles to Paris but was originally from Tulsa, where his Lebanese father—Darin referred to him as "the Ayatollah" —made his fortune in the high-end steakhouse business. Though we were about the same age, our paths never crossed in Tulsa because he spent most of his time in a Michigan boarding school.

He went to college in St. Louis and though he moved around after graduating, he eventually returned, having fallen under its spell. In 2009 he picked up a copy of the *Vital Voice* for the first time.

"It was in newspaper format back then and I'll never forget the headline was 'How to Survive Hep C,'" he recalled, making a sour face. "I wrote the owner, Lydia Rothenberg, and said 'I just picked up your little paper and it made me sad. Let's meet about me writing some fashion columns for you.' She was very receptive and the first time we met I thought 'This woman is going to change my life.' I've only gotten that feeling a few times, and I've always been right. I loved Lydia immediately. She's fabulous, Jewish, a lesbian, business and civic minded," he said.

He served as the associate publisher for a year, writing a fashion column, and working with her graphic artist to make the paper more visually appealing, but the improvements were coming a bit too late for Rothenberg, whose paper was drowning in debt.

"I don't know if I can make it," Rothenberg said to Darin. "We're one-hundred fifty-thousand dollars in debt, everyone wants everything for free. What would you think about making it a nonprofit?" she asked.

Slyman suggested they instead go to the community and lay it all out. "So she did. She was like 'Hey, St. Louis Community I've done everything to help you and now I need you to tell me if you really need *Vital Voice*. We've been working for you for fifteen years with no financial support and more work demanded. What direction do you think we should go?' and the community went crazy. People were like 'I had no idea *Vital Voice* was struggling!' while many others just bitched. *The Riverfront Times* ran a piece about us closing, and it was 2008 when everything was closing, so everyone believed them," Slyman recalled.

Not long after, Rothenberg turned to him and asked half-jokingly, "Do you want to buy this fucker?" and Slyman's interest was piqued.

"I asked, 'What would you want?' and she pulled out a four-year-old assessment document, which seemed out of date and way off."

He mentioned the offer to his mentor, Max Adonis, a handsome silver fox who was also one of the most powerful and influential men in the Midwest.

"Max was really excited about the idea, so I asked if he'd sit down with the two of us and help hammer out an agreement. He and Lydia go way back and he was like, 'Lydia you've busted your ass for years, and now you've got this kid who can take this to the next level. Let him buy the name only, and let the LLC go under.' And she agreed.

"After the September 2009 issue I shut it down and let most everyone go in preparation for the re-launch as a magazine. William Collins had done some writing for *Vital Voice* and I offered him a position, which he was really excited about. His strength was creating content and we were a good team, with him reporting news and me bringing the entertainment and razzle dazzle. I hustled my ass off for three months and was thrilled with the little seven-hundred dollars in advertising that came in. But in the whole time I've owned *Vital Voice* we've never gone in the hole. We pay as we go and have zero debt. Lydia, for her part, has been an incredible friend and our biggest cheerleader," Slyman said.

Slyman was relentless about recruiting talent, often from outside the region but he also went after local celebrities, including popular and classically handsome DJ Jimmy No Show, who he practically stalked to bring on board.

In only a few years he was able to expand to nearby markets, including Kansas City.


## 106. The Pretender

Rustin Winchell was the most feared man in LGBT circles. A towering young attorney and entrepreneur with political ambitions, he appeared to live fast and loose, but would rain misery down on anyone who so much as made a catty comment about him, beginning with a threatening Cease & Desist letter.

His threats had the chilling effect he desired—it was hard to get anyone to comment on him at all, regardless of how outlandish his behavior was—and it was pretty outlandish. Once, for instance, he couldn't pay his enormous tab at a Grove nightclub, and when the bartender tried to keep him from bailing, Winchell grabbed him and attempted to perform a citizen's arrest.

Despite his purported wealth, he often had embarrassing bouts of momentary impoverishment.

At his zenith he ran with heavy hitters in state Republican circles, and even arrived in a limo to pick up gubernatorial candidate Sarah Steelman, listed in a 2008 New York Times article as being among seventeen women who may run for president of the United States. She was looking for a donation from the successful young entrepreneur, the limo driver was looking to get paid several thousand dollars for services rendered, and both were left wanting.

He was a regular at the St. Louis County Courthouse, representing clients, passing out cards, and meeting with judges. The master log in his dam of lies was pulled, however, after he gave a made up bar number to a clerk. Soon he was arrested for practicing law without a license, and the public's interests in his pathology began, with St. Louis Magazine doing a major feature on him asking, "Why does somebody so smart need to spend so much time pretending?"

I ran a piece in the *Vital Voice* about his years of scams, with great stories from people in the community about his shenanigans. He was convicted and served about a year in prison, but conning was in his blood, and he'd continue to find new victims for his various ventures, which included every kind of pyramid scheme imaginable.

175

## 107. Holidays with Rustin Winchell

Friend and musician Jason Thompson read my piece on the arrest of Winchell, and decided to tell me about the time he dated him from Christmas to New Year's, which he described as, "One of the most fucked up traumatic things I've ever experienced and probably ever will."

"I met Rustin on Gay.com several years ago on Christmas night, and he'd recently turned twenty-five," Thompson began. "He was staying with his Uncle Cecil in south city near Interstate 55 and Bates, invited me over, and I am ashamed to say it was love at first sight. We drank a few beers with his uncle and had a great night. It wasn't until the next day I discovered the extent of his alcohol and drug abuse. He was taking at least four prescriptions, two of which were Oxycontin and Lorazepam, and he seemed to have an endless supply of money, which he spent on expensive liquor and wine. We got wasted and had a lot of sex. That night was fun, but I wasn't used to drinking that way," Thompson recalled.

Lighting a cigarette, he continued. "The next night was no different until we reached the bedroom again. I'm versatile in that way, and he is a top, so he had already fucked me three times that night when he all of a sudden decides he wants to bottom. When he tried to force my cock into his tight hole, between booze and exhaustion, I went soft. He got really upset and went into the kitchen. When he returned he told me he'd injected a large amount of morphine into his leg and that I needed to hold him down because he'd soon be going into convulsions because it was too much. He wasn't lying. I was terrified, but it was all just a big blur the next day."

Despite everything, Jason went back over there on the third night, although this time he didn't drink.

"Again he was wasted. We were in the bed and he started spilling his guts about his ex, then he went to a completely dark and terrifying place. Most of it was incoherent, but he told me that he was the devil and that I needed to kill him before he destroyed the world. He pulled out a shotgun from under his bed, showed me that it was loaded, and tried to blow his brains out. I screamed for his uncle, who couldn't hear me, and wrestled with him trying to get the gun away, to no avail. He finally passed out. The next day he called and I told him I didn't want to see him again. But he begged and pleaded until I offered to come over if he wouldn't drink. He agreed, and we had an evening together that was one of the most wonderful evenings of my life. He made me a wonderful dinner, and we watched movies and snuggled and had lots of sex.

"The next night I went out with my girlfriends and called him on my way home around two to check on him. He sounded sober and fine. Around six in the morning I received a call from his aunt telling me he was in an ICU at Barnes Hospital. He'd gotten drunk after we talked, got into a fight with his uncle, and stabbed himself in the neck with a broken bottle and a flathead screwdriver.

"I went to Barnes immediately and the room was a bloodbath. Something straight out of a horror movie. And he was hysterical. Insane. Once they finally got him calmed down he was transferred to the psych ward where I spent New Year's Eve with him.

"When they released him a few days later, his family wouldn't have anything to do with him. I picked him up and brought him back to my place so he could try to figure out what to do. I told him there was no way in hell he could stay with me because my roommates would have no part of it, and with nowhere to go, dropped him off at St. John's psych ward. I decided that my time had expired in this horrendous situation, and it wasn't until about a year or so later that he contacted me, claiming to be staying in Rolla, clean and sober ever since."

After that Jason would hear from Winchell every now and then. When Jason's band began getting more gigs around town Winchell offered to be their manager, and unsolicited, sent a contract.

"We looked at the contract he supposedly paid someone six-hundred dollars to create and graciously declined. He then tried to tell me that my band was crap and that I was the true artist and should leave them and go solo. We haven't spoken since."

## 108. Nautical Adventures with my Luxury Czar

Steven Fang was a high-end realtor in St. Louis, specializing in elite properties like penthouses and mansions, and he also owned a popular restaurant and entertainment venue in the Grove. We became Facebook friends through Miles, Archer Andronico's business partner, and he began following my posts and commenting on my stories.

One day, he posted a photo while boating near the confluence of the Mississippi and Missouri Rivers, where the bluff-lined river is really wide, much like a lake, and has many islands. "I've always wanted to go boating up there," I commented.

Two weeks later, on a Sunday morning, he sent me a spur of the moment invite for a nautical adventure. We met at his elegant University City home, which was a symmetrical two-story brick Tudor with leaded glass windows.

In typical realtor fashion he was on a business call when I arrived with Damon, and we stood in his foyer admiring the fine art until he wrapped up.

Fang was a thin, nice looking man in his forties, with sandy blond hair and blue eyes.

"Welcome! I've packed a picnic lunch and we're going to pick up Matt & Brian in Clayton," he said.

Matt & Brian were well-known architects who owned the boat.

Fang had several vehicles, but for occasions like this he brought out his large vintage Mercedes, and the five us rode to the marina together, where we loaded the luxury watercraft with coolers of champagne and food, then sailed out towards Grafton, Illinois, admiring the fall foliage on the limestone bluffs while drinking mimosas, eating hors d'oeuvres, visiting, and reading the New York Times.

I followed Fang to the padded bow where we spread out and enjoyed the view. He was a fun and relaxed man who was easy to converse with. It was after that first afternoon I dubbed him my "Luxury Czar," a title he lived up to time and again.

179

The Fangs made their fortune in the produce business, and in addition to their St. Louis properties the family owned a sprawling, exquisite oceanfront home on the highest point on Monterey Bay, a few hours south of San Francisco. Every room in the house had a thirty-mile ocean view, and the second-floor guest suite where we stayed also had a balcony. We'd sleep with the door ajar to enjoy the sounds of the ocean.

In addition to my hurried everyday life with Damon, our typical leisure activities involved driving somewhere, hiking for hours, etc. By contrast, we'd rarely leave the house while visiting the Fang Seaside Villa, and I'd come to think of it as the only place I could truly downshift and relax.

Matt & Brian were often there, as well as Fang's friend Seth, who was a chef. They all loved cooking and would spend the weekend trying recipe after recipe.

In the evenings he'd throw parties for friends in the area, one which included the ex-wife of a tech mogul who's a household name for his eccentric behavior. During a playful exchange the 50-something woman asked me to feel her fake breasts, which I did.

The home that previously sat on that hilltop lot was hurled into the sea during the 1989 earthquake, but Fang's father assured his wife and family that the Corps of Engineers shored up the hill, and the house was anchored by piers so "it wasn't going anywhere." On his deathbed, however, he confessed he had no confidence in the piers.

"What good does it to drill down into sand?" he asked.

## 109. Curry Favor

Back in St. Louis, Fang was in the midst of a fling with a slim, redheaded guy in his twenties named Jimmy Curry. We'd heard about Curry a few times before meeting him, including the disparaging remarks of Lawrence Landau, an elegant man in his fifties who was arguably the top designer in town, with headlines in the *Post-Dispatch* like, "Landau Designed Penthouse Fetches 4 Million."

Landau was a close friend of both Fang and Archer Andronico, and believed Curry, who hailed from a working-class North County suburb, was a gold digger, and nicknamed him Trixie.

Fang hosted a dinner party and mentioned that Curry planned to stop by when he got off work at the retail store he managed.

"I don't trust her. She's Trixie!" Landau began as he swirled his wine. "You know there's no future in this, Steven. The sooner you end it the better."

Curry seemed to be in mid-sentence as he walked in talking about his day, which included going off on a shoplifter. He was a live wire, full of energy with a bubbly personality. Fang did break up soon after, because they didn't have much in common, but the two remained friends.

Curry was devastated for months, and I don't believe he was after Fang's money. He'd caught on that the nickname Trixie was derogatory and blamed Landau for the relationship ending. When the normally fun-loving Curry would cross paths with Landau from that point on, which was usually in a bar, Curry would strive to make the interaction as uncomfortable as possible.

"Call me Trixie! I dare you!" an intoxicated Curry would say.

## 110. Campaign for King

The annual Metrolink Prom was approaching, which was a big party onboard the light rail trains. The transit system was constantly under attack by the anti-transit Tea Party, who'd prefer to scrap the whole thing, so a group of Washington University in St. Louis students began organizing events to build support and enthusiasm for the system.

Each year a King and Queen were elected at the event, and with Fang's help I mounted a vigorous campaign. Fang created advertisements with slogans like "ANDOE FOR METRO KING: He'll have your back when he's King of the Track."

The night of the event I arrived in full king attire, flanked to my left by Fang, introduced as my Political Advisor, and to my right by Kenneth, my urban exploring buddy, introduced as my Body Guard. I worked the platform, shaking hands and making my case. There were five candidates and during my speech I said, "For anyone else this will be a one night thing, but elect me and year 'round I'll pimp this shit!"

A voice vote was held, and it was a photo finish between me and a guy in a kilt, but I think my efforts swayed the judges to cast the deciding votes and name me the winner.

True to my word, I pimped the shit out of my King of Metrolink title and worked on a campaign to increase funding for the system. Most believed the proposition would fail because the Tea Party was organized against it, but our side, led by a group called Citizens for Modern Transit, galvanized college students and pulled a surprise victory.

## 111. Plain Jane & the Stalker

Me and Jane were inseparable from kindergarten through the second grade. I thought both she and her mother looked like Snow White with their fair complexions and dark hair, and each morning on the way in to school she'd greet me with a big friendly smile.

When second grade ended and I changed schools we lost touch, then over a quarter of a century later she sent me a friend request over Facebook. Being the nostalgic guy I am, I was happy to hear from her. We reminisced about our childhood, mutual childhood friends including Gloria Wholegroves, but other than that we had absolutely nothing in common. Nothing. I was an urbane liberal gay guy, and she was an isolated fundamentalist Christian living in rural Oklahoma.

Despite our lack of commonalities she would write constantly, although she'd never inquire about Damon or discuss anything that touched on my sexuality.

She began to express frustration or confusion that I wasn't responding to her in real time, and I got the feeling I was one of the only social outlets in her world. By contrast I had a lot of things going on. I'd recently been voted King of Metrolink and was busy campaigning for a ballot measure to increase funding, I had many other friends competing for attention, and I even had a new stalker.

I had been out boating at the confluence of the Mississippi and Missouri rivers with my Luxury Czar Steven Fang, when I received two messages. The first was a panicked call from Mom saying a man called asking about me as if he were an old friend. When she gave him my number he immediately took on a menacing tone, saying he knew I was coming to Tulsa and when I did he had some people who wanted to talk to me.

The next voice message was from this man, and he sounded like a disgruntled redneck:

"Chris AnDOUGH! King of the metROW! Can't wait for ya to get to Tellsa, 'cause when you get here, well, I've got some folks who wanna speak with ya."

He then emailed via a fake Facebook profile named James Matson. "Boy you ain't no King! You a pussy."

Why would someone in Oklahoma know or be concerned with this title? I started combing through his fake profile and noticed he was in a relationship with a woman in the Philippines named Analyn. I went to her wall and found she was getting love posts from a guy named Dick Lloyd Hunt in Tulsa.

That took me less than five minutes.

184

I sent Dick a message that I had cracked the mystery of his identity and he went nuts, doubling down on the threats. Then he called Mom again and told her about the bodily harm he was going to do to me. Minutes later he called again to tell her he was going to do something to her house. Minutes after that he called yet again and said,
"I'm getting in your house and am going to do things to you that HAVE NEVER BEEN DONE before!"

Exasperated, she replied "Why would you say these things to me? I've never even met you!"

He promptly hung up, perhaps himself realizing he'd gone too far.

I was planning to go to Tulsa within the week and wasn't going to cancel because of this deranged idiot. I worked with a military guy about my age named Scout. He was in charge of maintenance, and after his morning crew meeting I asked if I could have a word with him in my office.

He took a seat and I closed the door.

"I have a stalker in Tulsa, and I'm going to be there in a few days. I need to borrow a gun."

He sat calmly, silently and expressionless for a moment, then he started to think out loud about what kind of gun would work best for an inexperienced user and what gun wouldn't be traceable back to him. He decided on the right one and made arrangements for me to pick it up.

At that moment I was in awe of the efficiency of straight men. He didn't need or want the dramatic details. He didn't offer opinions. It was all about the business at hand.

185

Meanwhile, Mom went to the Tulsa Police Department to file a report. At first they seemed dismissive, but once she turned in her written account of the threat with the name of the suspect they spent a good deal of time with her. She got the feeling they were aware of Mr. Hunt.

"I have a pistol at home but I don't know how to load it," Mom began. "My kids don't think it's a good idea for me to have a loaded gun around the house."

The old, folksy officer replied, "Well if your kids won't show you how to load it bring it up here and I'll load it for you!"

Aside from dealing with the stalker I was making plans to see many friends back home and had even made arrangements to visit Jane. Not knowing what else to do with her I suggested we meet at the elementary school and walk the grounds together. It seemed like it would be a poignant moment, reuniting at the very place we parted a lifetime ago. And maybe that would help us remember more stories.

Days ahead of my arrival, Jane sent an odd request. "There's a guy at work who wants to date me but I'm not interested. Would you post something [on Facebook] about being my boyfriend? I've been telling him I have a boyfriend and if he sees that I do I think he'll stop asking me out. I COMPLETELY understand if you don't want to."

Much of her communication was odd to me, so I just put it out of my mind.

From my stalker's wall I was able to contact his sister, who was a professional woman working in downtown Tulsa. She tried to assure me that he brother was harmless but talked big, and she kept stressing the importance of Mom changing her phone number.

My family has had the same number since 1965, and Mom wasn't about to change it. I contacted the sister again when the stalker made more threats, and she got testy, as if we were negligent for not following her advice. I told her there was really nothing more for us to discuss, but she should know that her brother threatened to come after my family, and if he did we were ready for him.

My four-hundred mile road trip with my illegal firearm was uneventful, and on my first full day in Tulsa I had my reunion with Jane. When I met her at the old schoolhouse it was even more awkward than it had been online. She seemed much older than her years, wearing a giant gardening hat and mom jeans.
We walked around the building, and to our surprise the doors were open and teachers were inside preparing for the year. I asked staff if we could look around and we were allowed to roam the building. It seemed she was enjoying herself, yet hardly said a word. I was grateful I hadn't agreed to anything else and was able to say goodbye afterwards. I didn't hear from her for the rest of the trip.

I found an address for Dick Hunt. He was living in a subsidized apartment building near the river. I shared this information with my friend Chad over coffee. Chad was a local celebrity in Tulsa, regularly playing the lead in Rocky Horror.

"Oh my God! That's right around the corner from my house!" he exclaimed.

We decided to have a photo shoot at the building—complete with my crown.

It was an interesting couple of days, sitting around my 70-year-old mom's house with loaded guns, but all was quiet. I returned to St. Louis, returned the gun, and went about my life.

Within a few days I began receiving long, intensely personal messages from Jane. She went into great detail about her abusive ex-husband and how she had to leave everything behind to get away from him. I didn't know how to respond, and she would express irritation that I wasn't writing back immediately. Then one day she wrote, "Why did you want to meet me at the school?" and proceeded to make the case that I was emotionally manipulating her. My delayed replies were examples of "mind games" I was playing, and she decided I was laying the groundwork for sexual exploitation.

 I shared this over Facebook and my friends sounded the alarm.

"CUT HER OFF NOW!"

"WHAT A CRAZY BITCH! RUN!"
People were telling me I'm lucky she didn't cry rape at the school.

These sentiments didn't sit well with one of my acquaintances, Luella, who exploded about how insensitive we all were to mental illness—we were monsters for suggesting I walk away from Jane, and we should all be ashamed. I summarized it, but this finger-wagging tirade went on for many comments.

So there I was, a gay guy, and I had a lot of female trouble. Essentially I broke up with both Jane and Luella on the same day.

I wrote Luella to explain that I'm an often irreverent entertainer, my life is my art, and I can't comfortably write and my readers can't comfortably participate with such looming judgment and rebuke hanging over us. I was not and had never been a politically-correct guy. I said I respect her, but thought we weren't compatible over Facebook.

She proceeded to trash me on her wall.

I also sent Jane a letter that politely and sincerely told her she needed help. She replied that she had just been testing me to make sure my motivations were genuine. She now knew they were, so we could move forward, and continued, "The next time you're in Tulsa you should meet my MOM! Wouldn't that be FUN?!"

I began to connect the dots and now believe Dick Hunt was either the man pursuing Jane or a friend of his. I could picture Jane going on about how I was "King of the Metro," and was coming to Tulsa to see her.
Long after I stopped communicating she tried to engage me again, and I took that opportunity to ask if the man who was interested in her might know the stalker.

"I think I know where this is going, and I don't like it one bit!" she replied.

Shortly after she continued, "That's a real slap in the face Mr. Andoe. A BIG SLAP!"

Dick Lloyd Hunt didn't call Mom again, but he randomly contacted my childhood friend Mindy, telling her, "You look like you should be standing on the corner of Whore and Main."

189

A few months later he was spotted by another old classmate. I was at the gym and got a text that he was in the doctor's office getting a boil lanced. He was missing a lot of teeth and was flirting with the staff. Afterwards he waited outside for his mother to pick him up.

## 112. Weaving Time & Space

The first time I lived in San Francisco I walked the mile from my office at 24th and Valencia to my apartment near 15th & Valencia several times daily, and would often pass a woman who looked a lot like an old neighbor from Villa Georgia, with her bright red hair and wild outfits. I struck up a conversation with her one day and she told me her name was Heidi. After that we'd always say hello and smile as we passed, but nothing more.

I'd been back in the Midwest for a few years but flew out to San Francisco for a friend's wedding and was walking in the old neighborhood when I passed Heidi on the street. "Hi, Heidi," I said.

"Oh, hi! I didn't see you there!" she replied, and kept walking as she always had before.

In her mind, I presume, I was still part of the fabric of that place, and I found that comforting.

### Story Box 9: Ol' Patsy Pallbearer

My friend Mindy's mom Patsy was a funeral groupie. If she had any connection to the deceased—her mother's old coworker, her daughter's grade school teacher, an old neighbor's aunt—she'd be at the service just crying and carrying on.

She called Mindy at lunchtime to fill her in on that morning's funeral. "Oh, it was so sad!" she wailed, recalling the grief-stricken family and their touching displays of emotion. Then, noticing the time, snapped right out of it. "Uh, Mindy I gotta go! I've got another service at 2!"

## 113. An Emperor is Born

The organizers of the annual Metrolink Prom had all scattered to the wind after graduating from Washington University in St. Louis, but they wanted to see the event continue. As the last and most active King of Metrolink in history, they asked me to host the event and we decided I would do so as "The Emperor of Saint Louis."
With Steven Fang as the DJ we packed the subway car with well over a hundred festive people in zany formal attire, and by applause vote the People elected a new King and Queen.
The King was a gorgeous and charismatic young Black guy, and as I passed the crown on to this younger man, for the first time in my life I felt like George W. Bush.

I named my *Vital Voice* column *Tales from the Emperor.*

# The Tawdry Tales of Rotten Crotches

### 114. Meet Josh

"Dude! Amanda's vagina smells awful," Josh randomly announced during conversation. Strange as his pronouncement was, it didn't catch me off guard nearly as much as when he asked, "Do you think we're best friends?" only two weeks after we met.

I first laid eyes on this 19-year-old farm boy from Crocker, Missouri in an old and forgotten section of South St. Louis after he called my office looking for a cheap place to live. The best value I had was a one-bedroom overlooking a cemetery, and after one cursory look he was ready to rent it.

He had no idea how to conduct business, no credit or rental history, and only a handwritten note from his future boss at Taco Bell. It was pitiful, but he was trying really hard and going about the task seriously. He asked dozens of questions about the apartment, the application, the neighborhood, and would furrow his brow and contemplate every answer. He was out in the world trying to do things on his own, and I found all of his questions endearing. The kid was so green; he'd need some guidance to make it in the city. I rented to him, and the very night he moved in he began texting as if I were one of his buddies. Maybe it was because I was treated him kindly and gave him a chance, or perhaps that's the way things were done in the country.

He moved to St. Louis to be with a grubby high school girl named Amanda who he'd met online. Oh, she was dreadful. Short and squat with dark seven-inch roots mixing with stripper platinum, thick black mascara, faded pink lipstick, and chipped fingernail polish. She looked like a dirty girl, but the worst thing about her was the ever present scowl on her freckled face.

Amanda was intensely jealous and possessive. When she and Josh weren't together she'd call and text relentlessly to make sure she knew what he was up to. He'd spent a few months living with her dysfunctional family, and she'd grown accustomed to him just waiting in her bedroom while she was at school. She didn't like the idea of him being out of her sight, and if he didn't respond immediately to one of the hundreds of texts, she'd call screaming, "WHO ARE YOU FUCKING?"

Josh told me he had been fired from a previous job at a supermarket because he was always texting, and when he'd ignore her texts she'd call the store and demand to speak with him.

I cringed when I learned his mother was my age. At thirty-five, I wasn't old enough to be the parent of a grown man. He was the product of two horny teenagers in rural Missouri, the first in a frenzied breeding spree back on the farm resulting in something like twelve kids among the broken family.

Josh began following me around like a lost puppy, and since I didn't plan on having children of my own, I decided he'd be my project. He was going to languish at the bottom of society without some backing and support. I could change his trajectory, and it wouldn't be difficult, I figured. I was well connected; I could get him a better job. Me and Damon could help him with intimidating financial aid paperwork and get him educated.

This kid could have a whole new life.

So, I would accept this challenge and take him under my wing as if he were my own. But pouring energy into him while he was with Amanda would be like pouring water through a colander. No, in order for any of this to work Amanda would have to go.

## 115. Definition of Sex

According to Josh's reports, things continued to go awry in Amanda's poor vagina. The emanating odors were getting worse, and there seemed to be yeast sprouting.

Every visit included a vaginal update, so I was taken aback when he told me that he and Amanda had never had sex. She was underage, after all, and he didn't want to get in trouble with the law. I wasn't buying it until I learned Josh had a very specific definition of sex, which to him was a penis entering a vagina. He was knocking at the back door nightly and thought that didn't count. He also seemed to believe there was some sort of firewall between the vagina and anus which would prevent him from contracting the sexually transmitted disease wreaking havoc on the neighboring orifice.

I sat across the booth from him at a bustling Thai restaurant on South Grand. We were constantly interrupted by Amanda's texts and calls. She was really upset with him and he was riddled with anxiety, unable to focus on our conversation. "I'm sick of her shit," he'd complain, saying she stressed him out to the point of making him ill.

"You're consumed by this unhealthy relationship, and your life will never amount to anything as long as Amanda's in it," I began, and then I pulled two pennies out of my pocket. "If held close enough to your eyes, these two pennies could block out the entire Grand Canyon."

Josh loved to talk, loved to vent about Amanda, and loved to be listened to. He was separated from his mother too soon. They kicked him out in high school and he had lived with his grandparents and for a time in his car. He didn't respect his father, who was in prison, and desperately sought the illusive approval of his stepfather.

The Thai food was much too spicy and exotic for his taste, although he wouldn't admit it. I'm not sure if he took more than a bite before just playing with it between Amanda's frenzied texts.

An hour later he asked if I'd buy him a meal at Taco Bell.


### 116. Shower Show

Josh was showering while Amanda sat on the toilet lid talking to him. "Then she got all quiet 'n shit and I looked over and she had her hand up her skirt masturbating!" Josh recalled. When he asked what she was doing she replied, "I can't help it. You're just *so* hot!"

My friendship with Josh was taking up much of my bandwidth as I was consumed with trying to help him get established and break free from Amanda. Writer's block set in and I was often distracted at work. Then there was the drama. Being in the gay community I cut my teeth on drama queens, but had never been pulled in like I was with Josh. His drama came at you like a runaway semi-truck crossing the median.

Amanda would tell him she was messing around with somebody else and he'd call me or show up at my door crying hysterically. Complicating my efforts to help him get away from her was his own mother, who adored Amanda and would often come to her defense.

Amanda knew nothing made Josh angrier than the thought of her with someone else, and nothing got her off more than seeing Josh fight for her. She'd constantly set up ridiculous scenarios that ended with Josh beating up some guy, or she'd have guys call to taunt him. The latter was a lot harder on Josh. He wasn't one to match wits, and without the release of fighting he was left in torment.

I took the role of a father with him and tried to teach him how to be in control. That phone was a leash and she was jerking it. She was manipulating him constantly and making him her bitch. He took my advice and started turning his phone off for a few hours at a time when she was acting up, which would drive her crazy and temporarily give him the upper hand.

Apparently Amanda shared Josh's belief that what they were doing wasn't sex. I had taken Josh shopping for household goods and she kept sending him texts asking, "When are we going to have SEX??"

"The other day I was finally gonna do it but my dick went soft when I smelled that shit," he said.

Despite her issues, his attraction to her was intense. He'd sometimes describe her as being, "trashy and slutty" but said that really turned him on.

### 117. Amanda's Family

I had big plans for Josh, and Amanda was a real fly in the ointment, causing him nothing but heartache. My disdain for her didn't mean that I didn't see the tragedy of her circumstances, though.

Her mother was a junkie named Jane who hadn't worked in years and leached off the grandmother, Virginia. The whole gang lived in Virginia's suburban home, which according to Josh, looked like it was right off a Hoarders episode. Also living there were Amanda's obese brother and Jane's ex-con boyfriend LaMont.

Virginia's late husband had owned a successful business and they enjoyed an upper middle-class lifestyle for decades. I'm not sure how things went so wrong with Jane, but she was rapidly depleting Virginia's resources with her drug habit. Poor Virginia was pretty batty and lived in complete denial of the things going on around her. For instance, Jane would make up preposterous stories about needing money for surgeries and Virginia would do whatever she had to do to get her the funds.

197

## 118. Signs of Hope

Two detours before work. Walgreens to buy Josh something for jock itch and his apartment to give it to him. Yes, Josh was having problems with his crotch, and he'd never buy anything like that for himself.

This noble project of mentoring a promising disadvantaged youth had devolved to this. Zero progress had been made getting him enrolled in community college. In fact, little progress had been made in any area. I knew, however, that he was listening because he'd regularly regurgitate the pearls of wisdom I'd shared. I didn't know if he was actually listening or just parroting, but I had hope.

Another promising development was he and Amanda breaking up. On that front I was cautiously optimistic. Although he wanted to be away from her, he was still obsessed enough to monitor her online activity, especially her favorite white trash dating site where she claimed to be legal.

We were at lunch and I brought a pad and paper so we could map out what he wanted from life. "I wanna be single until I'm at least twenty five," he began. He wasn't sure if he wanted children. He wanted to marry a nice woman and have a healthy relationship, and cited my childhood friend Francis & his wife Edie as an example—he'd been very impressed with them. He thought he'd like to be a fireman. "And I ain't never going back to Crocker," he vowed.

I also wanted to see the world through his eyes. I asked about the mountains and the oceans. I asked if he knew how big New York was, how big Chicago and LA were, how big St. Louis was. He had no knowledge of the world, and was a little surprised Chicago was so much larger than St. Louis.

"I didn't know Chicago was that much bigger, but I still think St. Louis is more famous," he said.

I guess there wasn't much talk of Chicago in Crocker, MO.

## 119.   All Access Pass

I didn't want my boy to have a rotten crotch.

That damn Amanda was such a thorn in my side. Even if I did get him away from her he might remain permanently soiled. I wanted big things for this kid and had invested time, energy, and money. Well, at least at the beginning I wanted big things. My expectations were regularly adjusted, downward, but that's beside the point.

Of course I knew it was coming, and then he began to complain of excessive genital sweating and a rash on his scrotum. I'd been telling him, "You're going to get whatever she's got," and he'd always reply, "Well, if I got something I got something. I mean there's no use crying about it."

Like Josh's mother I had an all access pass to his life. Both of us knew how much yeast was being discharged from Amanda's toxic twat, if he'd smoked pot or had a sexual fantasy about a coworker, and if his nuts had a rash. Knowing so much gave me a strange sense of ownership of his issues.

This abundance of disclosure didn't mean he wasn't embarrassed, although it seemed the embarrassment didn't set in until the follow-up questions began. And I always had plenty.

He came over to use the computer, wanting to get on the white trash dating site where he'd met Amanda. Once online he was like a zombie glued to the screen, scrutinizing Amanda's profile while simultaneously instant messaging several girls.

I interrupted to research STDs with him. He was very uncomfortable so I pulled up a site that had descriptions and photos and left him alone to look through it. It took him about a minute to draw the conclusion it was merely jock itch before he resumed his online dating/stalking.

I found his dark and cluttered apartment depressing so I rarely visited, but I stopped to drop off something when he said, "Dude, my nuts stink. I'll get in the shower and really scrub and when I'm done they still stink!" This was disturbing, and like many of his problems it weighed on me.

The following weekend I was at a big cocktail party at Villa Ray and asked a few friends about Josh's symptoms. "Ooh it sounds like chlamydia," my friend Rodney said, while my exploring buddy Kenneth exclaimed, "That boy's got the clap!"

In my intoxicated state I was consumed with a sense of urgency and sent him a text.

His phone always took priority over anything else going on at that moment, even at work, so when it vibrated he stopped rolling burritos and stared intently at the screen trying to understand what I had written. Unfortunately, a nosy coworker also stopped to read over his shoulder.

The text began: "YOU HAVE CHLAMYDIA…"

## 120. Worthless

Josh had a cold and was complaining of a sore throat. Initially I ignored his text requests for help, refusing to compensate for the laziness of his trifling girlfriend, who was sitting there with him. He upped the ante with, "I thought you'd always be there for me."

Amanda was unpleasant, antisocial, dumb as a box of rocks, wouldn't help cook or clean, and couldn't even manage her own hygiene. From the very beginning I told Josh I wouldn't be around her, and I advised him against inflicting her on others. When he ignored my advice and brought her around people, she'd just glare at them in silence through globs of cheap mascara before she'd resume playing on her phone.

He kept asking me to bring him something for his throat. The barrage of requests and the attempts to make me feel guilty were infuriating, and I responded that she needed to walk to the corner store. "If you were alone and needed help that would be one thing, but I am not going to drive over when she's just sitting there like a lump on a log."

"I just thought you'd help me when I got sick," he wrote.

I went off. "I'm sorry that your girlfriend is so WORTHLESS she won't waddle her ass to the corner to help you, but I'm NOT going to play nursemaid. That's a girlfriend's job!"

To my knowledge, the sore throat went untreated for the night. We would have many more fights over the phone and over text in the coming months. They'd usually end when he'd call me and in a very calm tone say, "Dude, I don't wanna fight with you."

## 121. Sleepless

I had a dream Donald moved to St. Louis and bought a big old southern-style house, the kind with a porch that wrapped all the way around. He had a grand party and all of our friends were there, but I forgot to go.

That was one of many anxiety dreams about devoting too much time to Josh at the expense of everyone else, including Damon, who didn't see the appeal. My schedule was full before I met him and now this kid was cramping my style. I'd even missed Mardi Gras because he flaked out at the last minute, after my friends had already left.

I'd cut him off and then get roped back in by the drama, like the time he showed up on my doorstep at 6:30 in the morning with dark circles under his glazed over eyes and said, "Dude, I'm sorry for coming over like this but I need a friend real bad, man."

Amanda had some guy call and taunt him all evening, and he was beside himself, having paced, cried, and punched the air all night. He was so distraught and exhausted, and I wanted to comfort him. I put a big pillow next to me and he leaned in. While we talked I stroked his hair, and in that moment he was my kid.

That afternoon he told his mom every detail about the morning. Although Josh's life in the city seemed so foreign to her, she had a good sense of humor about it. Especially that he called me his "City Dad" and Damon his "City Mom."

Regarding his morning with me he said, "I'm not gay but it felt good to have someone give a shit about me."

While he and his mom were close, there was some lingering tension about his stepfather kicking him out.

Since he had her on the line he provided the obligatory update on Amanda's condition, and asked, "Hey, is it normal for a woman's vagina to smell like some nasty tuna?"

"Well, mine don't smell like no tuna!" she replied.

## 122. Squandered Opportunities

It was time to introduce Josh to people who might have opportunities for him, but first I had to get him clothing that fit as opposed to the grossly oversized outfits he'd swim around in.

I first took him shoe shopping. He wasn't sure what size he needed, but he thought he wore a ten. He tried on a pair and I asked how they felt but wasn't convinced they were the right size. Josh was a small guy, and I'm 6' and wear a 10 ½. I felt for his toe as if he were five years old, and the shoes were about three sizes too big.

"I just like bigger shoes," he said, and I didn't argue.

He wasn't comfortable meeting new people and had a bad habit of blurting out inappropriate questions and comments. Before I'd introduce him to someone, he'd nervously ask, "Are they nice?" I promised that everyone I knew would be nice to him, and they were.

I'd taken him to meet my friend Jimmy Curry, who managed a retail store, hoping I could at least get him out of fast food. Jimmy was slim and looked stylish in his form-fitting jacket. Josh filled out an application and visited for a few minutes, then asked Jimmy, "So, um, do you think I've got a pretty good chance of being hired here?"

After we left Josh said, "If I *was* gay I think I'd probably date someone like Jim, because I'd be more like the guy in the relationship."

At least he knew enough not to say *that* directly to Jimmy. While not particularly feminine, Jimmy was more fashionably dressed than any guy in the history of Crocker, Missouri.

Jimmy and Josh had a similar build, and Jimmy brought him a stack of nice, nearly new clothes. Between the two of us we had Josh looking like a new man, and he felt better too. Proud of his new appearance, Josh took note of how flattering the fitted shirts were and how nice the khakis looked.

"It feels like I fit in now, and people treated me with more respect."

Amanda, his eternal albatross, was threatened by his new look and berated him.

"Why are you trying to dress like Chris Andoe now?" she demanded. "Do you just wanna go be gay with Chris Andoe?"

From the start I thought Francis could be the one to give Josh his big break. He'd also moved to St. Louis from a small town but was now doing well for himself in the art publishing business. From time to time he had openings for assistants and I hoped he could take Josh under his wing. Francis could build a crate in the morning and comfortably talk with millionaire collectors in the afternoon. He had the patience and the skill to really mold Josh, I figured.

I began to sell Francis on the idea and his interest was piqued. I spoke to Josh about the possible opportunity and how it could lead to big things, stressing that he needed to make a good impression.

I'd located a sofa for Josh, and Francis helped us move it to his apartment. It was the first time the two of them met, and as usual Josh paid way too much attention to his damn phone. Me and Francis did most of the heavy lifting so needless to say he wasn't impressed with this kid, but kept an open mind. Noticing how bare the apartment was, he offered to give Josh a few things.

"I've got a basement full of stuff you could use. Come by this weekend and see if you want anything."

Josh and Amanda were broken up at the moment, but their relationship had a monthly cycle. It would be bitter and contentious, then they'd break up, and then they'd get back together and that phase was the fucking worst because Josh was so delusional about how everything was going to be different this time.

I had always stressed that on one side of the ledger was Amanda and on the other side was the entire world and what it had to offer, he had to choose, but during these honeymoon periods he desperately tried to find a way to have it all. During their break ups, his new life filled with good times and opportunity. If only he could somehow fold her into the equation.

So it was the following Saturday and Josh called to get directions to Francis & Edie's house. My stomach sank when I realized Amanda was with him.

"Josh, you should reschedule with Francis for a time when just the two of you can hang out and get to know each other," I said.

"I'm available to hang out. We can all hang out," he said.

I continued firmly, "Francis may want to discuss business, and it would be better if you went alone."

"I really want to get this done today," he replied bluntly.

Most of the time he and Amanda were together was spent playing video games or staring at the walls, so he was eager to be entertained.

Francis and Edie warmly welcomed them, but Amanda refused to speak, refused to sit down, and even ignored their friendly dog Shelby, who was trying to greet her. The items were in the basement so Francis and Josh went downstairs leaving Edie and Amanda alone. She didn't look up from texting when Edie gave her a soda, nor did she drink it. Of course Edie was offended, having never been treated so rudely in her own home.

Josh was giddy with excitement and seemed completely oblivious to Amanda's behavior. When the guys came back upstairs, Josh tried to settle in. "So how did you guys meet?" he eagerly asked, but Edie was expecting her mother any minute and wasn't in the mood to explain the dreadful creature glaring at everyone from the corner.

Picking up on Edie's cue, Francis started loading Josh's car. Josh took the hint and grabbed a box, then turned to Amanda, "Can you give me a hand?"

The miserable girl delivered her only word of the visit with an answer that stunned even Josh:

"No."

## 123. Fallout

"WHY DID YOU TAKE ME THERE?" Amanda barked when they got in the car.

Despite everything Josh thought the visit went fine, until he heard otherwise from me.

Me and Damon were antique shopping on Cherokee Street when I heard about the fiasco. I sent Josh a message that simply read, "You should have waited."

207

He immediately called but I didn't answer. He went into full panic mode. "Why? What happened? Call me," he wrote.

"SHE WAS RUDE AND DISRESPECTUL! SHE DIDN'T EVEN SPEAK! YOU SHOULD HAVE NEVER BROUGHT HER THERE. STOP INFLICTING HER ON PEOPLE!" I replied.

"Are you mad at me now?" he asked before trying to call me again.

I ignored the call and sent a message saying I was trying to spend the afternoon with Damon and I would talk to him later. He kept texting, wanting reassurance that I was still his friend. His last message said he tore into her for fucking things up for him and now she was crying.

Francis took a pass on Josh, but Jimmy Curry ended up hiring him as a favor to me—it didn't last long.

"Promise me you'll keep your phone off while you're working!" I demanded. He agreed, but it was obvious he was secretly talking to Amanda while in the restroom. He would disappear for fifteen minutes and then come out looking like he'd been crying and ask to take a smoke break. After he was fired I told him I knew he'd been on the phone with her at work, but he wouldn't admit it at the time.

He still had Taco Bell, and I told him I was no longer referring him to people. "I vouched for you, Josh, and this has damaged my credibility."

He hung his head and said, "I see what you're saying. I guess I did make you look like a jackass."

## 124. The Matron

Josh closed his eyes and tried to imagine it was Amanda going down on him.

"Does it smell down there?" he asked.

Sure it did, but the matronly young woman shook her head no and continued. While she was only twenty one, she had plain looks of a rural fifty-year-old mother of four. He ejaculated on her breasts and as it dribbled down her doughy torso he half-jokingly said, "I hope it doesn't get in your vagina and get you pregnant."

In a revealing moment the Matron replied casually, "If it does, it does."

Josh and Amanda had broken up again, and this break was looking a little more solid. Amanda had accessed his social media accounts, changed the passwords, and filled both profiles with long inarticulate diatribes about how Josh was gay and in love with Chris Andoe, was a user, and had a small dick.

Josh couldn't handle being without a girlfriend and within days had arranged to bring the Matron in from the sticks. They had gone to the same school but he was never attracted to her. Frustrated with the women on his white trash dating site who always flaked out, he figured the Matron was a sure thing. He wanted somebody around for the weekend, so the plan was to pick her up on Friday and take her home Sunday evening.

Anyone was better than Amanda, so I adopted a Pro-Matron stance. I had them over and we entertained them all weekend, really rolling out the red carpet.

"Chris Andoe likes you!" Josh excitedly told her. "Chris Andoe doesn't let just anybody in his house. I took Amanda over there once and he kicked our asses out!"

From the start I forbid Josh from bringing Amanda over, and the one time he tried I didn't let them get past the foyer.

Although a young woman, by rural Missouri standards the Matron was an old maid. In Crocker, high school is one's zenith, and it's all downhill from there. Single and dumpy, she seized on her chance at Josh and wasn't going to let go. When Sunday rolled around she dug in her heels, refusing to go home.

She worked at Walmart and called in sick three days in a row, then Josh called to say the Matron might just stay for good.

"She's still here and I might just let her stay," he began, sounding more resigned than excited. "She keeps the house clean, which Amanda never did. I hate how she calls me 'Baby' a hundred times a day though. And I'm not turned on by her so she just sucks my dick and shit."

My hopes and dreams for Josh were at a low-water mark. Now I just wanted to see him hold down his job, maintain his apartment, get treatment for his apparent STD, and stay away from that awful Amanda.

I said bluntly, "Josh, I think this is sloppy and isn't a good idea, but it's probably the only way you'll stay away from Amanda."

Josh had been clamming up about his rotten crotch. He'd grown tired of me asking about it and was still kind of sore at me for the drunken chlamydia text that was seen by his coworker.

I'm sure the Matron noticed the moist, foul-smelling rash on his scrotum and wondered if it was contagious, but then decided, "If it is, it is."

## 125. Shit Hits the Fan

I once told Josh he had the conversational style of a tennis ball launcher. An exhausting volley of questions with small pauses in between. He would ask if he could come over on a weeknight to check his dating site and wash his uniform. He would ask if I would go by and let his dog Maggie out. He would ask if I'd come over and talk to him because he was depressed. He'd try to build a safety net for himself by getting commitments from me, asking questions like, "I'm not planning on losing my job, but if I did, could I move in with you guys?"

He was good at overcoming objections and wearing people down. For example, he got a $25 parking ticket on a street cleaning day and called the City of St. Louis to dispute it. The bureaucrat explained that the street cleaning schedule was posted and that he'd have to pay it or he would incur penalties. He squatted on the line and went around and around with her. He asked her again what street cleaning meant and then said, "Well, I just moved here from the South and I never heard of that shit!"

"Fine!" the exhausted and defeated clerk said. "Consider this your one get out of jail free card." He started to thank her but she promptly disconnected.

He noticed that Edie and Francis always brought their dog Shelby over, and had been angling for the same privilege, but I told him it wasn't a good idea.

While I was invested in Josh, Damon had lost interest almost immediately and was increasingly annoyed by his visits. I'd attempt to balance my partner, who'd prefer Josh not come over at all, and Josh, who'd prefer to be over every day.

But now my defenses were compromised because I was reinforcing the theme that life is so much easier and more fun without Amanda. He asked if we could walk our dogs to the park together, and I agreed. We had only gotten as far as the corner when the first tennis ball was launched: "So do you think I can start bringing Maggie over all the time now?"

It was a warm and lovely evening in Tower Grove and the walk went fine. The Matron wasn't bright or interesting, but we tried to be as engaging as possible. Josh asked if he could check his email when we got back to the house, and as we were walking up the front steps he said, "Dude, I hope Maggie doesn't shit in your house."

"Has she been—?" I started before something interrupted us, and the next thing I knew Josh was firmly glued to the computer screen in the study as the Matron sat quietly in the living room.

Damon walked past Josh and noticed he was studying Amanda's dating profile. Seconds later he noticed Maggie had been squirting quarter-sized drops of diarrhea all over the hardwood floor.

"Josh, Maggie has diarrhea and I'm taking her to the yard," Damon said hurriedly.

"Oh, uh, okay," Josh said as he stared like a zombie at the screen, completely consumed with Amanda's profile.

The yard wasn't completely fenced so I stayed outside with Josh's sick dog while Damon went back in to deal with the mess. I wondered what was taking Josh so long. Surely he'd be out any minute to deal with Maggie. Damon came back out, having cleaned up all of the dog feces with a little help from the Matron. Josh had never left the computer.

My blood was boiling. I walked into the study and said, "Josh, it's time to go."

"Uh, okay, just let me check one more thing..."

"NOW," I interrupted.

Like an extra in an Old West shootout scene, the Matron broke camp, quickly rushing Maggie out towards the car. Josh seemed disoriented, having just awoken from a trance. He walked slowly to the front porch then turned back and asked, "So, um, what do you do when a dog has diarrhea?"

"I don't know," I curtly replied as I shut the door.

I only got angrier as I thought about him sitting on that computer, stalking that diseased whore, while my partner was cleaning up his dog's shit. I sent him a text that read, "I have never been so disrespected in my life."

He immediately tried to call back but I was not in the mood to talk to him. He left me an indignant voicemail. "YOU KNOW, I'M SICK OF YOUR SHIT. YOU NEED TO LEARN HOW TO TREAT PEOPLE. YOU THINK YOU'RE A REAL BADASS BUT YOU'RE NOT!"

At this point I was seeing red. Trying to keep a calm and collected front with Damon, I went outside to call Josh. He didn't answer and I was nearly choking on my own anger. My jaw was tight and I could feel the veins throbbing in my neck when I began, "YOU THANKLESS LITTLE FUCK! DON'T YOU EVER CALL ME FOR ANYTHING AGAIN!"

## 126. Wake up Maggie

And so I was done. After a few days Josh tried to call but I let it go to voicemail. It would be a few more days before he realized I had unfriended him on Facebook.

"YOU DELETED ME ON FACEBOOK! You're like a little girl!" he said in the message. Then things went quiet.

After a month or so he started to send me messages about doing drugs, which were clearly cries for attention.

"I love pot," a couple of them read. "Pot's my new girlfriend."

I ignored them until one Sunday night he sent a message about how he was in Crocker getting high all weekend. I knew he never brought Maggie to Crocker, and became concerned. I sent him a text.

Me: Where's Maggie?

Josh: She at home

Me: "You are so fucked up"

Josh: WHY?

Me: You left your dog alone in the apartment for several days!

Josh: I couldn't take her and had nobody to depend on

That last line, the manipulation and the avoidance of responsibility, infuriated me.

By this point the dog had been left unattended for about 48 hours. I was sick about it, and told Damon I wanted to let her out and make sure she had food and water. He advised against it, but I wasn't going to be able to sleep thinking about her. I sent Josh a text.

Me: I'm going to your apartment to let Maggie out.

Josh: Oh thanks man

Me: I'M NOT DOING THIS AS A FAVOR TO YOU! I can't sleep thinking about that abandoned dog!

Josh: Or be a bitch about it

I drove through the bowels of the city in the dark and the rain, wondering what I'd find. I never liked going to his forgotten part of town, where the old and sprawling cemeteries meandered leaving disjointed urban blocks floating in a sea of tombstones.

What was I going to find? Surely urine and feces, but Maggie was an older dog and I worried she might be dead or dying. The apartment was sure to be pitch black. Josh was very frugal about electricity, so all of the lights would be off.

Maggie happily greeted me at the door. I let her out first, then went in to assess the situation.

215

The first thing I noticed were the enormous piles of dirty laundry. He had always done his laundry at my house, and apparently had not done any since. Because of his rotten crotch he wore gym shorts instead of underwear, and had been washing them in the sink. They were hanging up all over the bathroom.

Surprisingly, there was so sign of dog feces or urine, but I noticed her food and water bowls were empty. I think he intentionally left her without food or water so she wouldn't have accidents.

"I'm so disappointed in you, Josh," I wrote, and I was. This was so much worse than anything that had come before.

He was partying with his uncle and a whole slew of rednecks out there in rural Missouri. They had just gotten back from a strip club where his uncle paid a stripper to have sex with him. He was riding high and I was a real buzzkill.

"Leave me the fuck alone and stop bringing me down. I'm happy with my life," he responded.

## 127. Return to Sender

A few weeks after his drug-induced backwoods orgy Josh called me at work, expressing remorse for leaving Maggie alone.

"I was just so upset when you weren't talking to me anymore and Amanda was fucking with me all the damn time. Dude, honestly I just had to get away. It was messed up of me to leave her."

216

I learned what became of the Matron. Shortly after I threw him out, they'd gotten in to an argument and he locked her out of the apartment, and her mother had to drive four hours round trip to retrieve her. As you can imagine, the jilted Matron was extremely bitter. She went public with her hostility, posting rants on his MySpace about what a piece of shit he was.

I couldn't fathom why he didn't just unfriend her, but he didn't even bother deleting her comments.

He claimed he was still broken up with Amanda, but his cell phone was on her family plan and she was threatening to take it back.

"I just want to take the fuckin' phone and throw it in the river," he'd say. He wanted to get a new phone with a different number so she couldn't reach him.

He never did anything on his own for the first time, so I agreed to go with him to get a new phone. I wanted to make sure he got something simple without a contract, and he settled on a phone that had internet access.

"Now I can throw her goddamn phone in the river!" he said.

"Josh, don't do that. Just send it back by certified mail. I'll go to the post office with you."

That phone was his digital collar. It's how she sent him hateful text messages daily and had strange guys call to mock him. I thought getting rid of it was going to be a step in the right direction, and was eager to see it go.

The next time I asked about it he said he had already dropped it in the mail to her. That didn't sound right and I started probing further, asking how he mailed it.

"Well, uh, I just put it in a Ziploc bag with a note saying to deliver it to her address and dropped it in the mailbox at the Kirkwood Post Office."

"Josh, they're not going to mail it like that. What were you thinking? I told you I'd help you!" I said, exasperated.

"It's just something I wanted to do myself," he replied.

When he was thinking hard about something he'd furrow his brow and wad up his face. Damon would say, "You can just see that hamster wheel turning."

Within the hour I anonymously called him on the old number several times. I knew it was taking all the discipline he could muster not to answer. He thought it was probably me testing him, but it could be Amanda or one of those guys. Eventually he succumbed to his curiosity.

"Hello...Hello...Hello," he said as I sat there in silence, disgusted.

I really had nothing planned to say, and started speaking softly but ended in an insane Molly Shannon-like shout, "I'm calling you from the KIRKWOOD POST OFFICE!" and hung up.

## 128.  Laundry Day

After I caught Josh in the lie about the phone he frantically tried to contact me.

"You're too dishonest for me to invest any additional time or energy," I said in a text.

"That's what you want? Well, if it's over I'll come and say goodbye in person," he wrote.

"BRING THAT DRAMA TO MY DOOR AND SEE WHAT HAPPENS!" I responded.

I didn't hear from him for a few days until he called me at work. He said he knew things wouldn't be the same but he wanted to work on our friendship.

"You and Damon never come over. I just want you guys to come over for dinner and hang out. When I was in Crocker my mom gave me all of this deer meat and we could cook that."

Well, all of that sounded just awful. His apartment was small and dirty, and I knew he couldn't cook. He always wanted me to hang out at his apartment but I only did a couple of times, but I couldn't relax in the squalor so I'd end up cleaning. One bright Saturday morning I visited and it was like a cave. I opened all of the blinds, washed dishes and helped him organize his closets. He was excited about how his place was shaping up and I said, "Josh, this is the kind of thing you and a girlfriend could do together. Your girlfriend is as useless as tits on a boar hog."

So no, I wasn't interested in going to dinner at his place.

"I'm not coming over for dinner but I'll meet you at the laundromat on my lunch break."

At this point I was under no illusions about Josh. I had no grand ambitions, didn't really trust him, but I wanted to leave him with something of value from his time in my life.

At one time I was going to get him educated, help him launch a career, and coach him to make healthy life choices. Now, as a parting gift, I would teach him how to do laundry and write a check.

## 129. Oh God, No

Of all the bad sexual decisions Josh made, I was most disturbed by his rendezvous with a seedy woman thirty years his senior, who he described as having "a face like a Bulldog."

She seduced him with erotic tales of her youth, when she was a hot biker chick. He wasn't attracted to her, but was initially aroused by the taboo situation.

"Wanna see my tits?" she asked.

She continued this game of show and tell by showing her vagina, which he found repulsive.

"Why? Was it all stretched out and canoe-shaped?" I'd later ask.

"Yeah, yeah it was!" he said excitedly. "It kinda looked like a banana!"

I scratched my head in bewilderment.

By the time her vagina was revealed, the sexual novelty was gone and Josh was no longer interested. She looked just hideous sprawled out before him, her stubby fingers straining to hold back rolls of pasty flesh to present her offering. But the wheels of fate had started to turn and Josh felt there was no way out. She was short of breath as Josh unzipped his pants, and then she eagerly went down on him.

Pausing momentarily she said, "Call me Amanda."

After swallowing, she seemed to bask in the afterglow, turning to him and confiding, "Josh, I feel so much closer to you now."

He was very much with Amanda at the time and felt horribly guilty about what had happened. He hoped she'd never find out.

I first learned about all of this when he was locked out of his apartment. I showed up to let him in and noticed his frantic energy as he took they key, looked both ways, and said, "Dude! I fucked Amanda's mom!"

## 130. Addict's Web

By the time Josh told me about sleeping with Amanda's mom, I rarely saw him. He'd been spending most nights with her family so he could drive them around. He was also buying their groceries.

Jane had bled the once affluent grandmother dry with her drug habit, and then Amanda's obese brother conned her out of her last few thousand dollars to buy a Jeep. The poor elderly woman had to be in her eighties, and may have been going senile. I met her when Josh and Amanda first came to look at the apartment. She was petite and frail with a classic helmet-shaped wig.

I knew how an addict's mind worked, and knew Jane would obsess about Josh's earnings. As meager as they were, she could get really high on a regular basis. My concerns were compounded when, despite working full time, he began asking me for money.

The stories about why he needed cash are really too ridiculous to write about. An example is the time he called and said an ex-girlfriend back in Crocker reported a cell phone stolen that she had loaned to him. According to Josh, the district attorney called saying he was going to issue an arrest warrant if Josh didn't either return the phone or pay $150. He couldn't return the phone because his stepmother had it and wouldn't give it back.

"Dude, I can't go to jail and I need to get this taken care of right away. If you'll loan me the $150, I'll pay you with my next check."

I denied these requests and his calls became less frequent.

"I'm worried Jane has you on drugs," I sent in a text.

He didn't reply, which only fueled my suspicion. If he were on drugs too, he'd be easier for her to manipulate.

I called him a few weeks later to see what was going on and I guess he thought it'd be cute to have me on speaker phone without my knowledge. I thought he was acting cold and cocky, but just figured it was because I didn't give him the money he'd asked for.

"So how are things with Jane?" I asked.

"Uhh, they're good...Yeah, they're fine," he replied nervously.

"So she hasn't been hitting on you or anything?"

Dead silence for a moment, then I heard some commotion and a woman's irritated voice in the background.

## 131.  Pride of the Clinic

Wearing my aviator sunglasses I strutted through the automatic doors of the clinic like I owned the place. My six-month campaign against rotten, festering crotches was coming to an end and victory was in my grasp, or in the grasp of a nurse practitioner wearing latex gloves.

I approached the reception desk and said, "I'm here with two people who need medical attention. The names are Josh Williams and Amanda Roth. Josh is complaining of occasional chest pains and both need to be screened for STD's."

This chain of events all began with a phone call from Josh at 8:30 on a Monday morning.

"So what's up? We haven't talked in a while," he said anxiously.

He always wanted something when he called but he liked to start off with pleasantries. He continued: "Hey, I'm going to send you a text in just a minute. I want you to read it and then call me. Call me as soon as you read it. Don't reply by text because I don't want anyone to see it."

Amanda had free reign to read his messages and the rest of her family may have had access too. I didn't argue.

"Can you take me to the clinic today?" he wrote.

I called to say I'd be available at lunch. He proceeded to vent about the stress he was under because of Amanda's family. They were out of money.

Thoroughly enmeshed in their dysfunctional family dynamic, he'd taken on the burden of supporting the sinking ship. He was carting around the three generations of women, buying groceries and even buying medication for the grandmother. Now he was tapped out and in need of gas, with payday a few days out.

Jane was desperately in need of a fix and was yelling at him for being out of money, and there was absolutely nothing left in the home that could be pawned. She got on the phone with her drug dealer and agreed sell him her car for $50. She blamed Josh for being in that position.

"Either all the stress or the smoking has caused me to start getting lightheaded and I'm also getting chest pains. Plus I'm still sweating a lot down there (his groin), even when the air conditioning is on. It's like a damn waterfall and still stinks like the worst tuna," he said.

224

He asked if Amanda could come to the clinic too. While I had a longstanding policy of not being around Amanda, in this case I owed it to the public to get her germinating genitals into the hands of competent health officials.

They followed me to the clinic in Josh's worn out economy car. Josh was frugal, so I'm not sure if the air conditioning didn't work or if he was just saving gas, but it had to be miserable riding around in the 95-degree heat coupled with the St. Louis humidity. They both looked a mess: raggedy, sweaty, and disheveled.

Josh couldn't pull off being unshaven because his beard was sparse, but he looked as if he hadn't shaved for weeks. He was wearing an old tank top and gym shorts. Amanda was still rocking those dark roots, but her mascara wasn't as thick as usual. She wore a hot pink baby doll shirt that was no match for her doughnut of fat pushing it up. Her white shorts were dingy and her drugstore flip flops showcased her dirty boxy feet and hot pink toenails.

In the parking lot they started arguing about who was going to hold on to the keys because neither of them had pockets.

Back at the reception counter, I was in the middle of the intake process by the time the two stragglers made their way in, just in time to hear me give the receptionist Amanda's name. Apparently she had not planned on seeing a doctor and was not happy.

This clinic catered to the uninsured but didn't look bad at all. The waiting room was relatively clean, spacious, and surprisingly wasn't crowded. The three of us sat side by side, with Josh in the middle. The two of them argued as discreetly as they could with me sitting right there.

Amanda must have received two dozen text messages, and Josh demanded a full report on each one. The main bone of contention, however, was whether Amanda would see a doctor. Josh kept urging her to go and I heard her say, "I have a doctor and I don't have anything. If I got something now I got it from you!"

When her name was called she approached the counter and told them she didn't need to be seen, then stomped across the lobby and sat far away from us. That afforded us space to have a real conversation.

Josh said he was depressed about spending all of his time at Amanda's house, but felt there was no way out.

"I'm surrounded by all these damn zombies and it's bringing me down. I miss my old life, like when me and you used to hang out. I miss spending time at my own apartment. I wish someone could just come in and rescue me or something."

I didn't bite.

He went on to express remorse for the way he'd messed things up.

"Well, Josh, you've held down a job for six months and paid your rent on time for six months. You've managed your bank account when your mom didn't think you'd be able to, and you've been able to do it all while spending most of your time in a snake pit."

Josh was called, and Amanda darted up to join him for his examination.

After less than ten minutes they came back out.

"It cost too much," Josh said in a resigned tone. "They want $175. That's like a car payment! Anyway, Jane called and is going to report Amanda kidnapped and have me arrested."

"Jane doesn't care if you live or die," I shot back. "Josh, we're here now and you need to do this. Your health has to be your top priority."

Josh was caught in the middle. Jane had berated him over the phone, Amanda was glaring at him, and I was hypnotically repeating, "Josh, you have to take care of yourself. You can make payment arrangements. Just get yourself taken care of."

He had big wide eyes anyway, but at this moment he really looked like a deer in the headlights.

"What am I going to go if I get behind on my rent?" he asked.

"What are you going to do if you let your health go and become disabled?" I replied.

"Well, uh, my stepdad wouldn't let my mom take care of me…"

"Nobody would take care of you, Josh! You'd end up in an institution or homeless. Chest pains are nothing to mess with. Go back in there."

He stood slack-jawed in silence, staring off into space, avoiding eye contact with both of us. The indirect sunlight was glistening off his sweaty face. He felt the weight of my stare and Amanda's.

"I'd have to go back up there and register all over again," he mumbled.

"That's okay, just go do it," I said softly. He stood for another few seconds, then slowly turned and approached the counter.

## 132. Wait for Me

The first call of my busy day was from Josh.

"Dude, I'm going to enroll in college today," he said proudly. "Yeah, either Cornell Brown or Advance Tech."

Both are the kind of schools that advertise during the worst of daytime television, presupposing their audience has a dead-end life that can be transformed with an exciting career as a massage therapist or dental assistant if they'd just get up off that couch and call.

I didn't know much about Advance Tech but I heard Cornell Brown was an expensive scam. Ray David was a department head at a major hospital, and they wouldn't hire medical coders from there, opting instead to recruit from the local community college. Josh was impulsive, though, and there was no getting him to wait or change course, so I just asked that he not go to Cornell Brown.

I later learned that Advance Tech wasn't much better. They were also obscenely expensive, their credits didn't transfer, and their advisers were like a cross between military recruiters and car salesmen. They gave him the old razzle dazzle and the next thing I knew he was padded up with student loans and beginning a criminal justice program the following Monday.

When Jane heard he was in school to be a cop, she flipped out, afraid that he'd turn her in.

"My mom said you can't come over here anymore," Amanda told him in a tearful call.

It really rocked Jane's world because the next thing we knew Amanda was being sent off to Creekside, a residential treatment center for troubled teens, until she was 18, which was months away. No phone, internet, or weekend passes. I didn't have the details, but the courts were involved, it was something to do with truancy and her grades, and something Jane had to sign off on.

Josh tried to brace himself for the loss by filling the void before she was even gone. He took a coworker from Taco Bell home with him and they messed around. He was ready to go all the way, but at the last minute she said, "I have respect for myself, so I don't do this on the first date." I wondered if she'd caught a whiff of the rotten crotch and aborted.

Amanda found the number of the coworker on Josh's phone and called her. "STOP FUCKING AROUND WITH MY BOYFRIEND BITCH!" she screamed.

The coworker was livid and the next time Josh saw her at work she yelled, "YOU TELL THAT LITTLE BITCH IF SHE EVER CALLS ME AGAIN I'M GOING TO BEAT HER ASS!"

All the employees were watching, so Josh just let her have the last word and kept his distance. Jane allowed Amanda go to the Cardinals game with him the weekend before she was sent off to Creekside, but all she did was complain.

"It's too hot." "I'm bored." "This is stupid, it's too hot to be here."

Both of them cried when he dropped her off after the game.

Monday morning arrived, and while Josh was in class, he'd receive the last text from Amanda: "I'm going to Creekside now. Wait for me."

## 133. Lifeboat

Josh was stuck in class when he got the text that Amanda was leaving for Creekside. His heart was racing as he thought about not seeing her for a year. She was the all-consuming focus of his life. Like a drowning man scrambling for a lifeboat, he began looking for anything to hold on to.

A few weeks prior he was telling me how disgusting and depressing Amanda's house was.

"Why do you stay there then? You have your own place," I inquired.

"They're all I've got, and I guess I'm kind of afraid of being all alone," he replied.

And things were very ugly in that house. Once Jane was demanding Josh give her fifty dollars but he refused. After being berated for an hour he threw a fifty at her and said, "THERE! That's all you're worth."

She slapped him and then Amanda jumped up before Josh could lay her out.

So back to the morning of Amanda's departure. Josh walked out of class and called me at work.

"Dude, I really need a friend right now. Amanda's at Creekside. I won't see her for about a year...I'm really having a hard time with this, man. Do you think you could come by this afternoon and hang out with me for a few minutes?"

My day was booked but I could let him ride along with me for a while so I picked him up. I accepted that he was a little redneck, but why did he have to come out in a green sleeveless Mountain Dew shirt? He immediately started talking about lunch. I had already eaten but said we could pick up something.

"Oh, dude, I forgot my wallet."

"Of course you did," I said as I forked out $7 for some dreadful Burger King meal.

He'd gone from being upset to being excited about the opportunities this break presented. While he was emotionally dependent on Amanda, intellectually he knew she was bad for him and stunted his growth. Plus, after he called me that morning, he'd hit on a girl in his class who seemed to like him.

"Dude, she's really hot! She can't weigh more than 90 pounds, has blond highlights in her hair, and blue eyes!" he told me.

I dropped him off and he seemed fine, but then the loneliness and anxiety kicked in later that evening. He sent messages asking that I come over, then he called.

"Dude, I really need a friend right now," He said choking back tears. "I can't stand being in this damn apartment because everything reminds me of fuckin' Amanda!"

He became harder to understand as he began crying and talking fast.

"I can't even sit on my couch because that's where me and Amanda used to have sex and I can't even play my fuckin' video game because (inaudible due to crying)…there's that little horse and Amanda liked that little horse!"

Despite everything, my parental instincts were still there, but I had to hold firm to my boundaries. I told him it was normal to feel sad, and that it would never get any harder than it was right now.

I did want to be there for him, but knew that was the wrong thing to do. I had worked hard to keep him at arm's length and couldn't go back to the days of dropping everything to deal with his drama.

Once he realized he couldn't get me to come over, he switched gears and called the girl from class. They spent hours on the phone that night, and he made plans to see her the next day.

"You're not a psycho bitch like my ex-girlfriend are you?" he asked.

## 134. No Pregnant Pause

Josh was working the busy drive-thru and had one of those customers who sits at the window skeptically surveying their order for accuracy. The line was growing longer and Josh was getting stressed.

"Ma'am, I want to say this as nice as I can, but you're going to have to get out of my drive-thu lane or you're fixin' to piss off a whole lot of people."

Josh had a way with words.

I coached him not to discuss Amanda with other girls, especially on the first date, but in his circles that's just the way things were done. The new girl from class, Sherri Lynn, just rolled along with the story of Amanda being a "psycho bitch" and vented about her recent breakup.

Sherri Lynn lived in a double wide with her parents in a small town about an hour south of St. Louis. Days after first talking with her, he went down there to meet the family and ended up spending four nights in a row, commuting back and forth to work.

"Her parents really liked me!" he bragged.

"Dude, she got off in my mouth!" he began. By the second night she was ready to go all the way. "I don't have any condoms," he said.

"Don't worry about using a condom because I think I'm already pregnant by my ex," she replied.

She was less than a hundred pounds, and he felt strong as he picked her up and held her against the wall.

"Dude, it was so tight it made my dick hurt! It was like sticking your dick in a..." he paused, trying to think of the right analogy, "small... wall hole...or something..." he trailed off.

"I'm not very good at analogies," he said.

After the fourth night she confessed to still being in love with her ex. Josh went to school the next day and asked another girl for her number.

"She's really hot! I was telling the class that I was a manager at the Taco Bell in Kirkwood and she said 'OH MY GOD, I'm the manager in Eureka!'"

With Amanda locked away, Josh enjoyed playing the field. I asked if he'd heard from Amanda and he seemed indifferent as he told me of a letter she wrote him, recalling it in a cool monotone:

"She wrote me a letter. Said Jane and her grandma came to visit her on the 4th but there were no fireworks or anything. They took them all to some park and a deer walked right past her and she cried because it reminded her of me. She said she wanted me to promise not to move on while she's in there because she's afraid I will. I don't know man. I, I don't know if I should even write back."

I learned never to underestimate the hold she had over him. These other girls were cleaner and prettier, but she knew how to get inside his head. If she got out soon she could have him back in a heartbeat. If she really was in there for a year it would just depend on the fortitude of the woman he was with at the time, I figured.

## 135. Getting Slick

Josh was really feeling his oats, having easily bagged Sherri Lynn and now flirting with Nicole, both of whom were classmates.

"I liked you, but thought you were shacked up with Sherri Lynn," Nicole said playfully.

"I liked you too, and the thing is, when I was fucking Sherri Lynn, I was picturing you. I mean, I was also thinking about Sherri Lynn but I was thinking about you, too," Josh replied.

Nicole laughed and said he would not be able to sleep with her so easily.

Josh recounted this story and said, "I'm getting slick, ain't I? Fuck this being pussy-whipped shit. I told my mom that I finally grew a pair of balls and I'm gonna use 'em!" he exclaimed, then after a brief pause trailed off, "Mom said it was kind of an inappropriate thing to say to her."

## 136. Obsession

Josh hadn't gotten around to writing Amanda back.

She had never been comfortable with him being out of sight. Regardless of what either of them were doing she would obsessively call and text him. When given the opportunity she'd even pop in at the job. But now, locked away with no phone or internet, all she could do was imagine all of the girls he was pursuing. The absence of anything from him in the daily mail was devastating and confirmed her fears that he was moving on.

Josh woke up to the phone ringing; the call was from a pay phone.

"Hey, Josh, I need you to pick me up," Amanda said in a frantic and screechy tone. He was surprised.

"Did they release you from Creekside?" he asked.

"Just come and get me," she said, telling him she was at a nearby convenience store.

"Amanda I can't go to jail!" Josh replied just as there was a loud knock on the door. It was the police.

The staff at Creekside found Josh's name and number doodled on everything in Amanda's cottage. They assumed she was with him and the police came inside to look for her.

"She's not here, she's on the goddamn phone!" Josh said as he handed it over.

The officer tried to reason with her but she just repeated "I don't know" and cried.

Figuring she had to keep moving, she hung up and ran to a nearby apartment complex where she proceeded to knock on random doors.

Josh called Amanda's mother, Jane. "I HOPE YOU'RE HAPPY BITCH! AMANDA'S ON THE RUN LIKE SOME WILD ANIMAL!"

Jane sounded high when she replied "Fuck you, Josh, it ain't my fucking problem!"

Finally, an older man let Amanda inside to use the phone, where she called Josh again.

"Why haven't you written me?" Amanda asked tearfully.

"I did write but just haven't sent it yet. Listen, you need to turn yourself in. I'm trying to be a cop and I can't get arrested! I love you, Amanda, and I'm sorry I didn't send the letter but you need to go back!"

She then hung up on him and ran out of the stranger's apartment.

Minutes later the older man hit redial. "Where did Amanda go? I want to help her get back!"

Thinking this old guy was a pervert that wanted to screw Amanda, Josh shouted,

"DON'T CALL MY NUMBER AGAIN OR I'M GONNA STICK MY FOOT IN YOUR NASTY OLD ASS!"

Defeated, alone, and out of options, Amanda turned herself in.

## 137. Misty Eyed

"Would you like me to supreme your Taco?" Josh suggestively asked Misty, a 30-year-old woman in his class. He was heavily influenced by Taco Bell, even when engaged in the art of seduction.

There have been a lot of women in play so let's try to get this organized. He dated Sherri Lynn, whom he had unprotected sex with because she figured she might be pregnant anyway. She went back with her ex, so he started pursuing Nicole, but she already had a boyfriend and decided not to cheat, so that was a non-starter. He was seducing Misty, who he described as "a hot old biker chick," but things were moving slowly on that front.

"My dick is like a roll of quarters just waiting to tear that pussy up!" he exclaimed.

He then got on his favorite dating site and met Britney.

"Dude, she's hot and has really got her shit together!" he began. "She's 23 and is a bartender in Cape Girardeau. She's got a three-year-old daughter named Haley and we spent several days together. I took her to the zoo last weekend, and next weekend we're going to have a barbeque in the park. You should come out and meet her!" he said.

The two of them had avoided sex in order to build something deeper. They shared their most intimate secrets. He told her that he'd slept with eleven girls and she confessed to sleeping with fifteen guys, mostly back when she was a partier.

"Do you think less of me now?" Britney asked. Josh assured her that he didn't.

Amanda did what she had to do to gain access to a smuggled phone at Creekside and called frequently, saying she was so depressed and was cutting herself. Josh had really been enjoying the break and was exasperated. He decided to tell her about Britney.

"Look Amanda, I just think I need to be with Britney right now. She's 23, has her own place, you know, you're a kid and she's an adult. She's in college. I'm trying to grow up. I mean, whose fault is it that you're locked up there anyway?"

"It's your fault that I'm in here because you kept me out all the time!" Amanda wailed.

"NO AMANDA IT'S YOUR DAMN FAULT! YOU HAD YOUR HEAD UP YOUR ASS AND WERE BLOWIN' OFF SCHOOL!" Josh replied.

Amanda's calls continued unabated, and her mother would even send texts.

"We miss you Josh! You should come around and see us sometime!" Jane wrote.

"Are you going to get pissed off that some bitch is blowing up my phone all the damn time?" Josh asked Britney.

"No, because I'm in the same situation" she replied. It turns out that her ex was a convicted felon in Illinois and called constantly.

Josh's heart was with Britney but he still had a roll of quarters for Misty, the 30-year-old biker chick in his class. Sitting side by side, they sent one another provocative messages.

"I could use a boy toy," Misty wrote. She confirmed she did want him to supreme her taco, "And I like to suck on things…" she added.

"Do you like sour cream?" he asked. "Do you like sour cream all over your face?" he continued.

"Ooh yeah! When it's on my face I just like to lick my cheeks and scoop it in my mouth," she replied.

"Man, I'm going to give it to her every which way! She's going to tell everyone the best sex she ever had was with a 19-year-old Taco Bell manager!" he boasted.

He went on to tell me what his mom had to say about it.

### 138. Badass Charlie

My buddy Charlie, a nice looking, well-built guy in his late thirties, owned a trucking business in East St. Louis, and had been interested in my urban exploration photos for some time when he asked for a tour. We met at 6 a.m. on a Saturday morning and hit the highlights.

I normally finished with the Murphy Building, a beautiful but partially collapsed masonry structure of about six floors. It was best accessed from the basement, which was ground level in the rear.

Flashlights were needed to find your way through the pitch black maze, over piles of clothing and debris from homeless people and prostitutes, to the rickety wooden steps to the main lobby.

"And this is as high as we can go because the marble stairs have been stolen," I announced. Minutes later, I saw Charlie jump out the back window, fifteen feet above the concrete below, and swing out three feet on to a rusty old fire escape.

"We can go up this way!" he said, as he proceeded to climb.

Well, holy shit. This place was shuttered in 1959, and Charlie was betting his life on a rusty fire escape on a crumbling brick building. I sat in the back window looking at the ladder hanging there three feet away and I could hear him exclaiming, "Wow, it's really cool up here!" Meanwhile, I was paralyzed by an inner conflict. The devil on my shoulder was telling me to get up there.

"You're the expert tour guide! People seek you out to show them these ruins and one of your guests is seeing places you're too afraid to explore!" while the angel on the other shoulder was saying, "Don't risk your life to climb that fire escape! What's worse than dying is becoming a paraplegic! What then?"

The two voices were equally matched. I couldn't make a decision and I couldn't move from the window, even when Charlie swung back in and was ready to go.

Finally, I decided I couldn't leave without going up, and it was like a religious experience. It was easily one of the most exhilarating moments of my life, especially looking out over the Gateway Arch, knowing I was up there because I'd overcome my fear.

As I carefully made my way down the fire escape, my friends Charlie and Roberta were cheering me on through the open window.

I replied, "Damon would NOT be happy with me right now!" —and at that very moment, I hear Damon's voice coming from my pocket "HELLO? HELLO?"

I had butt dialed him, or my grumpy, overworked guardian angel called him out of spite.

At some point in the next couple of years that rusty fire escape crashed to the ground.


## 139. East Side Horror

Across the river from the Gateway Arch, police discovered a pile of smoldering human remains on the levy. Their investigation took them to a rusty metal building at 650 N. Front Street on the East St. Louis riverfront, where the unspeakable horrors they found spawned reports in *The St. Louis Post Dispatch* and outlets around the nation of a "human slaughter chamber."

Two homeless men, Dennis "DJ" Iagulli, 41, and James Pierson, 36, were living at the warehouse. They befriended Zachary Irvin, 22, and lured him to the site where he was bound, sadistically tortured and raped for several days. Irvin had just arrived in St. Louis from tiny St. Elmo, Illinois, 90 miles east of the city, in search of a better life.

For years I'd explored the mighty ruins of East St. Louis with my friends Kenneth & Sara. The area began emptying out in the late 1950s and exploring it could be a post-apocalyptic experience.

We've climbed through old hospitals, most of the substantial downtown buildings where you could still find letters dated 1959, and made multiple trips to the massive crumbling meat packing plants. We'd even walked past 650 N. Front Street once after exploring the railyards between East St. Louis and Venice, but didn't bother checking it out because it was just a nondescript warehouse.

When I heard about the murder I felt compelled to visit the site. Kenneth & Sara had always been down for an east side adventure, including in the middle of the night, but they took a pass on this one.

My friend Rodney agreed to come, and we headed across the Mississippi. Not surprisingly the door was unlocked and we immediately saw signs of human habitation. Dirty blankets, clothing and trash. Most of the building was too dark to explore and our flashlight failed, but in a room with a window we found a tiled floor covered in dried blood. It's the landlords' responsibility to clean up these kinds of messes, so if the building is abandoned it's nobody's job.

The sensational headlines faded, but the tragic story stuck with me, and then nine months later I got a lead that brought me to a male-to-female transsexual named Autumn who had dated a close friend of the men charged, and had even done their laundry.

I found Autumn to be friendly and warm, living her life as a woman and working as a nursing assistant. She had only been dating her boyfriend Grant for a few months when she learned about the shady underworld he was involved with. He made his living stealing copper with DJ and Pierson, who lived in the warehouse with several other homeless people, including a young woman.

DJ was the feared ringleader. Pierson, as they called him, was the sidekick and always followed DJ's lead.

"Were they a couple?" I asked.

"No, No, DJ was openly gay but I don't know what Pierson was," she replied. "Pierson was afraid of him, and so was Grant. It was like he had some kind of mind control over people."

One evening Grant & Ronda were relaxing at home when Grant got a call from Pierson.

"Man, DJ's gone off the deep end!" Pierson began. "He lured some guy back to the warehouse from St. Patrick's Center and has got him tied up. He's been raping him and doing some crazy shit!"

Grant was on parole in Missouri and wasn't allowed to be in Illinois. He wanted no part of whatever was going on and decided to stay away from the warehouse until things calmed down.

"I didn't know if it was some sort of sick joke or what," Autumn said. "I take care of people for a living and kept wondering what I could do. Grant wouldn't talk to the police because that would mean going back to prison, and I couldn't call them and be like 'There's some guy tied up in an abandoned building in East St. Louis!'" she said. "I'd never even been there and didn't know where it was."

Grant picked her up from work at the nursing home on day two and she immediately asked for an update.

"Pierson keeps texting me and I've been deleting before I even look at 'em. I don't want to know nothin' about that shit!" Grant replied.

That evening Pierson called and Grant put him on speakerphone. DJ had left him alone with Irvin for hours that day. "NEXT TIME HE DOES THAT LET HIM GO!" Autumn pleaded. "GO GET A COP! GET HELP!"

"I knew it was serious. You know how you can sense a certain level of fear and anxiety. I could tell he wasn't thinking straight," she said. "He just kept saying DJ would come after him if he crossed him. He was afraid of DJ."

She tried to convince Grant to drop her off near the warehouse so she could call 911, but he refused.

"He knew they had guns over there," she said. "I reminded Grant that he's got tools over there with his fingerprints all over them."

Another day passed and Pierson called again. Autumn pleaded for him to intervene.

"You'll be the hero! You'll be the one who sets him free," she said.

The final call from Pierson was just after DJ shot Irvin.

"Is he dead?" Autumn asked.

"Yeah, he's dead," Grant replied.

It didn't quite seem real until she saw the story on the news while at work.

"I bet that's the dude DJ kidnapped!" she exclaimed to a coworker.

She heard Irvin was bound and raped, but during questioning the police told her the full extent of the torture and mutilation. She couldn't comprehend how anyone could do that to somebody.

Investigators wanted to tie Grant to the murder and grilled her about why she didn't call the police. Filled with shame and regret, she fell into a debilitating depression which resulted in her losing her job at the nursing home. She also broke up with Grant.

"I learned Grant had a problem with the truth," she began. "He came over to my house driving an RV he said his mom gave to him, and wanted me to run away with him. Somewhere down south. I walked out to look and saw he had to start it with a screwdriver! I told him I don't want a homeless life. I want a real home with running water. Not where I have to run to go get water!" she said in her folksy way.

Grant drove the RV to the warehouse to look for his tools and was arrested by investigators who were staking out the property. He'd written two letters from prison, but she didn't reply.

"The way I cope is that even if I called, the outcome would have still been the same. It wouldn't have changed what happened," she said, elaborating that the police wouldn't have searched all the abandoned buildings in East St. Louis because of her call.

Police indicated there could be other victims, and Autumn worried that the young woman who lived there might be one of them.

"One day they just said she got money for a bus ticket and went home. Her family in Hannibal was like come home and you can live with us and won't have to be homeless anymore," she recalled. "I don't know. That just sounds like a fairy tale to me."

After I left that space I often thought about returning to wash away Irvin's blood, like part of him was trapped in that miserable abandoned warehouse. I would want someone to do that for me, and I felt like I owed him something.

The warehouse at the end of that potholed road has since been demolished.

I closed my *Vital Voice* exposé with the following:

Many of us feel like cities are the answer. They're places of opportunity where we can be ourselves and find a community. Zachary Irvin, a friendly and free spirited young man of meager means, came to our city looking for this better life. He came looking for us.

He found Dennis "DJ" Iagulli.

## 140. Elaine's Delusions

Elaine's favorite grandmother was a lot like her: stylish and flashy with an irreverent sense of humor. She developed schizophrenia in her late fifties and even had her back windows boarded up, convinced people were watching her. Sadly, Elaine's battle began much earlier in life.

When Elaine was feeling like herself we were able to talk openly about what it was like for her in the eye of the storm. Once, in the dead of winter, she spent all of her money on a shopping spree and then overdosed on pills, causing her to be committed. She explained she was convinced she'd won the lottery, and that everyone knew but was just waiting to tell her.

In the hospital her world was truly magical. She believed I was sending her telepathic messages, as was a handsome patient in group therapy. She'd stare at him knowingly as he telepathically delighted her with his profound insights.

The hospital was like a vacation from the stresses of reality. She was dreading her upcoming release when she saw a big snowstorm outside her window. The roads were bad, so they weren't going to release her until the following day.

Damon knew she wasn't ready to handle the world outside, she thought to herself, so he made it snow to keep her safe.

## 141. The Non-Regulation Table

I was at a fledgling leather bar when I saw a table with ropes attached sitting unused. I find nothing erotic about the idea of being restrained, but thought sacrificing myself might liven things up.

An S&M aficionado was excited I was willing to be strapped down and was happy to do the job, but was embarrassed by the table itself.

"This isn't a regulation table," he sighed, shaking his head.

Again, during the knot tying, he apologized.

"I'm really sorry. This isn't a regulation table. If you want to do this on a real table sometime I've got a whole set up in my basement."

I was only tied up for a moment, then was released from captivity. On my way out a very intimidating-looking man who appeared to be a biker handed me a matchbook. In serial killer handwriting he'd scrawled his number with the message, "CALL IF YOU WANNA DO RAPE."

## 142. Political Ambitions

A few dynamic and interesting young guys were elected to the board of aldermen in 2009, including the smart and savvy Antonio French from the North Side's 21st ward, and the openly gay Shane Cohn in the 25th ward. These two were the talk of the town, always in the news and rubbing elbows at political shindigs.

Meanwhile in our district, the 15th Ward which covered Tower Grove, there was envy. We seemed to be stuck with competent but boring Ol' Angie Alabama, who reminded me of an elementary school teacher when interacting with her constituents. While people loved to complain about her, she often ran unopposed and this was a frequent complaint at neighborhood cocktail parties. It was at such a shindig when my friend and neighbor Jillian, who held a leadership post in the ward, said I should run and offered to coach me and work to get endorsements.

While my "open book" lifestyle may have been a deterrent in other parts of town, state Senator Mike Colona easily survived a last-minute smear campaign tying him to the porn industry a few years earlier, so Jillian didn't expect any problems in the liberal district.

I agreed to do it and met with her regularly to discuss strategy. The election was well over a year away, so I began participating in ward activities, attending meetings and canvassing. It was important that I become a known quantity.

## Story Box 10: May-December Weddings

First of all this isn't a story about an age difference. It's about a gay couple in St. Louis who, in a given year, would get married in May, then again in December. When Pat & Dan got their first taste of marriage attention it was like opium and they would never stop chasing that dragon.

I say "they" but it's really Pat. Both were awkward, out of shape, 30-something white guys but Dan was just along for the ride while wild-eyed Pat drove the crazy train.

249

"I'll say this one last time. Anyone who doesn't show up for the rehearsals is OUT! Anyone who's trying to run things is OUT!" Pat would announce to the wedding party, and as a reminder, post on Facebook along with numerous rants about how stressful it all was, how people weren't doing their part so he had to do everything himself, and how he just couldn't take it anymore and nobody understood.

Their online photos fell into two categories: professional wedding photographs and amateur wedding food photographs that included cases of Orange Crush and deviled eggs with ten times the normal amount of paprika.

"Once I started sprinkling I just couldn't stop!" Pat said.

The second wedding was a real letdown for Pat due to Dan's Best Man, who was much more effective than his own.

"He made the whole wedding all about Dan!" Pat lamented.

After several days of bitter public rants calling people out for ruining their second wedding extravaganza of the year, he decided the only way to remedy it was a do-over. Thus their third wedding ceremony was conceived. And so on.

And for each of these blessed events there was a core group that played along, took the abuse, cried and celebrated as if it were a once in a lifetime blessed event. That was the most morbidly fascinating part to me. When I inquired about this with a dear friend of theirs I hold in high regard she replied, "Look, Pat's a strange bird…but then who isn't, huh?"

## 143. 48 Hours

We'd moved so often that we hadn't even bothered unpacking our books the past few times. After a couple of years in our house on McDonald I finally bought a bookshelf and pulled the boxes up from the basement.

It was a beautiful fall day, the windows were open, and I could hear my friend Jillian talking to another neighbor outside. As I mindfully arranged the books I thought about how rooted we'd become and how much I enjoyed the sense of community. I stepped back and looked at the full bookcase, exhaled, and said to myself, "I'm home."

It was only a matter of weeks until Damon announced he had a possible opportunity to transfer to San Francisco. It was a long shot but he wanted to apply. A few months passed with no word, and in that time I did my best to put it out of my mind as I continued with my plans to run for office and went back to school to pursue a Political Science degree.

"Benny said you don't really wanna go back to school, you're just doing this because you think it'll impress me," Damon said dismissively.

Finally, the call Damon had been hoping for, and I had been dreading.

"We can use you in San Francisco but we need an answer in 48 hours."

It felt like I'd been on a dizzying roller coaster ride that was just coming to an end, and as I prepared to get off I felt a lurch followed by the sounds, "click click click." This ride wasn't over.

For years I'd been trying to make up for Oklahoma City, but still felt like I owed him. He'd moved for me in the past, so I'd do this for him. I started making calls, first to Peter, the President of Milpitas Management.

"I know this is odd," I began on his voicemail, "but Damon's needed in San Francisco, and we can only make it work if I have a job waiting. Do you have anything open?"

I then called the King & Queen of the Tenderloin, Leroy and Kathy Looper, to see if they had any leads. Kathy was ecstatic.

"We need you back over the Cadillac Hotel!" she exclaimed.

Within the 48 hours allotted I was sitting in class when I received a personal call from Peter telling me they had a job waiting. We were on our way back to California.

While I loved San Francisco, St. Louis was my home. I was honored that my San Francisco connections thought enough of me to make this happen, but the thought of telling my friends that once again I was leaving them, saying goodbye to the home and community I loved, and scrapping all of my big plans made my stomach turn.

## 144. Defying Benny

That despicable Benny Babbish didn't like anyone escaping his orbit and wasn't happy about Damon's plans. He feverishly worked to plant seeds of doubt.

"Financially, I just don't see how any of this is going to work. San Francisco is really expensive and only you have an offer. You'll be out there supporting Chris while paying that outrageous rent."

"Oh, Chris won't have any trouble getting work. He's got a good network" Damon replied.

"I doubt it'll be that easy," Benny said.

He couldn't even bring himself to respond when Damon told him I landed a good job within the 48 hours, and was forced to stew in his own stool.

## 145. Housing Options

The position open was a step down from the district-level position I held previously, but it did come with an apartment in one of the priciest parts of town, albeit in a building full of my formerly homeless tenants.

Having worked with that population in the Mission District, Damon was hesitant and anxious about taking the unit, so I began looking for a Housing Plan B and contacted my friend Pat, who owned the North St. Louis mansion and a mid-century home in the upscale peninsula community of San Mateo, south of San Francisco. I knew Pat had rented a spare room out in the past, and I asked her if it was available now.

"It sure is! And I'll be gone all next month, so you'll have the whole place to yourselves!" she said.

I went home and presented the plan to Damon, and he was much more comfortable with that option.

## 146.  Telling Ray David

Of all my close friends in St. Louis, I dreaded telling Ray most of all. We had a standing date every single Saturday night. We'd begin with drinks at Villa Ray, have dinner, then head out to our favorite bar, Clementine's, where we'd sometimes laugh until we cried.

Sitting at his basement bar with the sparkling granite countertop and neon lights, I was filled with anxiety about breaking the news. I'd held out as long as I could, but we needed to let people know and I wanted him to be the first. Finally, as if pulling off a bandage, I blurted,
"Oh Ray, Damon accepted a job in San Francisco. We're moving back."

A pained and disappointed look fell across his face. He was never one to meddle in someone's business, but he couldn't help remembering how just weeks before I told him I might need to move in for a while.

He struggled, "Chris, (heavy pause) I don't know if Damon's really interested in being in a relationship with you anymore," he said.

"I know, Ray, but if he leaves me I'll be better off financially there than if he left me here. My salary's good, and I'll have a rent-free apartment."

We hugged and went back to our drinks.

"How long do we have?" he asked, as if I'd disclosed a terminal illness.

"Two weeks," I replied.

## 147. Rotten Crotches Finale

Josh and Amanda walked in to find Amanda's drug-addled mother Jane sitting in a chair wearing nothing but a little T-shirt as blood tricked down her leg. "I don't have money for GOD DAMN TAMPONS!" she yelled.

Amanda rolled her eyes and mumbled, "My mom's stupid."

After a long hiatus, Josh's stories were flowing again.

I took him to lunch on his twentieth birthday, one year after I first met him, and our meeting had the feeling of an exit interview. I was returning to San Francisco in a few weeks, and he was on a trajectory that was unlikely to change. It wasn't all bad, though. I was proud of him for paying his rent on time every month, holding down a full time job, doing well in school, and maintaining his bank account. He was surer of himself than he was a year before.

For several months he had kept his distance because he didn't want me to know he was still with Amanda. I knew he was lying about being rid of her because she was still listed as his girlfriend on Facebook. "Oh, I just haven't gotten 'round to changing that" he'd mumble, before preceding to engage in some of the most mundane conversations I'd ever suffered through. He would talk about things like the mop his mom bought him that steams its own water.

The morning of his birthday he called and suggested we meet for lunch, and he came clean about being with Amanda. He wanted to get together and tell me everything.

"I want it all in the book," he said.

"Man, over the past year I probably gave them people four-thousand dollars," Josh lamented. "That could've been a new car right there."

They'd been bleeding him dry with requests for groceries and other living expenses.

He said he was no longer attracted to Amanda, and they haven't been intimate in months. I asked if she was running around and he blurted out, "Oh NOBODY wants Amanda!" then seemed to catch himself and try to clean it up with "Uh, she's just not out anywhere to meet people..."

His sex life was slow, although he did feel up a coworker in the walk-in freezer one day.

"Then I thought this ain't right. She's a crew member and I'm management..." he said.

"What keeps you with Amanda?" I asked.

"Well, that apartment is really big for one person and I like having someone around," he began. "We play Call of Duty together. I don't know why she plays it, but she's good. She's better than me!"

I asked where she fit in to his future plans.

"Well, when I get out of school and shit and if she hasn't pulled her head out of her ass and started doing something with her life, I'm leaving her," he said.

I have many amusing stories about people living crazy lives, but the stories can get sad after a while. Like the last few hours on the Midway of the state fair, when only a few stragglers remain in the litter-strewn aisles, and some of the lights have been turned off.

In Josh's case, he needed someone to fill the time. His biggest fear was being alone, and he took comfort in the chaos and activity Amanda's family provided. Nobody could ever feel alone among the flashing lights and dizzying rides. The sideshows were expensive, but for him the distraction was priceless.

None of us who have made it this far in the story can claim to be completely above cheap thrills ourselves. I've brought you all here and we've flailed from one sideshow to the next. Now I've rounded you up so we can leave together.

Even as Josh walked me out to say goodbye, he wasn't really in the moment. I could tell he was distracted. The noise of the Midway was calling.

### 148.   Elaine Passing

During an intimate conversation Elaine once shared the feeling of disappointment she'd get when she'd wake up from a failed suicide attempt, but one cold February morning, days before I moved back to California, she was successful.

While she did suffer from schizophrenia, I think she died from grinding poverty. The military guy who had fathered her son turned out to be a deadbeat who evaded child support and attended community college for nearly a decade.

Each job she lost was replaced by one that paid less than the one before. She wasn't wired to seek help, welfare, housing assistance, etc., but she sometimes would ask for a little money from me or from our friend Mindy, and we always gave it.

Mindy was to give her eulogy, and I helped her write it.

An historic blizzard hit Oklahoma when I was set to leave St. Louis, and her service was delayed repeatedly for a week, so I couldn't attend. Me and Damon travelled through Kansas instead of Oklahoma, then strangely enough had to track north again through Wyoming to avoid another blizzard from the south.

When we got to the dreaded Donner Pass in California, it was dry as a bone. It was time to adjust to our new life, and I never really mourned Elaine. I didn't see her in the casket, so it wasn't real.

I always thought once her son was grown I'd help her move to wherever I was living, and we'd resume the good times.

It still kind of feels like that's possible.


## 149. Greetings from Chatters

The last face we saw when we left San Francisco years before was our sweet Chatters, and as we arrived at Pat's we found Chatters waiting for us with a bottle of champagne.

The party was set to begin and Pat was a nervous wreck for several reasons. She was on thin ice with her adult children, who didn't want any negative feedback about their misbehaving kids, for starters, and the family didn't know she was still smoking. This would be a bombshell revelation considering she nearly died from lung cancer.

The patio party was lovely. Somehow Pat managed to hide her numerous ashtrays, and she held it together when her five-year-old granddaughter wanted to pick every lemon from her tree, only to forget them in plastic bags.

Enjoying her first cigarette of the night, Pat reflected on the event.

"She said 'I want lemons and I said 'how many' and she said 'I want *all* the lemons!" Pat recalled, then after a quick puff, continued, "Little bitch."

## 150. Old Man of Armour

I spent a great deal of time documenting the collection of ruins that made up much of the East St. Louis area. It's fascinating to see what happens to large masonry structures after fifty years of abandonment. The first couple of times the decay seems static, but after a few seasons your eye begins to measure the steady progression.

The site urban explorers long found the most intriguing was the Armour Meat Packing Plant, which was the first of East St. Louis's big three plants to shutter, closing in 1959. Visiting this behemoth was a religious experience for many, with its soaring smokestacks, towering ornate machinery—some circa 1902—incredible views, and endless areas to discover.

With a few flashlights you could descend into the labyrinth basement complete with oily black stone walls and deep watery pits. You could climb multiple levels, taking in the glazed brickwork and the old slaughter floor complete with a cattle chute, and check out the incredible views of the St. Louis skyline and the Mississippi.

One explorer documented his journey to the top of the smokestack, where bricks came loose in his hands and he nearly fell to his death.
The mystique around this place was accentuated because it was difficult to find, and you had to have a lot of street cred to even begin to look. You'd head north through East St. Louis, past the rough old prostitutes strolling Route 3, make a right at nowhere, make a left at nowhere, park along the nameless, overgrown and potholed road surrounded by the remnants of long vacated stockyards. Once on the property you'd trek the long convoluted pathways through thick vegetation, careful not to fall through open manholes, before finally reaching it.

Nature had taken back the site, inside and out. Trees were firmly rooted on the roof, vines climbed through windows, and a giant white owl waited in the rafters.

I'd visited the site regularly for a couple of years before metal scrappers discovered it and removed much of the flooring, and disassembled some of the ornate equipment. On an intellectual level I wondered why the thefts bothered me so much. After all the building had been steadily collapsing on itself for decades, and was well past the point of being converted into a new use. The condition was terminal, and after half a century of isolation, development was finally encroaching with the new I-70 slated to skirt the site. This hidden, mysterious treasure—long a beacon for explorers and thieves— would soon be laid bare as a dangerously accessible, intolerable eyesore on newly visible, valuable property. Its days were numbered but the dismantling bothered me nonetheless.

After being in California for seven months I was eager to see the ruins. With my friend Roberta in tow I visited the neighboring Hunter Plant, owned by my buddy Badass Charlie's trucking company and slated for demolition, several sites in downtown East St. Louis, and I saved the best for last. Sure enough the scrappers had stripped away even more of the personality, but in light of recent severe weather I was surprised that the structure hadn't fared too poorly.

I was in the main machine room looking around when my eyes locked with an old Black man in an official-looking uniform.

"Who told you you could be in here?" he demanded.

I'd always had ready-made replies in the event this would happen, but in that moment I felt like one of the 12-year-old kids in Stand By Me. I simply replied, "Nobody. I was just taking photos."

"Get your crew and get outta here."

My crew? I realized he thought I was a metal scrapper. I called to Roberta, and he followed us closely as we walked the long overgrown road littered with stamped bricks, scraps of wood, and broken, colored glass towards the property line. I shared that I knew about the scrappers and also thought it was a shame. He then opened up.

"They're who I was hopin' to catch!" he began. "They're tearing this place apart."

I'd found a kindred spirit. This man loved this crumbling monstrosity even more than I did. After inquiring further I was astonished to learn he worked at Armour during its heyday.

"When they said the plant was closing and everyone was let go the boss pulled me in and said they need to keep one guy on as the caretaker, and offered the job to me," he revealed.
In 1959 he watched his coworkers leave for the last time. He watched a solid facility slowly decay until entire sections of the roof crashed in, walls crumbled, supports failed, and people like myself climbed the building with abandon.

I had so many questions for him and asked if he'd speak with me for a piece I'd planned to write for the blog *UrbanReviewSTL*.

"I can't really say nothin', I've gotten in trouble in the past," he said.

He did point to a few areas and told us how many people worked in each. He spoke of all the jobs that were there.

The overgrown lot littered with brush, bricks, and debris gave way to the blinding white pavement of the brand new access road. We were off the property. The old man with gray stubble, one blind eye and a sharp, pressed uniform had done his job.

A few years back I had a dream that after a storm I went to check on the plant. As I approached I heard a snap, like a lone firecracker, then watched as the entire structure collapsed in slow motion before me, a spectacular sight, so vivid with the smokestacks splitting and a fire escape landing just feet from my body. That would have been a demise worthy of such a structure. Nestled in quiet vegetation, and in the company of someone who loved it.

Just before we got in the car, the caretaker pointed to a nearby dirt mound and said,
"That's where the new highway's comin'."

All of us understood what that meant.

## Story Box 12: Trouble in Technicolor

Levin & Sparkle were a polyamorous couple in Berkeley who ran with the Burning Man set and threw some of the wildest parties—which would typically begin as a garden BBQ but devolve into an attic orgy.

My first time at their home there was a tall young guy running around in nothing but a toga that looked like it was custom made for a dwarf stripper. His penis was just flopping about in the open air, and as he passed the buffet I heard what seemed to be fierce, whispered debate—the only part I could make out was "...but is it safe for him to be around food?"

While I didn't know the two people in the conversation, I knew a colorful character named Cornelius who was in earshot, and asked him what that exchange was about. Cornelius, a middle-aged man in the loudest outfit at a party full of loud outfits, spun around and began, "Oh, some people think he shouldn't be around the food, with his *condition*, but it's alright…" he tried to assure.

"Is it TB?" I asked.

"Oh no, no, it's…Look. Are you familiar with the author and activist Larry May? Well you know he's about eighty and I went to one of his book signings and kissed him and gave him tongue because that's just what I do, I give people tongue. A few months later I run into his assistant at Berkeley Bowl and ask him how Larry is and he said 'He's in the ICU! Some fan just came up to him at a book signing and gave him tongue, and he can't have that! He's eighty and immunocompromised!'"
With that, Cornelius rushed over to an arriving guest and gave him tongue—never returning to finish his thought.

When I was ready to leave I couldn't find Tatters, and someone suggested I check the loft. I climbed the ladder and there he was giving head to a lanky man named Basil, who was really well endowed.

With the low ceiling and carpeted floor, the loft was more for crawling than walking. I crawled up to Tatters and asked, "Whatcha doin'?"

Levin was a notorious power top, and while I didn't stay for the orgies I heard how he'd make use of the sling, often while Sparkle made out with someone directly below.

One of the most interesting plot twists at one of their parties was the time they invited some big woman none of us had met before—who initially struck me as a lesbian. She reminded me of Queen Latifah on testosterone, but despite her masculine energy she was definitely into men, and would look at some of us like we were pieces of meat—exactly the way a man who'd just gotten out of prison might look at beautiful women.

"Um um, I'd sure like some uh that!" she'd say lustily.

Towards the end of the night there was the exiting group, and the ascending group. I was in the former, but my friends who stayed said this gal got wise to the attic action and followed some guys in who were headed up the ladder. Levin cut her off at the pass.

"This is more of a gay guy thing," he said.

She went to the kitchen for a drink while Levin went on up. After five minutes she said, "Fuck it. I'm horny," and climbed up to get her some.

This next part is really something. An attic regular took one for the team. Although he was completely gay, he did his best to pleasure the unwanted guest and keep her away from the group.

"We could still hear her moaning really loudly, which was a bit distracting, but not too bad," Levin recalled.

## 151. Life's a Box of Chocolates

Lenny and Feather came out to San Francisco to visit us and we put them up in a four-star hotel on the Embarcadero. When I showed them our apartment on South Park, Lenny was clearly disappointed.

"Well, this is a lot different from your place in St. Louis," he said.

While I should've let it slide, I felt compelled to reply. "This is a three-thousand dollar apartment, Lenny." In other words, "You're not in Kansas anymore."

I'd set aside a day for sightseeing and braced myself when asking where they'd like to go. Feather nervously chimed in on Lenny's behalf.

"Lenny really wants to go to Bubba Gump Shrimp on Pier 39."

"Ok," I replied.
I was already resigned to the fact he'd want to do something ridiculous, so I just rolled with it, deciding we'd walk along the waterfront so we'd at least enjoy the scenery.

Due to hundreds of other Lennys, the wait at Bubba Gump was two hours, so we ate at a neighboring seafood restaurant. Lenny ordered the shrimp cocktail, and when it arrived, the color drained from his face.

"Is it even cooked?" he asked, face contorted.

He'd never seen shrimp that wasn't deep fried.

Whenever I'd feel myself getting too judgmental about his provincial ways, I'd remind myself that if civilization collapsed tomorrow, he'd probably survive while I wouldn't. We all have our own sets of strengths and weaknesses, I'd tell myself.

## Story Box 13: Dusty Drapes

There was a brief moment when the housing market was deflated, and Damon and I actually could afford a house in Oakland, at least in theory. We fell in love with a charming stucco bungalow on Ivy Hill, overlooking the Oakland skyline. In the Bay Area the asking price was just the opening bid, and the offers went up from there. We bid twenty-five thousand over asking, but there ended up being fifty other offers, many of them cash.

After missing out on several houses, our realtor explained that the cash buyers tended to be Chinese, and the Chinese didn't like to buy houses where someone died. Our new strategy was to only look at those properties, which was interesting. A lot of little old lady houses with gold shag carpet and dusty drapes.

Had we purchased something, anything, at that time it would have appreciated by a third in little over a year, but we were no longer equipped to make things like that happen. Our once amazing team dynamic was corroded. We couldn't agree on a house, and when a promotion came up, an opportunity that would mean giving up our rent-free apartment, I jumped at it, even though we'd actually have less money after paying Bay Area rent.

Benny's relentless narrative was that I was mediocre and lacked ambition. Even though the rent-free unit allowed us to put away thousands a month, I knew how passing up a promotion would be spun by him. Damon knew accepting the promotion would derail our one shot at buying a house, and although this caused him great internal angst, he wasn't comfortable advising me to pass up the promotion after berating me for my stalled career.

Some are held back by their dependence on alcohol, drugs, or gambling. We were under the influence of Benny *Fucking* Babbish, which was every bit as costly.

## 152. Josh on the Road

When I left St. Louis I didn't think I'd ever see Josh again. The entire mentoring experiment seemed like a failure, after all he was unable to shake Amanda, and he returned to the small town he came from with her in tow. Over time, however, he proved to be a loyal friend, and I began to appreciate him for the man he was, rather than compare him with my expectations.

Although he was fully immersed in rural Missouri, he stood firm in his beliefs. For example one day I saw the following post on his Facebook page:

"All of you talking about gays being against the Bible are talking out of your ass! I KNOW gay people and they're just like anybody else!"
In time he did manage to break free of Amanda for good, and he became an over the road truck driver. This was a great experience for him because he was able to travel to the lower 48 states, including California, where I had the honor of showing him the Pacific Ocean for the first time.

"This is all so much bigger and more beautiful than I pictured," he remarked.

I took him to lunch at the famed Cliff House, perched above the crashing waves of the sparking Pacific. When the waiter asked for his drink order he leaned in and discreetly asked,

"Do you have Mountain Dew?"

I wasn't the least bit embarrassed by this country boy, in fact, I was just as proud as if he were my son, and I watched his expressions of awe and wonder as he took in the view.

Josh was one of only a few people who could have me laughing to the point of tears without even trying, which he frequently did when he called to dryly relay the details of his life. Once, for instance, he mentioned having a new girlfriend.

"All she wants to do is suck my dick," Josh complained.

"You said you're not really into that, didn't you?" I asked.

"Oh, it's alright. But not the way she does it, with all the teeth and shit. I mean it feels like I'm sticking my dick in a goddamn beaver's mouth!"

## 153.   Immortal Style

I managed a couple of apartment buildings facing a lovely urban park near Downtown San Francisco. The properties housed formerly homeless people, and when the Dolores Housing acquired them for this purpose a couple of decades earlier the area was dilapidated and largely abandoned. Now South Park was among the most prestigious addresses on the West Coast, and was the epicenter of the dot com boom where companies like Twitter got their start.

After a few weeks commuting to and from San Mateo we ended up taking the manager unit on South Park, so there's the dichotomy of living among the formerly homeless but having a jaw dropping address with the richest tech millionaires as neighbors.

The oval park was the living room for the neighborhood, and while not seamless, my tenants mixed with the high-end residents better than I would have expected. People got to know one another, especially when both parties had the social lubrication a dog provides.

My most beautiful and elegant tenant was an African woman named Justine. She moved through the world effortlessly. Fine bone structure, fashionable clothing, and her trademark spiral curl wig. Men found her irresistible, from the white tech guru a few buildings down, who wined and dined her in the area's trendy restaurants, to her down and out alcoholic neighbor Teddy, a sixty-something Black man, who was also at her beck and call. Both of these men would regularly walk her dog Rusty whenever she requested, which was pretty much daily.

Teddy's adoration for Justine had to be rough on his old woman Connie, who, aside from being the same height as Justine and Black, was nothing like her. Homely Ol' Connie was a hot mess. Like Teddy, she was always drunk, and to borrow an expression from Josh, she had a face like a bull dog.

Justine had been battling health problems for some time and one evening the front desk attendant found her bent over in pain.

"I'm calling you an ambulance!" he said.

"No! I can't afford that" Justine struggled. "Just call me a taxi."

She left in an ambulance, and was dead within a few hours.

Whenever a tenant died in the SRO (Single room occupancy residential hotel) buildings the disposition of their belongings was often swift and shady. Inevitably, a trusted neighbor had a key and wouldn't waste a moment taking what they wanted and distributing the rest before we had a chance to padlock the unit and contact the family. This was certainly the case with Justine's place, as she had finer things than most.

The next couple of days were strange and unsettling. The smoke alarms in Justine's unit went off at all hours, for starters. After the unit was padlocked, neighbors would hear sounds coming from it. And then one morning I was leaving the building and stopped dead in my tracks. There was Justine sitting on the park bench!

Her back was to me, but it was unmistakably her, right where she always sat. The black and gold jacket she always wore, and her unique trademark wig. I approached her slowly, not believing my eyes.

She turned to look at me, and there was Connie's drunk old mug just a smiling.

## 154. Dropping In

There was a clearly marked loading zone in front of my South Park building, used by Meals on Wheels and medical taxis, but the entitled douches in that part of town would often park there anyway.

One afternoon a young woman in a BMW pulled into the loading zone and parked, heading to the Giants game a couple of blocks away.

"That's a loading zone. You shouldn't park there" said Gabriel, a formerly homeless man who bore a striking resemblance to Charles Manson.

The young woman simply brushed him off and went on her way.

It just so happened that a three hundred pound clinically depressed man decided to commit suicide that afternoon by jumping off the building. His fall was broken by the BMW, and he sustained only a few broken bones.

When the game was over the front desk had the pleasure of telling the entitled princess that her car wasn't there because it had been totaled, and was towed away.

The jumper was evicted, but was regularly at a sidewalk café on the block selling books of poetry.

## 155. Media Diva

It was an election year and I'd been contributing to a cheesy liberal blog as an outlet for my political pieces. It was run by Larry Less, a bitter queen whose claim to fame was being an intern for the Carter Administration, but I was excited about having a national audience for my work, and doing my part to motivate Democratic voters.

It was an unpaid position, so when I was asked to begin sending all submissions to his assistant, Paula Applebee, I felt it was fair to raise an objection. Applebee was a prolific creator of content, but there was no spark to her work and I felt like she wanted to lobotomize all of my pieces to make them more like hers.

Larry was infuriated by my request, and told me my ego was out of control and to take a hike.

I reached out to John Aravosis, who'd inspired me to organize the Dr. Laura protests many years earlier. He ran *AMERICAblog.com*, and if Larry's blog was a Ford, John's was a Mercedes.

I sent him writing samples, and after a few days he replied, "Your work is really good. Yes, I'd love for you to contribute, and thanks for asking."

While Larry also had a sizable readership, John's readers included many influential media elites, and a piece of mine on gun violence was tweeted by Andrew Rosenthal, Editorial Page Editor of *The New York Times*.

This came up in a heated argument about how Damon put so much weight on Benny Babbish's opinion of me. In a moment I find humorous in retrospect, we were in the middle of a heated exchange about his lack of respect for my work when I exclaimed,

"I'VE BEEN TWEETED BY THE *FUCKING* NEW YORK TIMES!"

## 156. Rise of the Fig Leaf

San Francisco's political Left, led by the ill-tempered and profanity prone Supervisor Weekly, had a decade-long run in which to save the soul of San Francisco. In 2003 their Green Party candidate, Matt Gonzalez, nearly became mayor, only narrowly bested by the far better funded Democrat Gavin Newsom.

I believe the photo-finish local election changed the course of national history because Newsom, in what I suspect was an attempt to win over a lukewarm electorate, became the first elected official in the nation to sanction gay marriage, just weeks after taking office. A move which even Barney Frank objected to, and which many say cost Kerry the election that year, but also would eventually lead to marriage equality nationwide.

And, after being elected by the slimmest of margins, it certainly made him wildly popular in San Francisco.

While the Left did get some things done, they largely squandered their legislative majority by not unifying around a cohesive agenda, and pursuing fool's errands like trying to overthrow the nonprofit Board of my parent company, Dolores Housing.

By 2010 their time was up, and the city was in a gentrification chokehold which was perfectly personified by Supervisor Scott Wiener.

The Castro elected the outward looking Harvey Milk in 1977, and went on to elect his bookend, the inward looking Scott Wiener in 2010. Milk was concerned with the international significance of his district as an island of misfit toys, a place where a queer kid from Kansas could seek refuge, a place on the forefront of societal change. Wiener, by contrast, was kept up at night by anything that made his affluent and increasingly straight constituently uncomfortable, which included adult items in storefront windows and public nudity.

"When I see an exposed penis I feel eye raped!" cried a hysterical Wiener supporter at a community meeting.

As the world became increasingly homogenized, I thought it important to preserve the character of the remaining unique places. If one was uncomfortable with public nudity, they had 88,000 American municipalities to choose from, and if they had to be in San Francisco, they could live just about anywhere except the heart of the Castro and not see it.

The real problem in the district was the mass displacement of longtime residents after crafty lawyers began holding workshops for investors on how to circumvent rent control laws. Thousands of long term LGBT residents were thrown out of the only homes they'd known for decades, and with absolutely no hope of finding another place in the city they loved, several, including travel agency owner Jonathan Klein, went to the Golden Gate Bridge and took their lives.

While in cities like Oakland and St. Louis, the media magnifies civic problems, in San Francisco it's the opposite. For example, three murders in a row in Oakland would be reported as a troubling pattern. Three murders in a row in San Francisco would be downplayed as three isolated incidents.

In the wake of Klein's suicide, the media tied themselves in knots to downplay his eviction as a factor, because that might make new residents uncomfortable, and we couldn't have that. Instead, they played up the general issue of "depression."

Friends of Klein knew better.

A makeshift memorial included the sign "Eviction = Death", and friend Cleve Jones issued a passionate statement:

"Everyone in San Francisco talks about the skyrocketing rent and the increasing evictions. It hits older and disabled people the hardest. Many of my friends have lost their homes, people like Peter Greene and Jonathan Klein, who operated the New Voyager Travel Agency on 18th Street since 1984. Peter and Jonathan have been despondent. The politicians talk and do nothing to protect us. Today I learned Jonathan has taken his life and am overwhelmed with sorrow."

The less gay the Castro became, the more rainbows they painted. It felt as self-conscious and desperate as the smile painted on a clown, and just when you thought there wasn't one more surface for a fucking rainbow, they painted the streets.

Supervisor Scott Wiener's Castro was to a gay neighborhood what Fisherman's Wharf was to a fishing village.

When Wiener was pushing his nudity ban, many devil's bargains were made to neutralize the likely opposition among groups like the organizers of the fetish events Folsom Street Fair & Dore Alley, with Wiener promising them they'd be exempted. But that's like promising to only melt eighty percent of an ice cube, assuring the remainder would be just fine. Still, the groups were more or less placated.

There was fierce debate when the nudity ban finally came before the Board of Supervisors, with progressive Supervisor David Campos saying, "I will not put on this fig leaf. I vote no" but a majority voted yes, while going out of their way to assure that this measure wouldn't take anything away from the character of San Francisco, just like they had with the other gentrification measures they'd passed.

The popular website *SFist* reported, "Today will go down in infamy as the day the Board of Supervisors stamped out one of the last vestiges of the Summer of Love."

San Francisco's gentrification forces felt entitled to have their cake and to eat it to. They wanted to soften and sanitize the city to make it more like where they came from, while claiming all of the street cred of living in the (former) counterculture capital. Few things irritated them more than being called out on this, which became my specialty. I received angry tweets from Supervisor Wiener, and impassioned, written rebuttals from the city's GLBT History Museum.

## 157. Anonymous

When I moved to San Francisco I found a familiar face on television, Linton Johnson, the former St. Louis newscaster who many years earlier danced shirtless at the Complex Nightclub every weekend. He was now the Chief Spokesman for Bay Area Rapid Transit (BART).

The agency was under fire after two shootings by BART officers, one which led to the 2013 acclaimed film *Fruitvale Station*. When BART Police shot a homeless man during the summer of 2011, the third shooting in three years, massive protests ensued.

On July 11, protesters shut down the frenzied Monday evening commute beneath San Francisco. For hours trains were held at the downtown stations by mobs of people jamming the doors and climbing on top of the cars. It took police in riot gear to disperse the protesters and get the commute under way.

In the middle of it all was Johnson coordinating and talking to media. *The San Francisco Chronicle* quoted him:

"They don't care about people who are trying to get home to their lives, trying to get home to their families."

The paper also reported the angry reaction to Johnson. "As he spoke to reporters, several white protesters called Johnson, who is African American, "Uncle Tom" and a "self-conflicted blackie." Anonymous, the amorphous political hacking group, targeted the agency, beginning with the infiltration of BART's website. They published the personal information for thousands of riders, then days later the group accessed the BART Police site and published the home addresses, email addresses and passwords of 102 BART officers. Then Johnson received his own ominous message from Anonymous:

"You're the party bitch of the Internet."

Hours later photos of Johnson on a gay cruise went viral, including one featuring full frontal nudity.

In the wake of the hacking, Johnson powered down his Oakland Hills home. No internet, no security system. During his career he had his share of stalkers, including one who was so persistent and unsettling he felt the need to install cameras. That gave them a sense of security, but now the cameras couldn't be trusted.

The FBI met with senior BART officials about another major service interruption planned for August 11, which would shut down all trains from San Francisco International to West Oakland. For several days BART officials tried to find a way to thwart the protest. While brainstorming, Johnson bounced the idea to shut off cell service in the stations just before the protest action was set to begin. BART had purchased and installed the equipment making underground cell service possible only recently, and believed they had a defensible reason to temporarily disrupt service in the interest of public safety.

Few outside the agency agreed.
In the eye of the storm many aspects of Johnson's life were collapsing at once. A fiercely loyal company man, he was now a lightning rod for controversy – criticized locally but also in the pages *The New York Times*, *Washington Post*, and newspapers around the world. A Taiwanese news program even aired an unintentionally comical animated short about the story featuring a cartoon Johnson slamming the "off button" in his corner office. He was under siege at home. His partner was traveling extensively for business and he felt isolated and alone.


### 158.  Chaos Stew

The protesters vowed to shut down the trains every Monday at rush hour, and a group of transit riders were organizing a counter demonstration. I didn't know Linton Johnson personally, but was outraged that in San Francisco of all places, the capital of the sexual revolution, personal sexual images were being used as weapons, not to mention the released images of he and his partner hugged up, as if merely being gay was supposed to shame and delegitimize him.

I issued a statement that began, "Puritanical shame based tactics have no place in the capital of sexual liberation" and announced I was organizing a demonstration alongside the protesters and counter-protesters.

It sounded like a complete circus, and the media was salivating.

I reached out to the counter demonstrators, expecting an enthusiastic welcome, but instead got radio silence. It turned out this group was primarily made up of conservative hotheads from far flung East Bay suburbs, not really interested in an alliance with sex-positive gay activists.
In an interview with KQED, the Bay Area's NPR affiliate, I described the release of the photos as gay-baiting sexual terrorism, and equated the actions of Anonymous with that of Republican operatives like Karl Rove.

Some posted comments suggesting I was a fuck buddy of Johnson's, "back in flyover country." I replied that I didn't personally know him back then, but if I had I probably would have.

"People have sex" I replied.

Anonymous consisted of countless individuals, a few of whom sent threatening messages about how they never forgive and never forget, but on their official Twitter feed they tweeted,
"Chris Andoe: We have nothing against the gay community."

Members of the group then reached out and explained that the photos were discussed in advance of the release, and the consensus was to not release them, but a rogue member did so anyway. I was given assurances, whatever they're worth, that the tactic of targeting someone with unrelated sexual images would not be used again, and was asked to cancel the protest.

Despite the sensational media coverage, our group was a ragtag assemblage of fearless Trans activists and myself. Few people were willing to cross Anonymous, and many people were simply indifferent.

I decided a good faith assurance from Anonymous was of more value than the demonstration would be, and released a statement that in light of their assurances the protest was cancelled.

A year later Linton Johnson sent me a message thanking me for all I did. I interviewed him for a *Vital Voice* piece titled Full Frontal, and we began working out together.

## Story Box 14: Washing Ashore

In high school I befriended a Japanese exchange student named Marcy Suzuki. She was a virgin when she arrived, but loved American boys, and they loved her. Her host family liked me so I often served as her alibi while she went on dates.

We sat together in art class where she'd tell me about the previous night's exploits.

"He pulled down his pants, and it was just, standing there. And it was so, pretty" she'd say, in reference to American penis.

One thing she didn't find pretty was fat. She didn't normally see fat people in Japan, and when a fat person walked in she'd lose her train of thought, wad up her face, and ask,

"Why she so, so, so *fat*? She like, *pig* or something!"

Almost twenty years later her family home was swept away in the 2011 tsunami. She returned to the bare foundation to mark the first anniversary and a neighbor who had been digging through piles of debris on the beach found a photo of us together.

## 159.  The Asian Kid

Sassy, an Atlanta art dealer who was a huge fan of Joe's, added me on Facebook, as well as my nephew Sam. After about six months she sent me a message saying she wanted to buy a few paintings, and I passed it along.

"I don't want to deal with her. If you'll negotiate and close the deal I'll give you twenty-five percent" Joe said.

His paintings ranged in price from eight to fifty thousand dollars, so that would be a nice commission. For her part, Sassy was excited to have the entire Andoe experience, and a Memorial Day Weekend in Manhattan was scheduled.

"Sassy, I'm being flown to New York to handle this sale. If you're not sure you want to buy anything yet you're welcome to go by the studio on your own to look at the work, and we can meet later" I said, wanting to ensure Joe didn't waste money on a tire kicker.

"Oh I'm certain, and I definitely want you there. I'm very familiar with his work. I have one of his horses. Plus I'm working with Sterling Gallery in San Antonio and they want several too."

She was exclusively interested in the horses, so Joe sent her a price list with a dozen paintings listed.

Sassy was a huge drinker, and loved to call me slopping drunk with big news. "Oh, my, GOD!" she'd begin. "I can't believe it, but, they're *all* sold. ALL of them. They're ALL sold" she'd say.

Joe didn't drink anymore, so he would've had no patience for her drunk dialing. I don't mind drunk talk though, especially when it's about a big pot of gold.

Sassy wanted Joe to go down to San Antonio and have a horse show, but he wasn't painting horses at the time and wasn't interested.

"Don't mention anything about a horse show when you meet him!" I instructed.

"Okay, okay, I won't. But he really should start painting them again. I could sell them all!" she said.

"Don't mention it, Sassy. We're only going to talk about the deal at hand" I coached. "He doesn't want advice on what to paint."

I flew to New York and Joe's space looked incredible. It was a working studio so it was always messy, but he'd really cleaned it up like a gallery space, with nothing but horse paintings on the fresh white walls. The plan was for me to meet Sassy in the lobby of the nearby Ace Hotel, visit over drinks, and then escort her to the studio. Once I secured the funds, I would call Joe, who'd be out and about, and he'd arrive to meet her.

283

When I arrived at the Ace, Sassy was a nervous wreck. Sitting in the back of the lobby, the puffy woman in her late forties sat jaw agape with big dark sunglasses. I greeted her and she replied, "What have you gotten me in to?" – which wasn't a good sign.

"Just relax, Sassy. Let's have a Bloody Mary" I said, determined to keep things on track.

She was accompanied by a heavyset man she'd grown up with.

"This is my high school sweetheart, Jack. Don't post anything on Facebook about him being here. My husband can't know!" she said.

The two of them began talking about the art show they wanted in San Antonio.

"If we can get him to do a show down there we can sell them all." Sassy said nervously.

"Sassy, I was flown here for *your* sale. Let's get that done and then we can discuss San Antonio. If there's no sale today, there will definitely be no hope for San Antonio" I said.

"Well, I can buy one today" she said in a resigned tone.

Entering the studio was a religious experience for Sassy, who walked in like she was in disbelief of the moment. Surveying the room she rotated until she saw a giant red horse elegantly positioned beneath a large skylight.

"OH!" she said as she threw her wrist over her head and fell into a nearby chair, dissolving into tears.

Her hand shook as she wrote out a check for forty thousand dollars, and then I made the call to Joe. She greeted him enthusiastically, clutching his arm as she discussed how much his work meant to her.

"Remember when your work was awarded in Savannah? I was one of the judges!" she said.

After about five minutes I escorted her to the door. We were walking out when she turned around and bolted back to Joe.
"Joe, let me be perfectly clear" she slurred. "You need to get back to painting horses…"

I rushed after her, grabbing one arm as her gentleman caller grabbed the other, and we ushered her out.

That afternoon she called from the bar in her hotel.

"Just got off the phone with San Antonio. They're all sold. They've been circulating the list among their buyers, and they're *all* sold. Oh my God. I can't even believe it" she said.

We planned to say our goodbyes over dinner that evening. I arrived to the only deserted restaurant on the island, an Irish place in her hotel. She was wasted, and was exuberant one minute and dissolved into tears the next.

"So where you going later tonight?" she asked.

"I'm meeting a friend at the Eagle after this" I said, and then to dissuade any thoughts of her coming, added, "It's a gay leather bar."

"Oh. Well I might meet you there" she said, as her more sober caretaker gave me a knowing look and nodded his head as if to say, "That's not going to happen."

The whole scene, from the empty, brightly lit restaurant to her crying spells, was really depressing, and I was relieved to say goodnight.

My young friend Lex, an attractive Mexican guy of twenty-two, who I'd met when he lived in the Bay Area, and who resembles Joseph Gordon-Levitt, was walking to the Eagle with me when I got a call from Sassy.

"WHERE ARE YOU? I'M HERE!" she said, shouting over loud music. Well shit.

"Looks like we'll be babysitting tonight" I told Lex. We walked into the Eagle and found two employees holding her up at the bar, which had no stools. Lex and I relieved them.

"Who are you?" she asked Lex.

"I'm Chris's friend Lex from California" he replied.

"Oh. Are you Asian?"

"No, I'm Mexican" he patiently replied.

"WHOO WHOO!" she yelled as she nearly fell backwards, her head thrown back and waving side to side.

On her best day her center of gravity was off, with her barrel-shaped middle and spindly legs, but add a day's worth of liquor and she was a total mess.

"This one's going to get you in trouble with Damon" Sassy said, pointing to Lex, then she turned to him and asked, "So are you Asian?"

We replaced her cocktail with water, and she asked
Lex about being Asian a few more times, and each
time he'd correct her to no avail.

"Sassy it's getting too crowded in here. Let us put
you in a taxi" I said.

"Ok ok, I'll go, but first I wanna see what's
upstairs" she said.

Damn. Upstairs was cram packed, shoulder to
shoulder and had guys sucking dick in dark corners.

"Ok Lex, I'll grab one arm and pull her from the
front. You grab the other and push her from the
back. We'll go up the back stairwell and bum rush
her to the front stairs" and that's what we did.

It was a wild ride for Sassy, and as we quickly
pushed through the crowd she tossed her head back
and swung from side to side gleefully yelling,
"WHOA! WHOA! WHOO! WHOO!"

I felt enormous relief when I put her in the taxi, but
she stopped me for one final thought. Holding the
taxi door she shouted, "CHRIS! Be a good boy.
DON'T *FUCK* THE ASIAN KID!"

### 160. Family Tree

A distant cousin who was about fifty-five, worked at
the post office, and was gay, found me while
researching the family tree. His name was Randall,
and he'd been researching the Andoe genealogy for
a long time, tracing us back to Norway's Andøya
Island. He said our people were Vikings who always
robbed the Irish at sea, and then decided to just
move to Ireland.

One Thanksgiving, me and Damon and traveled from St. Louis to the mountains of North Carolina to visit him and his partner in their eclectic rock home, which was full of antiques and unusual, kitschy items including flamenco dancer lamps and a white Christmas tree spinning on a turntable.

We kept in regular contact over the years, and Randall let me know he found more fruit on our family tree. We had a gay cousin in New York City named Eden, who he'd met with recently, and when I looked him up on Facebook I was taken by the family resemblance, especially his eyes, which were the same combination of green and brown as mine.

I sent Joe a link to Eden's photos, and he too was surprised at the family resemblance. Just days later Joe was waiting for the subway at 28th Street when the doors opened and there was Eden! Joe recognized him instantly but was too stunned to say anything.

I verified with Eden that it was indeed him.

"I'm rarely on that train or in that part of town at that time. What are the odds, in a city of eight million people, they'd stumble upon one another?" Eden remarked.

It was the weekend I'd traveled to New York to close the deal with Sassy, and decided to host a salon in Joe's studio. Guests included cousins Randall and Eden, my friend Lex, and a famous artist friend of Joe's named Walt, who'd done the cover art for the Rolling Stones.

We discussed many things that evening including the adventures with Sassy. Walt told us macabre tales of boating on the Ganges, where the Hindu faithful set the bodies of their loved ones adrift, and Randall discussed the Andoe family history.

Joe and Walt didn't drink, but the rest of us had plenty of wine, including Randall.

Joe was soaking it all in, and when everyone was leaving, he felt concerned he hadn't engaged with Randall enough. This man was a treasure trove of knowledge about our ancestry, and Joe wanted to make sure he knew that his visit was appreciated.

Warmly shaking his hand at the industrial steel door to the loft, Joe recapped some of what Randall had relayed about our Nordic and Irish roots.

Flushed from the wine, Randall poked his finger at Joe's chest. "If you have a stubby dick, that's the Irish genes" and turned to leave.

### Story Box 15: No Smoking

There have been a few splits in the Andoe Family over the years.

I remember a distant relative called me and wanted to know about the family history, saying her father would never tell her anything about the Andoes, only that something bad had happened that caused his branch of the family to break off. I referred her to Grandma, and the two had a nice conversation where they discussed many old and forgotten relatives.

"I can't really think of anything *bad* that happened" Grandma began. "Well, Connor *did* shoot his daughter for smoking."

### 161.  Sassy Goes South

When I returned to California, Sassy told me she and her husband were divorcing, and her funds were frozen. The forty thousand dollar check was no good.

289

## 162. Great Aunt Wilma

My great aunt Wilma was my kind of character, a big talking larger than life gal with a giant blond bouffant, diamonds, stiletto heels and an enormous fire engine red Cadillac. My family's own Cruella DeVil.

She met her husband Russell in Tulsa while working at a Utica Square dress shop called Irene Herbert's, a place that appeared to cater exclusively to daytime soap stars with its overwrought gowns. Russell walked in searching for a gift for his girlfriend and it was sabotage at first sight as she sold him the ugliest dress in the store. When he came back to return it she made her move and the rest is history.

"I was on a date at a really nice restaurant and we hear this woman in the bar just cursing like a sailor!" Mom once recalled, "looked around the corner and it was Wilma! I was so embarrassed I just slid down in my seat hoping she wouldn't see me. On the way home we see Russell pulled over by the police and Wilma standing on the side of the road with her hands on her hips."

My Great Aunt Norene cut Wilma out of her will after she said, while drunk, that Norene's second husband was just using her for her money. Norene had owned the only jewelry store in her town and when she passed she left her personal collection to Mom, including a dazzling diamond ring. Late one night Mom got a drunken call from Wilma. In her loud, slurred draw she said,
 "Lois Ann, how 'bout you give me that diamond raaang."

I always thought it would be fun to have drinks with Wilma, but she passed away shortly after I came of age.

Russell had always been in Wilma's shadow, a small, quiet man nobody ever gave a second thought, but right around the time Wilma passed Mom's boyfriend of sixteen years also passed, and Russell asked her out. He was only a relative by marriage, but it still raised eyebrows when she agreed to date him.

The Widower Russell found himself a hot commodity, something he'd never been before, because there just aren't many competing males in their mid-seventies. He was the cock of the walk and wanted to play the field, seeing several women at once. He was a cheap date and to top it off Mom thought he drank too much and he thought she drank too little.

I called her one day and asked how things were going with him. She told me it was over, but began the conversation with,

"Well, he traded in his Lincoln for one of those stubby nosed Chryslers…"

When it was done it was done, and the first Christmas after their short-lived romance she sent him a Christmas card signed, "Your niece, Lois."

### 163. Wanton Wanderlust: Denver

I had things in storage in St. Louis that I wanted to haul to our new place in Oakland.

"Donald, I'm thinking about renting a truck and driving from St. Louis to California. Wanna come?" I asked over the phone.

"My God that would be so much fun!" he exclaimed.

We made it a grand tour, holding court at stops along the way. In Denver we met up with a few friends for dinner and then went out to Wrangler, a gay bar, to meet several Facebook friends we'd never met in person. Heavy and hairy gay men are known as "bears" and when we checked in at Wrangler the bar name was followed with "THE BAR FOR BEARS."

A fun couple that I'd dubbed "The Duke & Duchess of Denver Debauchery" as well as a friend named Chuck, who'd been in a three-way relationship with a guy and a rodeo drag queen back in Oklahoma, were there. All were enjoyable company.

We were tracing back how we'd been virtually introduced and what friends we had in common when the name Mack Fantasia popped up. I'd never met Mack in person but he was a nice looking, masculine guy in his forties living in Oklahoma City.

As the drinks continued to pour Chuck talked about the orgies he and Mack had been in together where they were the only two tops in parties full of bottoms, which included the rodeo drag queen.

In a very thoughtful and serious tone Chuck said, "You know, Mack really contributed something to those parties, something unique" then staring wistfully off into space, trailed off, "He really did." The conversation started to move on to non-orgy related topics but I still had questions.

"So how did that work anyway, with all of those bottoms? Were they all just bent over waiting their turn?" I asked before Donald instantly shot back, "Chris it isn't Hungry Hungry Hippos!"

I later told Mack that he was quite the legend, and invited him to a Jet Set event. He ended up attending several over the years, and in St. Louis he wore a Hungry Hungry Hippos t-shirt.

## 164. Fifty Years Late

How remarkable and heartbreaking that nearly fifty years after the Summer of Love kids still flocked to the Haight looking for it. The Haight-Ashbury of 1969 was a vibrant place where one could just show up, find a commune, barter, smoke pot, fornicate, and live. Fifty years later there was nothing left, it had all been replaced by trust funder consumers and tourists shops, yet countless young people still made the pilgrimage.

It reminds me of turtles that continue to migrate to wetlands that no longer exist, or to beaches that are now overrun with tourists and trash. For the turtles and for the kids, the habitat is gone.

One night I was running around with Tatters and we found ourselves at the street's only gay bar, and afterwards we stumbled upon a large group sitting on the sidewalk, probably in their late teens to early twenties. I sat down among them, inquired about where they were from, most were from Texas, then I asked, "So what's it like to be fifty years late?"

Some laughed nervously but others knowingly nodded and shared their thoughts. I sensed they were projecting a relevance to the area that still made it worthwhile in their minds, and I didn't want to be a total buzzkill so I left them on a high note.

I wish I could remember what that high note was but I was pretty drunk.

## 165.  Crystal Clear

Miss Crystal, a male to female Trans woman in her thirties, met the much older Rita Revlon, also male to female, at a national Trans Activist Conference in Philadelphia.

In St. Louis, Rita had a questionable reputation as an ill-tempered, bridge-burning squeaky wheel with no real following, but she was in her element at national events, where she impressed people with her big ideas and was highly regarded.

Rita and Miss Crystal became romantically involved at the conference, and when discussing their activism Miss Crystal shared her frustration about Tucson, where she lived.

"There's a few seasoned activists who run everything and have been there for thirty years, and if you haven't been around as long as they have, don't even think about a leadership role" she complained.

That's when Rita presented her with what felt like the opportunity of a lifetime.

"I run Trans Central, a prominent advocacy organization in St. Louis, and plan to have my [gender reassignment] operation and retire soon. I've been looking for the right person to take it over. It's yours if you want it."

Miss Crystal was interested, and Rita offered to let her stay at her spacious exurban St. Charles County home until she got on her feet. While they were romantically involved, Miss Crystal was open about being polyamorous, having two girlfriends in Tucson, and about her stints as a sex worker.

Rita had her own entanglements as well, being married to a guy named Mark who'd fallen in love with her back when she was a macho guy, and stuck with her as she transitioned.

Looking back on her time in St. Louis, Miss Crystal began, "The longer I stayed, the weirder shit got."

She hit the ground running at Trans Central, reaching out to many organization and making connections. She was excited to share an email with Rita containing big news on the fruits of her labor.

"The National Coalition of Anti-Violence Project has invited us to collaborate with them!"

Rita read the email and her smile turned to a scowl.

"No, you've been invited. I'm going to call and give them a piece of my mind!" Rita threatened.

"I had to beg her not to call them, and I appeased her by delicately working to get her name added after the fact. But that's how she was, she always wanted the credit and flipped out if she didn't get it."

Miss Crystal continued making strides at Trans Central, building bridges, training rape crisis counselors, but Rita made progress difficult.

"She'd destroy everything I did" Miss Crystal lamented.

## 166. Rita Revlon vs. Simone Shasta

The iconic Simone Shasta was everything Rita wasn't, mainly beloved by the community. Adding the title Executive Director of the LGBT Center to her already substantial history, Simone was essentially the Queen of LGBT St. Louis. Rita didn't like it, but tried for a time to work with her.

Rita's husband Mark was a calming and stabilizing force in her life, and when he passed away, she became unmoored and her drinking intensified. She was increasingly obsessed with bringing Shasta down, and found a treasure trove of bad check charges and civil judgments she planned to hobble her with.

Miss Crystal didn't care for Shasta either.

"In front of others she was warm and interested in what everyone else was doing, but behind closed doors she was completely different" Miss Crystal began. "Once we were in a meeting and she said 'You two have it easy, just helping the Trans community. I'm here trying to serve everyone'" Crystal recalled.

Still, going after Shasta would be futile, she tried to explain to Rita.

"If you win, you lose. She has the support of the community and you don't."

Miss Crystal managed to keep a lid on Rita, but while checking Facebook on a flight she discovered Rita had dropped the bomb.

"I was thirty thousand feet in the air when I saw she posted Shasta's entire legal history, and just as I predicted, the whole town turned against her, and since everyone thought of me as Rita II, they turned against me as well."

As a bit of revenge, Simone Shasta did some online snooping of her own and discovered that the name Trans Central had never been registered with the state, so for seven dollars she registered it, then came out with a widely read piece in the Vital Voice announcing she was intersex. The piece held nothing back, even mentioning that she had a micro penis. It was the talk of the city, and Shasta was showered with messages of encouragement.

Trans Central now legally belonged to Simone Shasta, and she was more loved and supported than ever. Out foxed, Rita's bitterness grew, as did her enemies list.

*Vital Voice* Gossip Columnist Penelope Wigstock had the following to say about the feud:

"Not since the days of Knot's Landing and Dynasty have I enjoyed insane catfights like these! The only thing missing are a few shattered vases and physical assaults in a large outdoor fountain."

## 167. Bringing Out the Big Guns

Rita was armed to the hilt, and after a few drinks, loved to make veiled threats about shooting people.

"I don't know what she had against me, but she posted a pic of a gun in a garter belt and said I needed to meet her revolver!" said a female to male Trans man who lived in a rural community outside of town with his wife and children.

"Then one day I come home to find her 'Trans Van' parked down the street from my house! That was really scary."

Miss Crystal was still living with Rita.

"I couldn't afford to move, and was just trying to survive" she recalled.

Her two girlfriends came to town for Christmas and crashed at Rita's. Bitter and jealous, Rita was holed up in the den drinking.

"She was in a horrible mood, and when she's sitting in that little den with the door shut it's not a good sign – because you know she's drinking her vodka and things are not going to get better."

Miss Crystal and her girlfriends were drifting off to sleep when Rita finally emerged, and they could hear her angrily talking to herself in the neighboring room.

"She was just saying a lot of nonsense, and would yell and scream to herself. It was pretty scary, then she got eerily calm and said, 'I've got all these guns here. I could just shoot you all.'"

The girls were in fear for their life.

"My girlfriend Jill completely flipped the fuck out. I grabbed the phone and dialed 9-1-1 and said, 'I've got an actively psychotic person with a gun! Please come quick!' It still took them forever because it was St. Charles County – *everyone* is an actively psychotic person with a gun. I should have said I had a *black* psychotic person with a gun."

When the police arrived, Rita convinced them it was a simple domestic issue and they left.

"That was really stupid, Crystal" Rita sneered and went to bed.

Miss Crystal and the girls gathered their things and returned to Arizona, where they spent Christmas in a motel.

Not long after Miss Crystal left, Rita ended up in the hospital, and my activist friend Matthew Bryant went to see her, along with his friend Russ. He was taken aback that rather than appreciate the gesture, she acted as if they were planning to rob her of her guns.

"She was in rare form. She was both foul and paranoid. I'm not embellishing when I say that she mentioned two dozen times that although it was possible to break into her house, her guns were hidden so well that nobody would find them. I was very offended; I don't burglarize people plus I had just given up an entire morning to cheer up somebody that was essentially calling us a pair of thieves." Bryant recalled.

When they saw their visit was doing nothing to cheer Rita up, they politely said their goodbyes.

"Bye. You'll never find my guns!" Rita yelled as they exited the room.

## 168. Another Saturday Night

It was another Saturday night in San Francisco's industrial South of Market area and I found myself in the tawdry smoking alley with Tatters, Truman, and an attractive friend of Truman's from St. Louis, who was rather animated while getting head from a Filipino stranger less than a foot from us while we carried on our routine conversation.

"Aww yes! Umm, damn this is some good head. Umm, I mean I'd pay for this shit! *YEAH* that's it."

It was packed as always back there, and although the animated fellatio was a bit awkward, overall the scene almost felt pedestrian to my calloused sensibilities, not unlike waiting in line at the supermarket. But for some reason spotting a weathered old drag queen, with some 1980's news anchor wig, standing awkwardly in the middle of it all snapped me out of my trance, almost like I was watching the scene through a stranger's eyes.

I took a drink then dryly said to my friends, "Well, this is my life. Drag queens and blow jobs."

## 169. HOT MESS

Slyman later confirmed that it was in fact my Hot Mess event that made Collins, once my biggest advocate, sour towards me.

"You committed a cardinal sin when you upstaged his beloved William Lowe by getting the patio at Sensation. He was livid and kept saying 'This is all about ego! All of this is about Andoe's ego. He's not even raising money for charity!'"

"William Lowe's an alright guy, but I don't get why Collins thought he was enough of a draw to fill the patio. He's not an entertainer or anything" I said.

"To Collins, Lowe hung and the moon and he probably figured everyone else felt the same way and would pack the place. I remember him blushing and gushing one day saying, 'Everyone calls us the Williams.'"

Despite everything, though, Collins was friendly when I stopped by the office, and seemed genuinely amused by the Hot Gay Mess piece in *AMERICAblog*, despite the fact it was born as an end run around him. He even said I was just the man for the haunted bars piece they wanted for the October issue, and suggested I start by interviewing Gary Reed, owner of the city's oldest gay bar Clementine's, about Midnight Annie, the drag queen entombed in the wall.

I went to the Chase Park Plaza to pick up my friend and event planner Thurston Marks, in town from San Francisco, and headed to Clems. Soulard is dear to me, and I drove him by my first apartment and told him about how everyone sits on the stoops in the evening, drinking wine and visiting.

"This really is a great city" Thurston replied.

Gary Reed always reminded me of a funeral director. A solemn, quiet man with dark hair and his trademark sport coat, I found him doing paperwork at a table in the restaurant. I asked if I could have a moment of his time for a Vital Voice story. He nodded and extended his hand towards the chair.

"I'm here to ask about Midnight Annie" I began.

A surprised look flashed across his face, and then he asked "What would you like to know?"

Legend has it she got the name Midnight Annie because back in the forties she'd bribe a jailer to let her blow inmates after the midnight shift change, although Gary wasn't sure how much truth there was to that.

"She came from great wealth, but was estranged from her family. She'd get lump sums from time to time and would blow it all on seedy characters, taking men to Europe, buying them color televisions" Gary began. "At the end of her life she lived around the corner on Russell, and gave me power of attorney in the event I needed to make end of life decisions. Thank God that didn't happen, and she passed naturally. Her ashes sat on my mantle for years, but when we rehabbed the bar I decided to put her in the wall, and consulted with a Priest about how to do it properly" Gary recalled.

"I always say my only child was a seventy-five year old drag queen."

## 170. A Diva is Born

After years of rumors, questionable behavior and denials, Feather's husband Lenny finally came out of the closet, and not since Diana Ross has the world seen such a coming out spectacle. It was like a months-long Broadway production.

Over Labor Day I had the HOT MESS show in St. Louis. Lenny, Feather and the kids made the three hundred mile trek from Kansas and checked into the elegant Chase Park Plaza where our mostly gay guests were staying. Lenny was pumped and energized, making it clear right off the bat he was in no mood to be weighed down by the wife, kids, or in-laws.

"I'm not here to see you guys!" he snapped at Francis & Edie. "I'm here to see people I don't get to see all the time."

The criminally shy man who first sat across the table from me, Donald, and Damon years earlier, oddly giggling behind his phone, was now a confident, driven diva holding court. He was in his element, ditching Saturday plans with the in-laws to follow Lloyd Spartan's entourage to brunch in Soulard. And then there was Sunday.

## 171. Single White Female Brunch

Miltonia planned a brunch for half a dozen friends visiting from her home state of Kansas. Francis & Edie were included and Sunday morning they learned that Lenny, Feather and the kids wanted to join. Miltonia attempted to amend her reservation but the trendy restaurant was booked.

"Bring the entire party anyway. We'll make it work, but you might have separate tables" the hostess said.

The restaurant managed to seat everyone together, not that it meant much to sit by Lenny since he was absorbed with his phone, at least until he noticed two parties leaving. At that point he sprang up and began moving tables around like he was at the local smorgasbord.

"Lenny! What are you doing?" Francis asked.

"Well I've got some people coming and need to make room" he replied, without looking up.

This was news to everyone. "You can't just move tables around. They have reservations and a wait list" Francis said to no avail.

Back at the Chase I got a Facebook notification when decorator Robert Hayden tagged me: "I'm at Chris Andoe's brunch and he's not even here!"

Hungover and disoriented I threw on clothes and rushed over thinking I must've forgotten this event. I arrived fifteen minutes later to see twenty-five of my friends finishing their meals, and a bright-eyed Lenny working the room.

It wasn't until weeks later I learned he'd hijacked Miltonia's plans and my name to throw himself a debutante ball before returning to the doldrums of the rural plains. Miltonia didn't know most of these people, and I wasn't aware "Chris Andoe's Brunch" was even going on.

The 1992 thriller *Single White Female* came to mind, a movie about a woman whose roommate becomes so obsessed with her she tries to *be* her.

### 172. Lights, Camera, Action!

By November 5th Lenny was essentially, if not officially, out on Facebook. He'd been posting photos of himself hugged up with a gay guy back home named Ryan, who was living at the Salvation Army while recovering from meth addiction. The photo gave me and Donald pause, not only because the two were so snuggly, but because Ryan looked a lot like the drug addict known as Crankles who had stolen Donald's wallet six years earlier.

Fresh from his seven month research project in Uganda, Donald sent Lenny a message asking who the guy was, and Lenny replied, "I guess I have some explaining to do."

Lenny came out to Donald, telling him Heather didn't know yet, nor did I. Ryan was his boyfriend.

"We both smile ear to ear when he's around, he makes me giggle like a little school girl. I have never been so happy Donald!" Lenny gushed.

"Well, this is crazy! How are you going to handle this with Feather? It's going to turn her life upside down" Donald asked.

"Yes it is" Lenny began. "I'm thinking my best play with Feather is to separate first. With everything she has going on with the kids I don't think she could handle the me being gay bomb. I've fought it since high school."

Despite announcing he was gay, Kenny oddly put some of the blame for the relationship collapse on Feather.

"Her not wanting to come to Florida for my family get together hurt me. She had every chance to be there and didn't want to. It's time to do what LENNY wants to do to be happy and Lenny is *going* to do it. Ryan does it all for me. I have had more feelings in more places than I ever have in my life. It comes over kind of selfish but I'm ready for happiness." Lenny said.

Donald asked when he planned to tell everyone.

"I've already told my mom, and the other guy I had sex with knows. I've known him for 18 years, and there are a couple of friends in St. Louis who know like Jeff, Michael, Robert Hayden, John Talbot, John Zachary, and Ron…"

After rattling off half of the gay guys in St. Louis, he continued, "And I've told Monte and Anthony. Feather and I need to move along with splitting up very soon. I'm going to try really hard to do that through this coming weekend. Going to be very hard moving on with the Feather situation."

*If you caught the part about the guy he had sex with who he's known for 18 years, just wait.*

The following day, Wednesday November 6th, Ol'
Limelight Lenny invited his social network to follow
along as he left his wife. Minutes before she got
home he posted:

"I am going to confess. Support me."

Feather found a crying Lenny curled up in the fetal
position. He said he couldn't live there anymore -
he had thinking to do and had to be alone. Feather
didn't quite understand what he was getting at,
other than he needed space.

"Do you want to stay in the camper for a while?"
she asked.

"I can't think here!" he replied, still weeping.

"Honey I've got to pick up the kids. Let's go
somewhere and talk when I get home" she said,
patting his back.

When she returned he was gone. She checked his
Facebook page and saw his confession update with
every country queen in a 500 mile radius chiming in
with the messages of support he'd solicited.
Feather chimed in too.

"I can deal with you leaving me with all the bills. I
can deal with you leaving me while I'm injured. I
can deal with you not wanting to be there for me
emotionally while one on my children had severe
emotions issues & the hospitalizations that were a
result of those issues. But if I lose custody of my
child because I no longer have a stable residence I
won't ever be able to forgive. I know this is me
being a bitch airing dirty laundry. But right now you
deserve this."

Well, that pretty much killed that thread, it was crickets. Nobody wanted to follow that- until his loony friend, a janitor in suburban St. Louis named Jay Best chimed in.

"BESTIES FOREVER! I SUPPORT FOREVER!"

On Friday November 8th, after days of cooking up this masturbatory mess, it was finally time to add the final ingredient to his social media soufflé.

## 173.  The Announcement.

"Just to make it all clear. None of this is Feather's fault. This is all me. I apologize for what I have done to her and the family in my confused state of my life. I do not blame her, the kids, her friends, and her family for hating me at all. I should not have gone about it all the way I did. Now that I am OUT to her. I'm now coming OUT to the rest of you! If I loose [sic] a few of you due to this I understand.
Thank you, and have a wonderful day......"

Again, Feather weighed in:

"I'm glad you finally stopped lying to me & giving me false hope. I don't care who you choose to be with. The worst part is that you cheated on me. You might as well repost the pic of you & Ryan. I've had to look at it every time someone liked it or commented on it wondering why you guys looked so intimate."

Lenny had invited the world to participate in the shedding of his family, and understandably the world felt at liberty to weigh in. Mostly the messages were ones of qualified support - many mixed messages were posted from people who hardly knew either one of them. Comments like that of Gloria Wholegroves:

"Oooh. Well I'm happy you came out, but I don't condone cheating."

Then here came Jay Best.

"for those of u that think he cheated? i know for a fact he didn't! some of u are just hearing n seeing 1 sided story"

I saw where this was headed. Gays and allies often see "coming out" the way Christians see a baptism, everything that happened before is rinsed away and irrelevant. There's nothing left to do but celebrate, and Ms. Lenny was in full parade mode. Plenty of confetti cannons were going off. Sprinkle a little victimization talk of Feather "hating" him, muddy the waters with insinuations there actually was no infidelity, and voilà! A clean slate.

Considering 90% of his gay friends were my friends, many wondered when I was going to say more about it. I wandered in front of the parade and essentially said, "Not so fast."

I posted an open letter to his wall.

*Lenny,*

*For the most part you're not going to lose friends over coming out of the closet. Everyone's been cool about that, even your wife. Sure the public way you went about it raised eyebrows, but it is what it is.*

*You'll be judged on what happens next.*

*Will you own that you've entered into an intimate relationship with Ryan while married and living with Feather? You pretty much have, but your nutty "bestie" Jay Best is publicly insinuating Feather isn't telling the truth, and that there's "two sides" to this, which there aren't. Will you allow this, or will you step up and unequivocally defend Feather's character?*

*With your departure, 2/3 of the household income is gone without notice, and just before the holidays. We'll be watching to see if you do right by Feather and the kids by not leaving them high and dry.*

*The confetti is being swept up from your announcement while Feather is sifting through the rubble of a wasted decade. You've invited hundreds of people to watch this drama unfold and now the audience is waiting to see who you really are. They'll be watching Feather's struggles to see who you really are.*

*The jury's still out.*

*Chris*

Lenny commented, "I am the bad person in this. I did cheat. In the end of it all I am guilty of it as charged. I am GUILTY."

Jay Best chimed in with more nonsense, and I replied as follows:

"Jay Best: Fifteen hours ago you claimed to know for a fact that Lenny didn't cheat and then lectured people who said he had, even though the fact that he cheated isn't in dispute by anyone, even Lenny! You're a grown man posting misspelled gibberish filled with "bestie" this and "bestie" that. You pretend to be an authority on Lenny & Feather's marriage and the intimate details of Lenny & Ryan's sex life. Not only have you made a complete fool of yourself, you've revealed yourself to be a dishonest, low class drama queen without an ounce of credibility. I honestly find it embarrassing you're even part of this discussion."

Jay Best had an epic meltdown and told me to fuck off half a dozen times, in his own misspelled gibberish fashion.

## 174. A Bit Much

My boy Josh had been trying to reach me for days and I was finally able to take his call on a Saturday night. For some bizarre reason Lenny called him of all people to share explicit sexual details about how he was the top in his relationship with Ryan, and how he was able to ejaculate inside him during sex, something he said he could never do before.

The conversation made Josh a bit nauseated.

"Well I'm happy for you man, but I don't need to hear all that shit."

While Josh wasn't interested in hearing about man on man sex period, it didn't help that he thought Lenny and Ryan were very unattractive.

"Damn they're an ugly homosexual couple" Josh often said shaking his head. "And Ryan looks like a big jolly sack of potatoes."

As his conversation wrapped up with Lenny the topic turned to alimony and complaints about Feather's financial demands.

"Hey man, I'm not tryin' to piss you off here, but you need to help out your wife. Being happy being gay doesn't mean you don't have to live up to your responsibilities" Josh said.

Lenny got snippy. "Helping her out doesn't mean giving her everything she wants!"

## 175. Woman to Woman

Bevan, a portly gay guy in Feather's town, ran a website selling country crafts. With her household income now decimated she was looking for more exposure for her creative work and met with him to discuss options. Although by all accounts Bevan was madly in love with his partner, he often talked about his plans for when the man was dead.

"He's got Type II diabetes and won't be around forever, and when he's gone I done told him I'm taking that life insurance and getting lipo and a tummy tuck and a chin lift and I'm movin' to California to marry me a rich man!"

While Feather discussed business, all this queen could think about was the secret he knew, a secret she'd be mighty interested in, and it was just killing him. He quickly broke with the classic opener, "Well, don't tell him I told you, but…"

A few months back a distant relative they called Uncle Bruce stopped by Lenny & Feather's house. Ol' Bruce was a character. With a reputation around town as a horny old goat, he was married but everyone knew he was bisexual- although it seemed his days of getting action had long passed. He appeared older than his sixty years.

Scrawny and pale with a scraggly beard, he was plagued by medical issues and was prone to seizures. He made no secret of his insatiable horniness though. Noticing Lenny's new slim and muscular physique, Bruce stared for a few moments, jaw agape, then fanning himself and holding the wall for support he looked Lenny up and down, and, right in front of Feather and the kids, said lustily in his raspy country twang,

"Oh Lenny your body's just callin' out to me!"

After that Bruce began popping in regularly asking Lenny to repair his car, and once he called saying he was having a seizure and Lenny's was the only number he could call on his speed dial. This made no sense to Feather, and although Lenny agreed it was odd, he went over to see what he could do.

Well, it turns out what Lenny could do was pound Uncle Bruce's old booty. Which he did. A lot.

Feather was only able to sit on this information for an hour, then confronted Lenny over the phone.

"I've got people coming out of the woodwork telling me they've either slept with you or they know someone who has. I deserve to know the truth."

After some prodding Lenny admitted that he'd slept with Bruce, but denied sleeping with anyone else.

"I should've known people would talk, this is Ottawa!" Lenny said, indignant and disgusted about his gossipy low-rent hometown, as if people in more cosmopolitan locales would have kept such information to themselves. Fuming, he continued, "I didn't want anyone to know about that!"

Lenny's voice was quivering with anger.

"I can't talk about this right now. I've got to go" he said.

"All of these people know. Don't you think I have a right to know?" she asked, before continuing "How many DATES with GUYS have you taken me and the kids on Lenny?" she demanded, reflecting back on strange brunches with new "friends" who seemed surprised her and the kids were in tow.

"I haven't been on any dates!" Lenny exclaimed, before again stating how angry he was.

He disconnected and Feather was overcome with a sense of calm for having squeezed out the truth, but this crack in the dam would lead to a flood of new revelations.

Uncle Bruce, it turns out, wasn't just some one time rendezvous for Lenny. According to him, he was Lenny's longtime lover.


### 176. Uncle Bruce Tells All

When Lenny was sixteen his family lived a few doors down from Bruce, and Bruce remembered the awkward boy he'd defend from the bigger kids in the neighborhood.

"He was bullied because he had a funny walk and I would not put up with that" he recalled, "I've known he was gay since puberty."

A friendship emerged and when Lenny was about twenty-four they had their first intimate encounter, which he describes as, "rubbing and touching". This kind of light play went on for some time, then one night during heavy kissing Lenny pushed for more.

"We had sex, but he started it, not me, and it was just what he wanted to do. I do not apply myself on other males they come to me."

As far as what they did in bed, he offers "I will put it this way: He's the only one to penetrate me that way since I was raped in 1975."

Lenny bought a used camper that became their love nest. During their rendezvous he'd play Show & Tell, scrolling through the dozens of St. Louis penises on his phone. He asked if he could take sexual photos of Uncle Bruce to show a special friend in Rolla, MO, but Bruce said no.

In late October, about two weeks before he left Feather, Lenny told Uncle Bruce he'd met someone. He awkwardly and quietly delivered the news, avoiding eye contact. After he came out to Feather he stopped by one last time to tell Bruce and his wife JoAnne that she'd kicked him out with nowhere to go. They offered to let him live on their property in his camper but he declined.

The truth was he wasn't kicked out. He'd already rented an expensive two bedroom in the nearby college town of Lawrence, where Ryan was in rehab.

Uncle Bruce dissolved into tears thinking about Lenny leaving him for Ryan, and admitted to sending emotional emails about Ryan being bad news, and the persistent rumors that he was HIV positive.

"I'm pissed but I'm hurt more than anything" he said.

When word about the love camper started spreading through Ottawa, a livid Lenny issued a threat.

"If I hear one more person talk about what we did in the camper I'm going to tell your WIFE all about it!"

"She already knows so you can't hurt me like that!" Bruce replied.

Feather, for her part, found herself being oddly empathetic to Bruce.

"Well I guess Uncle Bruce was with him longer than I was" she said.

Such empathy stood in stark contrast to the absolute lack of concern Uncle Bruce showed for Feather or for his own wife- who was his sole source of financial support. This dovetailed with Lenny's flippant disregard for Feather's emotions during his grand reality show coming out spectacle. To Lenny and Bruce, it seemed these women were little more than wallpaper.

After Lenny got with Ryan, Bruce said Lenny repeatedly scolded him about talking too much. Although he'd already blamed Feather for leaving Ottawa, claiming she threw him out with nowhere to go but the pricier pastures of nearby Lawrence, he came back for a second bite of the apple by blaming Uncle Bruce.

"You and your mouth are the reason I had to leave town!" he barked.

Sad Ol' Uncle Bruce didn't want Lenny to be angry with him. This Lenny wasn't the relatively masculine, quiet mechanic he loved. Seemingly overnight he'd transformed into a 1990's gay stereotype with his rainbow flags and his dropping of the word "fabulous" at every opportunity, but I could tell Uncle Bruce hoped somehow things would go back to the way they were. Completely irrational as it was, maybe the genie could be put back in the bottle.

Bruce said Lenny's Facebook addiction had gotten him into trouble at work to the point he was on probation, "But he's still on there all the time! I see that green notification light on- he could really get into trouble!"

After a couple of months of the cold shoulder from Lenny, Uncle Bruce decided to call his boss at the auto dealership and tell her all about it.

"Hi, I'm Lenny's ex-lover Bruce, the one from the camper" he began.

## 177. Fall of Prop 8

*Americablog.com* 7/2/2013

Thirteen years ago I was attending a gay church service when I saw Damon walk in.

He was an attractive, conservatively dressed, fresh-faced Black man of twenty-three. With his excellent posture, serious expression and weathered old Bible he looked like a young preacher. Considering four churches were at the same intersection, all I could think was "OMG HE'S IN THE WRONG CHURCH!"

It was three weeks before the LGBT Pride celebrations, and the service was even gayer than normal but he kept sitting there, so I figured he knew where he was. When service let out I hopped and elbowed my way up the aisle so we'd exit at the same moment. "Hi I'm Chris," I said as I shook his hand. I invited him to stay for the potluck, but he politely declined. I assumed he wasn't interested, and didn't think anything more about it.

He attended the next three services, I found out later, looking for me, but I wasn't around. Then came Pride Sunday. I was working a booth when I saw him in the crowd. "Damon!" I yell. I'm horrible with names, but I remembered his.

He walked over, dressed more casually than last time, but still very well put together, and we had one of those conversations where the butterflies drown out anything the other person is saying. He took off his mirrored sunglasses and asked if I'd like to go out sometime.

Four years later, in 2004, we found ourselves living one mile away from San Francisco City Hall when Mayor Gavin Newsom surprised everyone by ordering city officials to issue marriage licenses to same-sex couples. It was cold and dreary out, but couples from around the world came to wait in the rain for the opportunity to get married. But not us. Damon had a cold, and we correctly figured the marriages would be nullified.

The decision not to participate in that historical moment was always something we regretted. We ended up moving around the country for five years before returning to California and waiting out Prop 8, which repealed California's new-found legalization of same-sex marriages in 2008.

I was optimistic Prop 8 and the Defense of Marriage Act (DOMA) would fall, and expected to be excited. But when the rulings came down from the Supreme Court last Wednesday, and I read Justice Kennedy's decision, saying, "DOMA singles out a class of persons deemed by a State entitled of recognition and protection to enhance their own liberty," I broke into tears. The reaction surprised me. It came from somewhere deep within.

There was still a great deal of caution, in light of the 25 day stay (initially we all believed that the court's decision wouldn't go into place for 25 days) so we kept our enthusiasm in check. But then on Friday evening, I was sitting in the park with my dogs, when I read the California Federal Appeals Court issued a late order: "The stay in the above matter is dissolved effective immediately". A few minutes later I read "A jubilant San Francisco Mayor Ed Lee announced that same-sex couples would be able to marry all weekend in his city, which is hosting its annual gay pride celebration this weekend." And the marriages began.

Damon and I had another chance, and this time we had the federal government behind us.

Saturday morning we decided thirteen years was long enough to wait, we were going to get married. We already had non-wedding plans with our friend Chatters, so I needed to inform her things had changed. Chatters and I only text in rhyme, so I sent the following:

*This weekend's plans have somewhat varied*
*Pride tomorrow but today get married.*

*We're heading to SF City Hall to stand and wait*
*We'd like you with us. That'd be great.*

She threw on a dress, jumped on her bicycle and rode the fifteen blocks to meet us. She was so excited she got dizzy and had to sit down. None of us could really believe this was happening. It was so surreal.

We stood in a line that began outside City Hall and snaked through the corridors. Hundreds of couples were there, many who'd been together decades longer than us.

The love, camaraderie and jubilation was like nothing we'd experienced. Cars driving by honked in support. People took photos for strangers. Stories were told. Pens were exchanged as forms were filled out. Questions like "Where was your dad born" echoed through the halls. Smiling volunteers were everywhere.

Two elderly gentlemen in their eighties were among the couples. One of them had mobility issues and his partner fussed over him and made sure he was comfortable. I thought about how critical being married was for them; they don't have to worry about being split up in a nursing home, and won't be burdened with unfair end of life complications. The surviving partner won't be treated as just "a friend."

In the grand rotunda Damon and I vowed that we'd always look after one another. We are a family. Chatters took us out for brunch at a lesbian-run restaurant. Afterwards we celebrated with "bottomless mimosas," and the earthy waitress held us to the "bottomless" part, in light of our big day. Full and happy we nearly fell asleep in the booth.

Everyone we encountered on our way home seemed able to tell we'd just been married, and all we got was love — from the streets of San Francisco, to the new neighbors we met in our Oakland elevator — people struck up conversations with us and shared in our joy.

Californians had been humiliated by the fluke which was Prop 8. Funded and backed largely by Mormons in Utah, it was never who we were.

In the corridors of San Francisco's palatial City Hall, the building that rose after the catastrophic 1906 earthquake, the building where Harvey Milk made history, and where a young Diane Feinstein appeared before gasping reporters to deliver the unbelievable news that Supervisor Milk and Mayor Moscone had been assassinated in their offices. The building where brand new Mayor Gavin Newsom made history by issuing the first same-sex wedding licenses in the United States, and where his successor Ed Lee invited couples to marry all weekend in the wake of the Supreme Court rulings.

In that building we didn't do things the way they wanted us to do them in Utah, or in Mississippi, or on the Plains. We were free to make our own way, make our own families, and it was beautiful.

## 178. LGBT Center Shitstorm

William Collins and William Lowe, both on the Board at the LGBT Center, came to ask for Slyman's help one day. Simone Shasta was the Executive Director of the Center, and things weren't smelling right.

"There's been some issues with the Center's credit card lately, and we wondered if you'd mind looking over these charges and seeing if they make any sense to you" Collins asked.

Looking at the statement, familiar patterns emerged.

"This $162 at Walgreens every other week looks like Simone's estrogen" Slyman began. "And Uncle Bill's Pancake House, that's where she and her boyfriend have breakfast every day" he continued.

"Oh wow," Lowe replied as his stomach sank.

The Center conducted an internal investigation that took weeks. Meanwhile, Shasta was still working alongside everyone at *Vital Voice* part time. It was during this period Slyman discovered discrepancies of his own, mainly that the company bank account was nearly empty.

"I called my accountant and asked, 'What happened to my money?' and he said 'Well, there haven't been any invoices issued in sixty days.'"

That was Simone's job.

321

"And I was like 'What the fuck, Simone? No invoices!' and she said, 'I'm so sorry, I've just been so busy running the Center, and dealing with my boyfriend. I'll stay late every day until I'm caught up."

The Board was finally wrapping up the investigation, and Slyman decided it was time to cut ties with Shasta.

"I walked in to her office at the Center carrying a box of her things and her jaw dropped. She asked, 'I'm fired aren't I?' and I said 'Why don't we just say you're going full time over here' and she said okay and we hugged."

Collins decided to get ahead of the story by running a brief piece about the 'misuse of funds' on the *Vital Voice* website.

"It was a puff piece" Slyman began, "and the community saw through it and then came after *Vital Voice*. Making matters worse, NPR ran a more detailed story with William Lowe quoted saying the amount was under five thousand dollars. If you're trying to keep the lid on something you never mention a number! People went crazy. For a minute it looked like this was going to bring down the Center and *Vital Voice*!"

Embezzlement aside, Shasta ran the Center like nobody else could. She raised money, she was the heart of the agency, cooking large dinners for the community on Thanksgiving and Christmas, and she set firm boundaries with volunteers and visitors – critically important since some were homeless and used the Center as their daytime home.

"Put your shoes on. You're in public" Shasta snapped when she spotted someone walking around in socks. Often the homeless or marginally housed would be at the Center in the guise of volunteering, and Shasta would put them to work cleaning or setting up for events.

The following Director, a bleeding heart named Amy Marsh, was no Simone Shasta, and things completely unraveled in a matter of months.

I met an eccentric former volunteer named Clint on a quiet upper floor of the grand Central Library to discuss those final months. He spoke of how two homeless lesbians, one who'd punched a volunteer, basically took over, as if the Center was their personal home – and it turned out it was.

"They were secretly living there at night. Everyone seemed to know, but it wasn't really talked about. Then one time one of them went up to Amy's office and told her that she'd left her lights on, and asked for her car keys to turn them off. Amy gave them to her, and the women took off in her car! Neither even had a license. They were gone for thirty or forty minutes. We were all standing on the sidewalk wondering what to do when they finally returned."

This was quite a tale, so I took another former volunteer, Lucas, out to dinner in Soulard to get confirmation.

It was all true.

Lucas, a fit and attractive veteran in his forties, had essentially worked full time at the Center, although he was unpaid. His motivation was helping people, and the Center provided him with many opportunities to do that.

"People who were new in town would often call or come by, but there were also young people in desperate need. We had a fourteen year old kid who had a falling out with his mother and slept in the gangway between ours and the neighboring building one night before asking us for help. I was able to talk to his mother and work with them to sort things out."

Lucas also recalled a situation where, despite their differences, Simone Shasta and Rita Revlon came together to help someone in need.

"A Trans girl who was about eighteen had moved from Indianapolis to East St. Louis to live with a friend, but was kicked out. At the time there weren't any appropriate shelters or temporary housing options for Trans people, so Shasta called Revlon for help. Revlon drove in, and the two of them worked for six hours to find a solution."

While it did feel good to help people, Lucas was often frustrated by the petty politics of the place, and how many of the Board members didn't seem to do much other than show up for photo ops.

"The Williams, as I call them, Collins & Lowe, would volunteer on Thursdays but they did nothing but sit out back and chain smoke like Patty & Selma from the Simpson's. Then they'd finally come in and say, 'Well, you've got this under control. We're going to dinner.'"

Lucas wasn't a big fan of Shasta, who he described as moody, but he agreed with Clint that while the house of cards was wobbly in the wake of Shasta's embezzlement scandal, it fully collapsed under Amy Marsh's leadership.

A petite white woman in her fifties with salt and pepper hair, Marsh was the epitome of white guilt, according to Lucas, and she bristled at any talk of enforcing rules or setting boundaries.

"We had these two bad girls from the neighborhood. They were in their early teens, and they weren't LGBT, they just learned we had free computers with no time limit, so they'd get in fights at school, have someone take videos of the fights, and then cut class and come to the Center to watch the videos online. I raised my concerns to Amy, adding that I wasn't comfortable being the only adult in the building and I thought it was putting the Center at risk. She accused me of being anti-youth!"

The Black lesbian couple who used the Center as their daytime home "volunteered" to close each night, and it soon became apparent to everyone they were living there.

"They tried to be sneaky at first, but then they started changing into their pajamas thirty minutes before closing!" Lucas exclaimed. "And when I'd bring this up, I was labeled a racist. So over Marsh's tenure I wound up being labeled an ageist, a racist, anti-Trans, anti-woman…"

Lucas was also there the night the lesbian couple ran off with Marsh's car.

Amy had been out back with the Williams and then said she was leaving for a Birthday party. She walked out the door and walked right back in. She was like, 'Oh my God, my car is gone. I don't think I ever got my keys back from the girls!' and William Collins was like, 'Are you fucking kidding me? They took your car?' Oh, he was livid."

On the front sidewalk Collins kept saying they needed to call the police, but Marsh held him off.

"I'm giving them fifteen minutes, and then if you don't call the police I'm calling them for you!" Collins said.

"Just in time, literally fifteen minutes later they pulled up and Amy said, 'I'll handle it' and walked over to the car. Collins walked away in disgust and said 'I'm outta here.'" Lucas recalled.

Marsh saw racism everywhere at the Center, and was grating the Board's nerves with demands they make major reforms.

"Shasta's Black and never complained of racial issues at the Center" some countered, but Marsh would reply, "Well, maybe it wasn't happening when she was here."

After Marsh blew up at the Board about racism, both Lowe and Collins quietly stepped down and in a matter of months the Center closed its doors, becoming an online only entity. The building was owned by former *Vital Voice* publisher Lydia Rothenberg, who'd been subsidizing the Center by letting them pay half the rent they'd agreed on, which didn't cover her mortgage.

"There's grumbling about Lydia selling the building like she's some greedy landlord when she gave more to the Center than anyone!" Slyman exclaimed.

For six months Slyman didn't speak to Simone Shasta.

"Simone was my rock. We'd gone way back and I felt so betrayed. But after six months she invited me to lunch and offered the most heartfelt apology I'd ever received. There were no excuses, she came clean about everything and asked for forgiveness" Slyman began, "And she's suffered enough. It's amazing how someone can fall so far so fast. She was the biggest celebrity in town, known by everyone, on the cover of magazines, in meetings with the Mayor, and now she's the salad girl at Sensation."

As far as the community goes, in a few weeks the vast majority forgave her the way a family might shrug off the antics of a quirky aunt. She was still very much beloved, which made her detractors, chief among them Rita Revlon, fit to be tied.

When Rita got up in her cups the Dark Mistress would emerge on Facebook and mock the community for their love of Shasta, and she'd threaten to bring Shasta and the entire city down.

A source of civic pride was the city's ranking as a top ten place for LGBT people, and like some sort of queer comic book villain she'd sit on her veranda and plot ways to revoke that ranking. According to Shasta, the threats went even farther.

"Rita once threatened to run me over with her Trans Van!" Simone said.

Speaking of running folks over, while meeting with Lucas I noticed his black T-shirt had five car icons running over five man icons.

There was a local character known as "Speedbump Sally" who had been run over by five different men, and Lucas was one of them, which entitled him to the shirt.

## 179. Out to Sea

Overlooking the ocean at a loungey, 1960's-era seafood restaurant in Pacifica, California I sat with two people I loved dearly: Peter, the President of Milpitas Management, and Kathy Looper, who was a big client, but was also like a mother to me. It was one of my going-away lunches before moving on to my new job, and it was bittersweet.

"You and Chris are really close" Kathy remarked.

"He's like a son to me" Peter replied.

A highly competent Director named Karen Thatch had left the company, but remained a friend and mentor of mine. Karen was statuesque, attractive, and always impeccably put together, normally wearing all black with fashionable high heel boots. She could be an intimidating presence and commanded respect when she entered a room.

Peter went the opposite direction when Thatch left for a bigger position, hiring a folksy woman named Latrice – who, it soon became apparent, was in way over her head, and for some reason decided I was after her job. Her paranoia was exacerbated by the fact I was close with her predecessor as well as Peter.

Things were really stressful around the office and weren't getting better. I'd always been careful not to take advantage of my friendship with Peter, so I didn't go to him with the issues until things had gotten unbearable.

She was intentionally letting a position in my portfolio go unfilled, which meant for months I had to cover it – along with my own position. I was getting calls at all hours of the night regarding issues like alarm trouble signals and lock outs. Adding to the stress were the bizarre meetings she'd call with me to discuss her feelings.

Milpitas had the culture of a family. On Christmas Eve each year Peter would prepare a huge Swedish feast for all of the employees. Few ever quit, and almost nobody was fired. I knew Latrice wouldn't last, but her departure wouldn't come soon enough for me, with my sleepless nights and dramatic days.

I decided it was best for everyone, for the time being, if I moved on. I sat down in Peter's office and told him I'd accepted a position in the East Bay. He was disappointed, but understood, and reiterated that our friendship transcended the company's walls.

I'd later regret so easily letting go of something so very special, but the office dynamics were already souring as a result of the tension, with Latrice insinuating to coworkers I was getting special treatment, and my efforts to smooth things over had failed. Had I stayed to fight, I might have damaged my friendship with Peter.

I'd been so young when I first met Peter, Kathy, and Kathy's late husband Leroy – and they took my under their wing with a parental kind of care. Leroy was now gone, and Peter and Kathy would someday retire or pass on as well. Life had once seemed static, but I understood its ephemeral nature more than ever.

Back at the oceanfront table I looked at their faces, present in the moment, and I looked out the window and saw a ship heading to sea.

## 180. Six Inches of San Francisco Real Estate

I apply a three strikes rule to social invitations. If someone declines an invitation three consecutive times I think it's best to abandon the effort, otherwise it just becomes awkward. Since moving to the other side of the bay, tensions had developed with my San Francisco-centric happy hour crew, The Castro Consorts.

They gathered around five, but with my new job in Berkeley I could rarely make it before seven. After several failed attempts to connect, arriving just as everyone was leaving or after they'd already left, I was feeling disenchanted and started to think it wasn't worth the effort. Plus they were only rarely willing to come to Oakland.

I'd declined two invites for events in the city when Truman sent the make or break third, which was the worst of all. He wanted to meet for a drag show at the Midnight Sun, which had always been my least favorite Castro establishment for a variety of reasons. I felt it had terrible feng shui, for starters, and it only had two standing tables, if you could call them that, which were only about twelve inches across.

The name of the game at the Sun was claiming a table for your group, otherwise you'd wind up standing there holding your drink and getting jostled around all night. Me and Damon felt we had to go, and decided to arrive early to claim our territory.

Upon moving to the city years earlier the Crab taught us how to go about this task, and we followed his instructions precisely. The tables were never empty, but you chose the one with two or more parties utilizing it, often two couples distracted by the campy videos high on the wall. Then, standing a few feet away, you'd place one cocktail, arm extended fully, on the table. Instinctively people will allow for a little room, then a little more, and then when they leave the table would be yours.

A wrinkle in our masterful plan was not accounting for Truman's trademark tardiness. After all of our strategic planning, the two of us were unable to defend our conquered territory, and a group of rough and tumble rugby players laid claim to half of it, six inches to be precise.

A cold war quickly emerged as we struggled to hold the line in an increasingly lopsided struggle, as their population grew. All parties tried to act nonchalant as each of our elbows were deployed at the line of scrimmage.

By the time Truman and the others arrived, they found four men facing opposite directions while pretending not to notice their triceps and shoulders were firmly pressed against the triceps and shoulders of complete strangers. Finally, a bearded stocky white guy flipped around and exclaimed, "STOP! Would you PLEASE just STOP you've been trying to push us away from the table ever since you got here!"

"HEY we've been here since SEVEN!" I shot back.

"NO YOU HAVEN'T we were here first!" he countered.

The guy's buddies calmed him down, and although he turned away to watch the show, our cold war stance continued as his friends anchored their elbows on the disputed territory. The lights had gone down for the show, featuring my friends Anna Conda and Mutha Chucka, and I began to gather cocktail lemons from old drinks to fill the pocket of their leader's jacket, which was hanging below the table.

I'm not sure what the spark was, but the alpha of the group ended up grabbing Damon by the lapel. I threw a drink in his face then lunged over as one of his buddies returned fire with a drink in my face. The house lights went up, the show stopped, and all of us were tossed out into the night.

On the sidewalk Damon extended an olive branch, which was warmly received, and we all decided to go to Moby Dick a few doors down. It was like we were old friends as we patted one another on the back and laughed.

"I'm sorry man, but I'm Irish and don't take any shit!" the alpha of the group said.

"I'm Irish too!" I exclaimed, then he pulled me in and kissed me. We got shots, he kissed Damon, all while a young friend with us sat in disbelief.
The next day I received a Facebook post from our new buddy:

"You put lemons in my pocket didn't you?"

I replied in two parts. First with, "People ask me the strangest questions!" followed by, "OH, but yes."

## 181. Marriage Bus

In the wake of Iowa legalizing same-sex marriage, my old friends Reggie and Emanuel in St. Louis began organizing Marriage Bus trips to the state.

"Then these Marriage Bus fund drives started popping up in strange places that we knew nothing about, and the money never made it to us" Reggie recalled. "One day I get a call from Cole Bertman saying there's a thermometer on the wall at Bernie's showing how much they'd raised, and I should get down there."

Bernie's was a sleek and stylish bar frequented by the twenty-somethings, and the owner, Bernie Marks, had quite a shaky reputation. There was a persistent rumor he'd burned down his Central West End bar for the insurance money, employees were always complaining about not getting paid, and there were accusations of embezzlement from Hamburger Mary's, a crime for which he later pled guilty and was ordered to pay tens of thousands to his former business partners.

When Lady Gaga came to town Bernie announced the official after-party would be at his bar – and Gaga herself would be there. People packed the place, I'm sure well past fire code, but of course she never arrived.

"Gaga drove by and her people saw all of us packed in here swinging from the chandeliers and were like 'No way we're letting you go in there!'" he posted on Facebook, followed by "But we sure did have a blast anyway!"

Reggie, who knew nothing about a Marriage Bus fund drive there, took Cole's advice and went straight to Bernie's. Sure enough there was a fundraising thermometer on the wall showing the six or seven hundred dollars they raised.

"Bernie wasn't there but I made the bartender call him" Reggie began. "Uh, we already gave that money to someone who came to pick it up' he told me, and I said 'There's nobody else involved, just me and Emanuel, and I'm here to pick up the donations, and I'm not leaving without them.'"

Flustered, Bernie had the bartender hand Reggie $250 from the safe if he'd call it even.

## 182. Collins Goes Off

While things looked calm on the surface at the *Vital Voice* office, tensions were developing over Slyman and Collins's differing visions for the direction of the magazine, and over the rise and increasing influence of Jimmy No Show, a local DJ who joined the staff as a fresh faced intern who often donned the brand's squirrel mascot costume, but over the years rose through the ranks to become Associate Publisher.

Once the notorious and controversial bar owner Fancy Slovak finally closed up shop after several false alarms, including the big thirty dollar a head "final night that wasn't" fiasco I'd mentioned at the beginning of the book, rising star Jimmy No Show pitched a feature on her – an idea Collins was dead set against, calling it "tabloid material."

Collins loved to write about drag queens, history, and history involving drag queens. Slyman felt the magazine was way too heavy on drag stories, especially the upcoming issue, and was intrigued by Jimmy's provocative idea. When Slyman decided to run with the piece, Collins was irritated, and only more so when he had to cut back a drag queen story to make room for it.

The team was at a client's event when Slyman mentioned the upcoming story.

"That piece is a *fucking* mistake!" snarled Collins, who'd had several cocktails at this point.

Slyman was startled by his surly demeanor, and after some back and forth Collins continued, "You know what Darin? Everyone in St. Louis can see through your glossy bullshit!"

"Well if this is the way you feel maybe we should revisit your role with this magazine" Slyman replied.

Collins slammed down his drink and yelled, "You can't fire me! I *AM* VITAL VOICE!"

He then stormed off.

"William, don't go" Slyman yelled.

"FUCK YOU!" Collins replied, then took to Facebook to trash Slyman, who stayed at the event and tried to smooth things over with the client who witnessed the ugly scene.

The following day Collins reported to work and was greeted with dropped jaws that he'd actually shown up. He found Slyman out back, apologized and offered to resign.

"I have to wrap my mind around all of this. I'm not firing you, but I'm suspending you for a month while we figure things out" Slyman said.

Late in the evening, while drinking, Collins would post vague, negative Facebook updates about Slyman and the magazine, and then delete them in the morning. It became clear there could be no reconciliation.

Collins and Lowe started their own gay news blog called #*blast*, designed to go head to head with *Vital Voice*, only without the paper magazine component. This violated a non-compete clause in Collins's contract which required some legal wrangling to sort out.

Collins and Lowe promoted their brand by attending events where the two dressed alike. Collins' long term partner, Rex, bankrolled the effort, but expressed concern over Lowe's influence over Collins. He knew Collins was completely under Lowe's spell, and blamed Lowe for encouraging his drinking, which had become problematic.

### 183. A Tale of Two Hoes

Ed, an acquaintance from St. Louis, moved to the Bay Area, and we invited him over to our place a few times. A flamboyant Black guy in his thirties, Ed stood at about 6'3" with a muscular build.

We were with a group of friends at a restaurant overlooking the waterfront when the topic of gay relationships in San Francisco came up.

"I think it's hard for couples to make it out here, with all the choices" Ed remarked.

"People say that, but Damon and I don't have any problems" I replied.

"Well that's 'cause you a ho, and he a ho!" he quipped, in what was intended to be good natured ribbing.

Nine months earlier I might have shrugged it off, but it didn't feel good. I'd always thought of our arrangement as civilized and urbane. We often boasted about our lack of sexual hang ups. But maybe Ed's assessment was closer to reality.

We were a family, we loved and cared for one another. I didn't correct Ed because his lack of reverence for our relationship was just a symptom of a greater issue we needed to address. I wasn't sure what that would look like, but I didn't want the world looking at our marriage as a union of hoes.

## 184. The Juggernaut

Sarah Monroe, Executive Director of a Berkeley-based affordable housing developer called People's Housing Development, was approached by a Board member of her organization's rival: East Bay Development.

"Our E.D. is leaving, and we'd like to offer you the position."

East Bay was about a third larger and had more lucrative assets, but Monroe had been with People's for some time, and felt a lot of loyalty to the plucky organization. In a savvy move she countered with a proposal of her own.

"I'm not interested in leaving People's, but we should discuss a merger."

With that, the largest affordable housing developer in the East Bay was born: People's East Bay Development.

The new Board put a lot of thought into how to best blend the two teams. They decided since the Executive Director was from People's, the department heads beneath her, which oversaw Property Management, Human Resources, and Maintenance, would all hail from East Bay. It's my opinion they overcompensated with that arrangement, creating what I referred to as "the Juggernaut".

Monroe's interest lied in development and long-range planning, not daily operations. The department heads, by contrast, actually created the corporate culture – which was one of fear and anxiety, unless you'd been part of their inner circle at East Bay.

"I remember the first All Staff Meeting after the merger" recalled a manager from People's, "Right off the bat they announced there'd be a new supervisory position called 'Maintenance Lead', and then named the three chosen for these positions – and they were all from East Bay. It was a kick in the gut to the People's guys. Everyone knew it was a bad sign."

And the bad signs kept coming.

When I came on board six months after the merger, employees from People's, some with nearly two decades of service, were routinely dismissed - leading most everyone else to wonder if they'd be next. Those who were in good with the Juggernaut were invincible, including a lazy maintenance man in my portfolio who bragged to coworkers that he could get his supervisor fired with one call.

"I'm in with Zain, Jose, and Marissa (the Juggernaut). My influence goes all the way to the top!" he boasted.

I reported to Kate Longfellow, who'd been the Director of Property Management at People's, but was demoted to Associate Director after the merger.

Kate was a scrappy lesbian who'd worked her way up from a maintenance position eighteen years ago, and it was openly discussed she and Zain, the Director she reported to, didn't like one another – at an All Staff Meeting they'd even announced they were working with a counselor about their issues. In a prior senior management meeting I'd recommended against such an announcement, and then reiterated my concerns privately with both Zain and with Kate, but for whatever reason they thought it was a good idea. As I predicted, however, it only made the rank and file more uneasy about the stability of the organization.

Everyone knew the knife was at Kate's throat, and her anxiety made the lives of the District Managers below her, including me, really difficult. Delia, my friend and coworker who'd helped me get hired, would often break down in tears after meetings with Kate – who she'd nicknamed, "Crazy Town."

Monroe paid for an outside firm to survey the employees about their feelings on the merger, and was horrified by the results. Morale was in the toilet, people didn't feel secure in their positions, and many were actively looking for other employment options.

All kinds of strategies were implemented in response, but none that addressed the Juggernaut.

"FOURTEEN MANAGERS! WE'VE HAD FOURTEEN MANAGERS IN TWO YEARS!" a feisty elderly Tenant Association President yelled during a meeting I held at Piedmont Pines, a property for seniors.

The company relied heavily on temps, and sometimes there'd be four temps in a row before a "permanent" hire came on board. Once a good team was in place, which included a manager, maintenance person, custodian and a social worker, the Juggernaut would decide to move one or two people elsewhere – infuriating the tenants who were hungry for stability.
I liked the tenants and agreed with them, and I tried my best to be a buffer between my tenants/staff and corporate's whims.

"Chris, Pedro says Marcus is no good. I need you to go by the property and relieve him" Kate urgently instructed over the phone as I'm sitting in the doctor's office. Pedro was the lazy maintenance man who'd boasted about being able to get people fired, and apparently he was right.

"Kate, please let me discuss this with you when I get back to the office. I don't want to continue this revolving door staffing pattern at Piedmont" I pleaded.

For those as the site level, it felt like one of those reality shows where obstacles are thrown at participants to keep things interesting. Teams would become bonded by fire as they worked under enormous pressure to get things done despite corporate's chaos, only to have the rug pulled out from under them. That was certainly the case at Piedmont Pines, where I was able to push back against the Juggernaut's desire to fire Marcus – who the team and tenants adored – for only a couple of weeks until the final order came down to terminate.

I arrived to find him meeting with the social worker and the custodian, and since the decision impacted everyone, I didn't ask them to leave. I told Marcus I was sent there to let him go, and that I was grateful to him for the long hours and for pulling through for the team. He was clearly upset, but did his best to hold it together.

"I know this wasn't your decision, and I really appreciate the way you've handled it – letting me say my goodbyes and leave with dignity" he said.

Dana, the social worker, sat red eyed shaking her head.

"Unbelievable. We just get a good team – I don't know how much they think we can take. Do they even think about us?" she said.

Darius, the custodian, was silent and glassy eyed.

Marcus told me what he was working on, and what needed to get done. Everyone was choked up when saying goodbye.

"Now, now, don't do this to me" Marcus said as he hugged his coworkers for the last time.

The second the door closed behind him, Dana and Darius fell into an embrace and sobbed. My God they were such kind and hardworking people, and I felt so horrible.

The stress was impacting my health in all kinds of ways. I was having chest pains, my feet would fall asleep and I tripped over my foot at work – which was why I was at the doctor's office, I was passing blood in my stool, I was getting joint pain, and I was often unable to perform sexually.

341

Not only was I earning more money than I ever had, I was earning more than I'd ever anticipated. Combined with Damon's excellent salary, our household income put us in the top 5% of earners nationwide, yet he was riddled with financial anxiety. Since he handled the finances and would express irritation when I'd ask for details, I didn't understand this, although we were living in one of the world's most expensive markets, and were paying an obscene amount in rent for our luxury apartment. Still, our income and expenses didn't vary from week to week, so it seemed when he was in a good mood, we were rich, and when he was depressed, we were poor.

Dad died of a heart attack as a result of work stress in his early forties, just a couple of years older than my age during this period, so mortality was always on my mind, but I didn't know what to do about it. I was firing on all cylinders, killing myself, and it wasn't enough, and certainly hadn't earned back the respect I'd lost from Damon seven years earlier.

I was drowning while he was soaring. Comparatively speaking, his career was on cruise control. He was in best physical shape of his lifetime, and his life was filled with new people and interests.

For me, failure wasn't an option, and I knew talking to Damon about my struggles too much would only serve to pleasure and arm Benny Babbish, who was always making the case that I was a lazy, mediocre failure who was only holding Damon back.

There was no alternative but to suck it up and try to survive.

## 185. Disconnected

I'd never felt more at home than in St. Louis, but there also was much I loved about living in San Francisco, where I could always walk to happy hour and find friendly faces and warm greetings. By contrast I felt cut off and lonely in Oakland. Not only was I a long way from social outlets, I had no sense of belonging, around town, at work, or at home.

Damon had been somewhat lonely his entire life, and felt a little cut off in Oakland but overall he loved the place and was always meeting new people. A capital of Black culture, he began making many acquaintances of color, which was unusual for him, coming from an all-white college in Wisconsin and typically being the only Black guy in a room. While his Black friends came in all shapes, sizes, and genders, the few white friends he'd make were really pretty boys, usually couples who could easily have been models in ads for upscale condo developments. I didn't ask where he was meeting them.

He went out regularly with all the new people in his life, normally without me.

"I've just been making my own friends because all yours do is hang out in the Castro" he said.

"My friends are two thousand miles away" I quipped.

He didn't respond, and I settled into my office and wrote the following:

*Two thousand miles away from friends, family, and the city that gave me a sense of purpose. My job wasn't impressive but my life was rich with art and camaraderie and family. I had roots.*

343

*I hate this meaningless rat race, working so hard for this worthless monopoly money that simply allows us to tread water in some soulless apartment building surrounded by people you couldn't get to know if you wanted to because it's little more than an extended stay hotel. It's a land of illusions.*
*But Damon was cruelly pulled away from California twice in his life, as a boy happily walking on the beaches of San Diego one day only to find himself in a miserable apartment beneath the St. Louis airport the next. Then there was the time I pulled him away, my family was loved in Oklahoma. And we'd be welcomed and would prosper, I promised, only for him to find himself again in St. Louis, scrubbing Archer Andronico's toilets.*

*Two sides of a coin. He doesn't know the city I love and I don't know the city that's the pit of his despair.*

*I might take some consolation if he felt as fulfilled in Oakland as I did in St. Louis, but he feels the void like I do. The loneliness, yet he says he's never felt so at home. The happiest a sad man can be perhaps.*

*We sit here, disconnected.*


## 186. Married Life

Sitting in Berkeley traffic Damon stared out the window at an eyesore apartment building where every balcony was being used as storage.

"You just can't give poor people balconies" he sighed.

I broke out laughing and then he did too. In the politically correct affordable housing circles where we made our livelihoods, such a statement would be considered heresy.

344

We had our moments, and despite all of our problems, being married was something I was proud of, and it helped to give me the sense of permanence that I'd always longed for. We were officially a family and were responsible for one another, which was comforting.

So many guys seemed addicted to apps and were perpetually single because the grass was always greener, and Mr. Perfect might be one refreshed screen away. But I had a man who chose me, and I felt fortunate.

For a dozen years I had a big night out every weekend while Damon, more of a homebody, stayed home. Sometimes, at the South of Market bars in San Francisco, the lights would go out towards the end of the night and I'd partake in the ensuing debauchery.

Before we were married, though, I slowed way down, maybe going out once a month for happy hour and then coming home. At first it was the logistical complications of getting to the city that deterred me, but then I found I just enjoyed being home with him and Brawny. Even though Damon had a busier social life than before, he was normally home at a reasonable hour and we had a comfortable routine.

I decided every relationship had problems, and we'd just needed to find a way to fix ours. Damon was going through a phase and I'd wait it out.

## 187. The Unraveling

We were on the bed talking one evening when I took note of my changed outlook.

"A few years ago Joe remarked how when you're young and have sex with someone, it's like a handshake, but when you get older it feels like you leave a piece of your soul with each person."

"I've always felt like that" Damon replied.

"I find I don't want it anymore. At the end of a long week I just enjoy hanging out at the house with you" I said.

Damon fell back on the pillows, threw the heels of his palms over his eyes, arched his back and groaned, "Life is so fucked up."

It turns out there had been a role reversal, and not only was he not interested in a monogamous relationship with me, he was falling in love with somebody else, a man ten years younger, and was hoping we'd transition to more of a housemate situation.

I was too late, and I really couldn't be mad at him. The man who liked to be at home with me died on the vine, and was replaced with someone new. At any point in those seven Pre-Benny years he would've been elated to have me to himself. Only when the old Damon was fully gone did I realize the how unique and irreplaceable that sweet man was.

He'd gone through a rapid transformation once his braces came off. Filled with a new sense of self-confidence, he became absorbed with fashion and fitness. Much like the scene from *The Sixth Sense* where Bruce Willis realizes he's dead then is flooded with all the signs he'd been ignoring, I thought back to the dinners Damon had been running off to with new friends while I sat at home. I remembered when I tried to join him at Cross Fit, and when they'd ask everyone to find a partner he'd scan the other faces as if I wasn't there.

For years I thought each day we remained together was a victory against Benny, but it was now clear Benny had won this battle long ago. The Babbish Plan, I'd later learn, was much more sinister than a mere break up. In light of my stress induced sexual problems, my fate would be that of the palace eunuch, growing old and plugging away at the corporate job that was killing me in order to maintain our Bay Area lifestyle, while Damon pursued a younger man who earned half of what I did. Benny was even encouraging him to take on a third partner.

Aging and broken, I was headed out to pasture, which is just where Benny wanted me.

## 188.   The Sleepover

The guy Damon was seeing was named Patrick, and the two of them were closing down the bar one night when Damon sent me a message.

"Patrick forgot to book a room so he'll need to sleep over."

The air mattress motor was loud so I went ahead and set it up, complete with sheets and blankets. I was in the darkened bedroom when they got home. Damon got in our bed, and I let him believe I was asleep. Old habits die hard, and in his sleep he rolled over and put his arm around me. The whole time I laid awake with uninvited guest Bonnie Raitt singing "I can't make you love me" in my ear.

The next morning I woke to an empty bed, and opened the bedroom door to find Damon and Patrick in a partial embrace. Patrick jumped nervously.

"Good morning. Staying for brunch?" I asked as I walked to the computer.

"No, I've got to get back to Santa Cruz" he said, without making eye contact.

Damon was a founding member of a group called The Oakland Queer Brunch Club, and it was his turn to host. I told him I'd pick up anything he needed, but I wouldn't be there to eat. I was working on a big project and would spend the day at the office.

He was angry with me for not staying, which he conveyed nonverbally though negative energy, pregnant pauses and sighs.

### 189. Vanity Smurf

I referred to the flippant new fitness, fashion, apps, and selfie Damon as "Nuevo Damon", but he referred to himself as "Vanity Smurf," an attempt at self-deprecation, but so spot-on it came off as unabashed ownership of the new personality.

348

Each day brought at least one new selfie on social media with a hashtag reference to how good his biceps looked (#themguns) or how cute his meticulously planned outfit was.

The topic came up and I gently suggested he eliminate or at least tone down the captions.

"The photos speak for themselves; I think you should leave off the references. You look hot in the pictures and while confidence is sexy, vanity isn't, at least in my opinion. I think it's sexier to act less aware of, or concerned with, your aesthetics."

He seemed open to the suggestion but didn't really reply.

After a nice brunch with Chatters and her new gentleman caller we were all going to take the train to the city, Chatters and her man to go home, and Damon to pick up his designer eyeglasses that had just arrived. News he greeted with a happy dance.

"I can't go the city wearing this!" he exclaimed before catching himself and acknowledging, "I guess I've become *that* guy."

He asked if I wanted to go, and although I didn't, I said I did and asked where Brawny's bag was since we were taking him. He rattled off a few different places to check as he hurriedly put together his ensemble and rushed to our oversized bathroom, which was larger than some San Francisco apartments.

"It's not here" I said.

"Check the car" he replied through the closed bathroom door.

I took the elevator downstairs with Chatters and her man, but the bag wasn't there and I wasn't going to carry Brawny around without it. I kept the two company on the sidewalk while we waited for Damon to finally emerge, polished and well put together.

"I couldn't find the bag so I'll just walk Brawny around the block and take a nap" I said.

From blocks away I could still see the three of them making their way to the train. How I missed my familiar Damon. I'd always imagined I'd die first, but if I lost him it would be due to death, be it old age or a tragic accident, but this was its own kind of death. The person I loved had become someone else, seemingly overnight. His true love was now himself.

Brawny was staring into my face. "Soon it'll be just the two of us Brawny" I said. "But we'll be alright."


## 190. Liberated

After years of being the main one flexing the flexibility in our relationship, I didn't think I deserved anything more than the outcome I was living with and I tried to be as accommodating as I could, like making up a bed for his boyfriend, for instance. But despite all of this I was still vilified and disparaged.

"Dude, when you're not there Damon dogs you, man!" Chatters confided after a bit too much to drink. "And then the next time I see you two together he acts like everything's fine."

He'd left his computer unlocked, and like a moth to the flame I trolled through to see if he was still speaking ill of me to others, despite how well we'd been getting along under the circumstances, and he was. With both Benny and Patrick he painted me as a loser who he was staying with out of pity, and then there were the discussions about taking on a third partner.

In a strange way the sheer hopelessness of it all was liberating. There was nothing more I could be, do, or give to make him happy. I was at my maximum earning potential for the time being, I was the youngest I would ever be, and I couldn't have been much more accommodating. And it still wasn't even close to being enough, nor would it ever be with the constantly moving goal posts and Benny reframing everything in a negative light. Knowing how he spoke about me to others, I thought about how he probably wouldn't even speak highly of me when I was dead.

There were many times I wanted to leave over the years, but stayed out of a sense of obligation due to the promise made to that despondent 23-year-old kid sobbing in my bed. I felt no such obligation now. Damon was on top of the world with a six figure income, a great new body, and a handsome young love interest. And the thought of life without that loathsome Benny Babbish was exhilarating, like being released from a dirty cage.

Always looking for the silver lining in any situation, I decided I was now free. Free to reinvent myself. Free to break the shackles of the corporate job I hated, and free to move to New York, which was the great unfinished business of my life. There I would attempt to earn a living from my creative pursuits. I'd take ten days to cross the country, visiting friends and family along the way.

First, though, I had to survive the last five weeks of our lease with this man who was a painful reminder of what was lost. This guy who looked like Damon, but was a stranger.

When he came home I sat him down on the sofa.

"You're afraid to make the decision to let go because of all the years we've invested, but at this point in your life you really need to be single, and I need to be in New York."

A pained look crossed his face revealing a level of concern I hadn't seen in months.

"I didn't intend for this to happen" he said.

## 191. Lunch with Nuevo Damon

I sat across the table from Nuevo Damon at a sushi restaurant on a classic San Francisco street above Union Square. We'd been congratulating ourselves on the healthy way we'd communicated over the past few weeks and how glad we were we didn't drag our friends and family into a nasty break up. It was all very civilized.

He was simultaneously familiar and unfamiliar, looking at me without an ounce of the love or reverence that once lived in his eyes. I decided to explain what this whole experience was like for me.

"I feel a lot like my partner died- it's strange how much like a death it is. I look at you and you're not familiar. I like this person, you're friendly, but you're a stranger. You look at me like a stranger, an affable stranger, but a stranger. There's no recognition. No connection. The look of love, interest, and reverence is gone."

"When do you think the change happened?" he asked casually while twirling his straw in his teacup.

"I wish I could point to an exact moment, and one may come to me, but generally it was around the time your braces came off. Your personality and interests changed. Meanwhile I'm drowning at this corporate job while you're flying high. I'm getting chest pains while thinking how my dad died of a heart attack around my age, I'm shitting blood, I assume from an ulcer, all to live up to these performance expectations you have. My body's in revolt and then my dick stops working reliably. You get into Cross Fit and push me to do it, but I didn't know how to add one more thing when I was about to drop dead as it was."

I continued, "You'd made comments about transitioning to housemates, sharing expenses but becoming romantically involved with others. Then you began dating Patrick and when I learned you were still under Benny's influence I realized there was nothing left to work with, all hope was lost. That's when I decided I needed to move to New York and reinvent myself. I was at rock bottom with nothing left to lose".

 "You know you've never really talked to me about a lot of this" he replied.

"I tried, but you've always showered me with disapproval whenever the topic came to stress at work." I said. "I feel like we're having opposite kinds of mid-life crises" I began, forgetting for a moment he loathed any talk of approaching middle age. "You're looking for youth and I'm looking for what's real. This is a world of illusions, and I feel like there's no more time to waste. I want to spend my time on things that are real"

"I don't think I'm having a midlife crisis. I think it's just a delayed self-discovery" he began. "I thought you were no longer interested in me sexually, since our sex life had waned, and all these things I wanted to do, like Cross Fit, you didn't want to do so I just started doing my own thing" he said. "I get sad at what could've been, but less so than before. I'm accepting it."

I thought that flip response was *so* Nuevo Damon.


## 192. Mom Keeps it Real

The family joked about the great luck Mom's always had with men, with the exception of Dad passing, of course. Even at 79, an age where women outnumber men two to one, she had a gentleman caller who was so fond of her he kept her photo on his dashboard, even though she'd often tell him he was cheap for not taking her to nicer places, and would break up with him. (Since he was hard of hearing, he normally didn't know she'd broken up, and when he'd ask her out to the Casino again she figured she might as well go).

I called to let her know things were over with my man. He'd fallen for someone else.

"Well, I thought something might be wrong because he hadn't come home with you in ages."

After talking about it all for a few minutes she said, "I know how you feel. Well, I don't actually *know*, because that's never happened to *me*, but I empathize."

## 193. The Brawny Discussion

I'd been dreading the topic because I knew it would be a major conflict, but during a sad but otherwise pleasant conversation Damon brought up the question.

"What about Brawny?"

"I plan to take him" I replied.

He sat quietly for a moment, and then said, "I'm going to miss him, but he's more attached to you. When you're gone he just waits at the edge of the bed, and won't even sleep, but when I'm gone he's fine. That dog wants his Chris Andoe."

With that, the last big issue was resolved. Damon loved the little dog immensely, and while I walked him more often, Damon made sure he was bathed and groomed, and he extensively and perhaps obsessively researched his food. He took excellent care of Brawny, and I was so grateful to him for not fighting me.

In turn, I tried to make sure Brawny was cared for as well as before, and one way I did that was to take him with me as often as possible.

## 194. Painful Poetry & Rants of Rage

"I'm weeping in the barren fields for crops that were never planted" my poem to Damon began. As much as I wanted sole possession of his heart and mind, I hadn't made those investments. In all the years we were together only once did I initiate a serious discussion about monogamy, and that was long after the insidious Benny Babbish had become the squatter tenant in our relationship.

"I would not support that at all!" Benny exclaimed at the time, before asking me "Do you want him so bad because you can't have him?"

My reflections inspired Damon to open up as well.

"I love you and have always loved you, in my own way. But that love was not healthy, giving or supportive because it was contingent upon you being 'something,' whatever that was for me. As trite as it may sound, I may not have known how to love you the way you deserved because I never loved myself. I didn't think I was worthy of you so I tried to keep you close so you wouldn't get away" he began. "I've been unfair for years. I've made you own each setback we experienced and whipped you for them. We made many of those decisions together and I should have shouldered the burden more fully by forgiving myself and you. I felt abandoned when we returned to St. Louis, and I think our common core started to fade then. I got focused on healing our balance sheet, you were focused on healing your badly damaged self-esteem. You told me many times how painful the Oklahoma City experience was for you, but I didn't or couldn't hear what that really meant. I decided that we were on different pages and kept moving."

For years Damon acted like I was crazy for distrusting Benny, but he finally acknowledged Benny's destructive role, which meant a great deal to me.

"We needed help when we returned to St. Louis, but we didn't know it. I turned to Benny, who wasn't invested in us as a couple and became like a tree root busting through our foundation."

He spoke of a magazine article he read about the seven ways women emasculate their men, and realized Benny had advised him to do all seven. He brought up a couple we'd befriended in Oakland, who treated us like family and had us over every Christmas.

"I wish we had had friends like Michael and Teresa who could have listened to each of our stories with love and helped us reconcile."

I replied, "If you want me to stay, just tell me. Even if it's at the last minute, if you think we can work things out I'll stay" but he was painfully honest about what he called his divided heart.

"Chris Andoe and Patrick Frugal. I love one and have a butterfly crush on the other. I have a divided heart. I want you to pursue your passion and return to me the confident Chris I met thirteen years ago, free, full of life, energy, and passion. I also want you to be near me, to talk to me, to hold me and reassure me but I am an emotional sink for you. New York will reinvigorate you but I'm not adult enough to let you be you. My sister was saying how we could have changed our life to allow you to pursue being a writer here, but my love isn't giving enough to allow that to happen.

"Patrick makes me feel wanted, and I've wanted to feel that way for a long, long time. I have no idea what is going to happen. He likes me to be sure, but he knows nothing about me; my bouts with depression; my body's history; the mean streak that I can't seem to shake.

"Your greedy man wants it all. Attention from a new man but the security of my man who knows and accepts all of my bumps, warts, and craziness. I can't have it all and just like the dog who drops the bone he has to steal the bone of another dog, which happens to be his own reflection, and thereby drops his bone in the water and has nothing, I too may end up with nothing.

"I'm asking for your forgiveness for all the regret and doubt you hold for yourself. Live in New York City, thrive in New York City, succeed in New York City. I am already proud of you, I already love you, just not the way that is healthy. I'm committed to supporting your dream and your success, and think that's the best legacy for all the time, energy, and love we've put into our relationship" he said.

The following weeks were turbulent. We were more open and honest than we'd ever been at times, and more dysfunctional than ever at others. It was at a low point when I again went snooping and found that Benny Babbish was still working his voodoo and injecting his poison. After Benny's exchange there was an email to our old friend Suzanne in Kansas City, channeling Benny's toxic energy as if Benny himself was writing her.

"Chris was never interested in being married, he only married me as a publicity stunt so he could write about it. He's so narcissistic he can't handle me having friends so he's decided he needs to be in New York to be happy" Damon wrote.

358

I don't think any words had ever hurt me more.

When I first wrote about our marriage he was moved to tears, but just like everything it was spun into something ugly. It was a kick in the gut and I felt like such a fool for all of the feel good discussions we'd been having.

In the heat of the moment I send Benny the following message:

*I should've known nothing that flows from Damon could be pure when he's hooked on your vile poison, you miserable troll! You like to sell yourself as some sort of spiritual guru, meanwhile you pay desperate married men to allow you to fuck them. You're a nasty, sick, and wretched hog and I'm so fucking thankful to be cutting all ties with you. I hope you burn in Hell.*

Damon was out and his phone was dead, so he came in with the pleasant demeanor we'd enjoyed for the past few days, and was surprised to see me beside myself with rage.

"I'M SO FUCKING STUPID to think you could be sincere when you're still listening to that GODDAMN BENNY *FUCKING* BABBISH!" I screamed, throwing pillows across the room and then breaking down, barely able to choke out the words as I was convulsed, "The life Benny's got planned for you is filled with so much loneliness…"

I was the one who pushed Damon into the light, away from his natural inclinations to pull away from his family, discard old friends and isolate. I'd often worry about what would come of him if I died first, and dozens of times told him if that should happen, not to waste any time mourning, but to go out and find happiness and companionship.

359

Benny was a dark force. He proved masterful at stoking every negative instinct Damon had, and I was devastated at the thought of the crippling loneliness and despair such a life would bring. But just being present wasn't enough to protect him, I'd discovered.

Over the years I had repeatedly given up power in penance for our financial collapse in Oklahoma City, but that power was transferred to Benny and I was too diminished to serve as a counterweight. Rather than pulling Damon out of the darkness I was enveloped in it as well.

## 195. Cancelling with Chatters

It was my last evening in California and I was receiving guests at the crookedest bar in the nation, Heinold's First and Last Chance on the Oakland waterfront. The pilings underneath the saloon sank into the mud during the Great San Francisco Earthquake of 1906, leaving the floor and bar tilted.

Friends who came out included a Castro Consorts member and several staff members from Piedmont Pines.

Damon's phone was chiming like crazy the entire time. I will say he did a marvelous job of engaging in conversation while simultaneously texting Patrick, but I was growing frustrated. It was my last night, and I wanted him to set aside a few hours just for me. For our final hours together in California I just wanted him to be fully present.

Chatters was heading over shortly to take us to dinner, and I sent her a message asking to cancel.

"Damon's probably sent two hundred texts in the last hour. I'm spent, and am not feeling social. Please don't come."

## 196. Fall of the Queen

It was our final night together in the apartment, and a few days earlier I had asked Damon for a favor.

"Damon" I calmly began, "I've developed a sad association with the instant message chime. Would you mind turning it off for these last few days? You don't really need it since you're on the computer anyway, and can see you have messages."

His face was friendly if maybe a bit puzzled. He didn't really respond, but he did turn it off, for one day, then it was back to nonstop chimes, each one like a paper cut.

I was being punished. While he did want to pursue a romantic relationship with Patrick, he felt I owed it to him to maintain our household and financial situation. Benny Babbish and, ironically, even Patrick, cast dispersions on me for leaving. In an earlier fight I said,

"I should be considered the *hero* of the Damon and Patrick love story for so politely getting out of the way, and Benny *FUCKING* Babbish should throw me a GODDAMN PARADE!"

That final night I was still packing, and had three large paintings from college I was removing from their stretchers to make them more portable. The last one was the giant, smirking queen who'd hung so prominently above the bar when me and Donald were roommates some eighteen years earlier, and had most recently hung above the oversized oval tub at our luxurious, if soulless, Jack London apartment.

She came to be at the end of a horrible semester in art school, when my studio class was filled with sorority girls and a professor who loved them. After each critique I'd get so upset I'd destroy my painting, but she was the finale, and had such a look of confidence on her face.

She was ready for them.

During the critique, again everyone was confused.

"What's she supposed to be?" one girl asked.

"What is she to you?" I demanded, before continuing "Maybe she's an upscale prostitute. Maybe she's a drag queen. Maybe she's a drag queen prostitute."

"Well, if she's a prostitute I think she should be on a street corner..." one sorority girl timidly began.

"Look, life doesn't always come with an explanation. The fact is she feels good about herself, and she doesn't like any of you."

It was past my bedtime and my nerves were shot with the constant chime, every twenty seconds. Chime! Chime! Chime! Why was he being so mean? Why was this necessary? Chime! Chime!

The Queen was born as a "fuck you" to the soulless drones in my studio at the University of Oklahoma. She'd risen above their baseless opinions and confidently looked down on them with amusement. But eighteen years later, in that moment of torment, I decided that just as The Queen was born to send a message, she would die for the same purpose. Knowing how much she meant to me, Damon was surprised to see the canvas crammed into the kitchen garbage can.

"You're throwing her away?" he asked.

"Yes" I replied, without looking up from packing.

With the chime of his computer he resumed his virtual communication with Patrick Frugal, Benny Babbish, Truman or whoever.

## 197. Goodbye

I don't remember anything about how we slept during that last night, but in the morning I was collecting a few toiletries and thought to myself, "In five minutes I'll say goodbye to my husband, to the man who was my family all these years." It was surreal, and I was so very sad.

He was standing in the kitchen packing and I approached without warning, threw my arms around him and sobbed, "I'm so sorry. I'm so sorry for everything."

He didn't cry, but it felt for a moment like the wall between us was gone. We took the final load to the rental car I'd be crossing the country in, where he said goodbye to me and to Brawny.

## 198. Adam & the Apple

When I decided to move to New York I reached out to everyone I knew in the Bay Area with ties there, including my friend Adam, who was a New York native and a Broadway producer. While he'd flown back and forth between the east and west coasts countless times, he'd never made a cross-country trip by car and offered to accompany me as far as Oklahoma.

Adam had been coaching me on all things New York, and was probably the most urbane and cosmopolitan man I'd ever spent time with. A few weeks earlier I asked,

"When you lived in New York, where would you go for weekend getaways?"

"Paris" he replied.

In addition to producing plays, Adam owned a tech consulting company and travelled the world teaching teams ways to better work together. In the car he gave me the Myers-Briggs personality test, coached me on my strengths and how to sell them, and we travelled vast expanses listening to *The Power Broker: Robert Moses and the Fall of New York*, so I'd know my history.

He was enthusiastic about my talents, which felt like basking in the warm sun after seven years in the cold, and it was great to have someone to talk to during those long stretches. Driving through the drought stricken Central Valley I said,

"See how most of these fields are barren? I think it's fucked up people in the suburbs can water their grass but farmers can't grow crops."

"Oh I'm sure that's not true" he began. "Surely they're not letting people water grass…well, I don't know anyone with a lawn."

## 199. Return of the Iron Doorknocker

Since being removed from the wide front door of
the Oklahoma City house, the iron door knocker
Dad made in the fifties had been shuffled around
from place to place in a box. I didn't affix it to our
house in Tower Grove because there was no place
for it on the ornate millwork, and of course we were
renting in California. I always found it unsettling to
have it packed away. It was a constant reminder that
I didn't have a real home, and it was at risk of
getting misplaced.

Bill and his fiancé had just bought a home in Tulsa,
and I decided I would give it back to him when I
passed through. He was thrilled to have it, and I felt
a sense of peace and closure seeing him affix it to
his front porch. It looked like it had always been
there.

## 200. The Regent of the Rustbelt's Detroit

I'd been trying to get to Detroit for years so finally
exploring it was a highlight of my cross country
adventure, and I couldn't have asked for a better
tour guide. The lovely Claire Nowak-Boyd, who I'd
dubbed "The Regent of the Rust Belt", was one of
the organizers and judges of the Metrolink Prom
where I became King of Metrolink. She'd recently
accepted a position as Executive Director of
Preservation Detroit, and set aside the afternoon to
show me around the post-apocalyptic metropolis,
culminating with an event she planned at a local bar.

There's nothing like getting a tour from a guide who
really knows and loves the place, and her affection
bled through the most when showing me
Hamtramck, which is the most densely populated
part of town.

"Hamtramck is an independent city surrounded by Detroit, in the same way Rome surrounds Vatican City" she said, possibly the only person in history to compare hardscrabble Hamtramck with Vatican City.

We rode past stately mansions with tarps strapped to the roofs. We walked by the ruins of the 40 acre Packard Plant, which was the size of a small city. I wanted to sneak into the abandoned Belle Isle Zoo, but understood a woman in her position couldn't really do that. Besides, she explained how the once cool art of urban exploring had become mainstream, played out, and frowned upon. Terms like "ruin porn" were thrown about, and violent criminals were in on the act, mugging explorers.

I didn't want to leave Brawny alone in a strange hotel room, so she pulled some springs and found a Hamtramck bartender who agreed to let me bring him. It was a homey, old school blue collar dive. About eight friendly people came out to meet me, which was quite an honor for some guy just passing through town. As the three dollar cocktails flowed so did the local stories.

"Our Emergency Financial Manager assaults people with her torpedo titties" one hearty gal began. "Seriously! If she doesn't want you in the room she'll just ram you out with those crazy boobs!" she said, referring to the unelected woman the Republican Governor appointed to manage either Detroit or Hamtramck. I wasn't sure which one.

The bartender had made peanut butter and jelly sandwiches on white bread for everyone, and I learned she also ran a jewel of an independent radio station that featured interviews and specialized in classic Detroit artists.

"The signal only covers about two square miles"
Claire said.


## 201. Grand Arrival

I double parked on West 27th to unload. Joe was
outside waiting with a video recorder and my nieces
Lilly and Madalene, both in their mid-twenties, ran
down to greet me. Everyone grabbed something to
take up, suitcases, plastic tubs & Brawny. I set
additional items at the open door for their next trip
down, then Joe jumped in the rental car so we could
return it.

Afterwards the whole New York family, including
my nephew Sam and his girlfriend, met at a
Szechwan restaurant.

It had been a long time since I lived near family and
it felt good to spend that time with them. Back at
the loft, however, everything started to catch up
with me. The cross country trip had been a grand
distraction, but now reality was sinking in. The place
was dirty, with the feel of a garage, and Brawny had
gotten into a trash bag on the floor and ate
something. I anxiously wondered if he'd survive in
this working artist loft, among the mess and toxic
oil paint and chemicals.

My room doubled as the office and television room,
so I had no real personal space and was so tired. A
harsh fluorescent overhead bulb illuminated the
narrow space. I thought back to the clean, proper
home in Oakland, and was angry at Damon for
changing his mind about what he wanted this late in
the game.

I began sorting through my pile of belongings, looking for the things Brawny needed before bed. His food, favorite toys etc. My stomach sank when I realized many things never made it upstairs.

I had assumed Lilly and Madalene were coming back down to retrieve them, and they weren't aware there was anything more to get. Hours had passed and while I suspected it would be futile I ran downstairs and frantically looked around. Next to the garbage I saw the opened tubs and Brawny's toys strewn across the dirty wet sidewalk. One of my suitcases was missing.

I carried my molested belongings upstairs and worked to maintain my composure. It was my first night there and I wanted to maintain a celebratory vibe, although inside I was melting down. I'd taken so little, and now many of those things- including family heirlooms, were gone.

The bright spot was that Brawny's toys were recovered. He liked to ritually groom them before going to sleep, and after all of the changes I wanted to maintain that shred of continuity for him.

Joe went to his room, and I was finally able to turn off that ugly light and go to bed on the black vinyl sofa. With Brawny comfortably resting, I pulled the curtain back so I could drift off to sleep while looking at the Empire State Building.

## 202.  Well, That's That

I hadn't even made it to the Grand Canyon when
Patrick, Damon's love interest who aggressively
pursued him, calling the house phone every few
hours and texting him nonstop, lost interest and
decided he wanted to pursue someone else. I told
Damon I was dumfounded and speechless. All the
wheels had been set in motion with him as the
catalyst, and he just flaked.

"We had problems already. We can't blame him"
Damon said.

"I wish just once I could be shown that kind of
grace, or just once I could be on the other end of
your complaints. Maybe just one time you could be
on my side, or complain about Patrick or Benny to
me" I said.

Benny and Patrick had each heavily influenced
Damon to upend his life, but I knew they'd take no
responsibility in the end, which was irritating.

## 203.  Can't Tame the Chelsea

Like in San Francisco, but on a much larger scale,
artists were being purged from New York City, and
there was no better example than the Chelsea Hotel,
which was long home to countless artists, musicians
and writers including Mark Twain, William
Burroughs, Stanly Kubrick, Jimi Hendrix, Bob
Dylan, Janis Joplin, and Iggy Pop.

New owners decided to evict the artists and instead rent to tourists who'd pay a premium for the novelty of staying where the artists once lived. Joe moved out before the purge, and I was fortunate enough to stay there a few times- the last being fifteen years earlier with a passionate Dominican boyfriend.

Joe's hair stylist was among a dozen or so who'd lawyered up and refused to leave. I accompanied him to get his haircut, entering the largely vacant building and taking the elevator to the top floor.

The tall, slender, attractive man in his fifties, but with youthful vibe, greeted us at his front door, and from there we climbed a flight of stairs to his colorful nest in the sky, with the same southern views of Downtown I'd once enjoyed, sans the twin towers, and windows to the north which accessed the rooftop where he once had a garden, until he was forced to remove it.

"Their latest offer to Vivian was half a million" the stylist began, discussing the constant negotiations between the latest owner and the last remaining tenants. "She said no. By the time she paid the taxes that would be two fifty, and with rent what it is that wouldn't go far" he said.

The building was eerily quiet, with half illuminated hallways where it appeared construction crews just walked off the job one day and never returned.

On our way out we took the stairs rather than the elevator. "See this dent?" Joe asked, pointing to the brass railing on the staircase. "See how it repeats on every floor? A guy committed suicide by jumping, and hit each rail going down. I'm sure these owners don't even know that. Several owners have come and gone since the ones who first kicked everyone out, and this place ruins them. It sits here empty except for the people who refuse to leave. Something always goes wrong with this place. It can't be tamed."

## Story Box 16: Christopher Street Flashback

Joe was the first family member to give me the cue that it was alright to be gay. The year was 1989. I was fifteen and was visiting him in New York. We spent hours exploring the city and one stop on his walking tour was Christopher Street, the original gay area. He told me about the Stonewall Riots and we walked through a few stores.

I thought I was being nonchalant by not offering much of a reaction, but I've always grossly overestimated my poker face. That evening I somehow managed to break free from the family to wander the city on my own. Of course I took the subway directly to Christopher Street.

I revisited the same stores again, seeing as there wasn't much else for a fifteen-year-old to do, and noticed a tall muscular man in a sleeveless shirt watching me. Probably 30, this guy was attractive but seemed really dangerous and predatory. As I wandered the area I noticed he was following and I ducked into an adult movie theatre where, surprisingly, they let me in.

I expected to find a traditional theater, except of course it would feature gay porn instead of *A Fish Called Wanda*. Instead I found a maze of booths painted black from floor to ceiling, each with a loitering man and a small screen showing porn. Then I found a stairway to a lower level, and proceeded cautiously to the dungeon, which was only lit by the flickering of one television. As I entered the main room I witnessed a mob of fifty men in the throes of carnal pleasures and my heart raced with fear. Just then I felt hands caress my waist. I flipped around and saw it was the man with the sleeveless shirt!

I blurted, "I'm not from here!" and flailed out of there as if my life depended on it.

And perhaps it did.


## 204. Cast Iron Skillet

When I returned from Brawny's morning walks in Madison Square Park I'd fry a few eggs in the cast iron skillet, and at least half a dozen times I walked off and left the burner on. My mind was on Damon and my old life in California, it was on my dwindling bank account, it was on the latest job prospect, it was on my age, it was on how much longer I could hang on and what to do next, and it was on trying to maintain an upbeat façade.

I was sensitive to the fact I was in Joe's workspace, and tried not to taint the energy with my forlorn mood, but I was a horrible actor.

"You seem like a deer in the headlights here" my always direct twenty-nine year old nephew Sam, a New York native, began. "You're someone who makes groups gel, and we were expecting you to bring cohesion to the family, but it's kind of like you're the third sibling, and we don't need a third sibling" he said, standing at a gallery opening in Chelsea.

"Well Sam the rug's been pulled out from under me, and I don't know where I belong or what I should be doing anymore. Damon was my bedrock, and seemingly overnight that bedrock turned to sand, and it's been a difficult adjustment."

"I didn't really know what happened there" he replied.

I was in a fog for weeks, and was doing a horrible job of hiding it. Forget how my mood was impacting the space. Joe was concerned I was going to burn down the building.

## 205. Celebrity Soiree

I sat in the Tribeca loft of Robert DeNiro's beautiful daughter Drena, who was part of Joe's core group of friends. She and a well-known designer were preparing to launch a fashion line, and I was invited to accompany them to the designer's birthday party in Brooklyn.

There had been serious discussions about turning Joe's 2007 memoir *Jubilee City* into a screenplay, and casting Drena as our mom, circa 1955-1995, with Tulsa native Larry Clark directing.

Playing with her fluffy little dog I contemplated her in that role, and then the topic turned to September 11th. She shared her story of watching everything from the roof.

"The neighborhood has never been the same, there's a heavy energy down here" she said.

We went down to find a taxi and she pointed to the intersection at the end of her block.

"One of the airplane engines landed right there. The tops of these buildings were covered with debris."

The party was at an exquisite Brooklyn brownstone, and the basement was like a nightclub where everyone was dancing. There were famous people including cast members from Game of Thrones, but I was most excited about dancing next to Fred Schneider of the B-52's.

"Is that Fred Schneider?" I asked Drena.

"I think it might be" she began, "but I think Fred would be a better dancer."

Upstairs at the bar I introduced myself to the man, but he turned out to be a neighbor named Dave. One of Diane Sawyer's writers, a thirty-something Jewish woman, struck up a conversation with me and the next thing I know we're doing a steamy photo shoot together. Guests raved about what a good looking couple we made, and I got the feeling that in her slightly intoxicated state she might be up for working around the whole gay thing.

Back downstairs I danced with Drena and an attractive blond woman who said she was a Lyme disease spokesperson. When we took a break Drena asked how I was adjusting to New York.


"I thought going from San Francisco to New York would be like going from seventy miles per hour to a hundred, but it's more like seventy to four hundred." I began.

"It's the difference between barreling down the highway and flying in a jet. This really is the world's stage, and it first hit me when I sat forty feet from Neil Patrick Harris performing Hedwig while the Obamas were around the block watching Raisin in the Sun. My niece's apartment over looks Taylor Swift's loft and the home where Dominique Strauss-Kahn was under house arrest. Jay Z and Beyonce live around the corner. And of course I've spent the evening dancing with Drena DeNiro."

"I need to hang out with you more" Drena began. "New York has kind of lost its magic for me. I like your energy and how you see things."

## 206. Going Mad in Manhattan

Damon was the unchanging bedrock of my life, and when that turned to sand I felt like a piece of Styrofoam swept out to sea. I wasn't sure who I was or what I was even doing in New York. I couldn't focus or prioritize, and my money was rapidly evaporating.

He confided that Truman had been trashing me since I left, saying he could do much better, among other things. It didn't surprise me because I knew the two spoke ill of me, but it really stuck in my craw considering I'd been a good friend to him, and all I'd done helping him get set up in San Francisco.

Consumed with bitterness I wrote the following, rambling thoughts to myself:

*Thinking about running again. Maybe upstate. Maybe Detroit...but how can I run when I don't even have a car- the first time I haven't had a car since I was sixteen.*

*No place of my own- no place of my own to live. No place to belong- no career, no job, no partner. All I have is Brawny and some clothing. How did this happen? It happened because I lived for other people. I moved away because that's what they wanted. I took the jobs they wanted me to take. I left the jobs because someone didn't want me there.*

*Now I'm out of road, out of the opportunities youth provides. Have to rebuild from nothing. And when I do I'll be a tough son of a bitch. I'll slit the throats of my enemies and anchor like a stone.*

*Yet so much glitz and glamour. The Facebook show would go on. Parties with celebrities, views of the Empire State Building...*

*Thought going from SF to NY would be like going from 70mph to 100, but more like a 70 to 400.*

*I remember those last months in Oakland. Newly married we were on the bed talking when I said how I was no longer interested in casual sex and Damon threw his hands over his eyes in horror and said, "Life's so fucked up".*

*How do I stay true to my optimistic, friendly, helpful, laid back self when it's led me to the point where I have nothing?*

*People I've gotten jobs, like Truman, are pissing in my face while I sit here unemployed. I feel like I've been rolled time and time again. I'm so angry, bitter and tired.*

*I'm never getting out of anyone's way again.*
*Latrice made my life Hell then flamed out. I should have fought her to the bitter end.*
*Patrick pursued Damon then flaked out. I should have beat his fucking face into the counter.*
*Now I'm here feeling like I've been rolled. I have nothing and I mean nothing. A dog and a few clothes.*
*I've gotten people jobs and they've pissed in my face.*
*I feel growing hate and bitterness. I wish that sick grotesque Benny Babbish were dead. I hate that he walks the earth.*

376

*I can't be true to the guy who got me here. Fuck him. I'm a different man and I embrace it.*
*I'll slash the throats of my enemies. I'll get revenge. I'll fuck anyone who fucks me.*

*The Devil on my shoulder makes some good points. "Where has being nice got you? Does the punk ass bitch who threw a match on your relationship appreciate how politely you got out of the way? Does he even think about it? FUCK NO. He took your house and decided he didn't even want it- moved on without looking back. What about Truman? You stuck out your neck for him, got him a job with an apartment in SAN FRANCISCO and he pisses in your face. Talks shit about you. Look at you. You're 39 and all you've fucking got is a dog and a suitcase full of unremarkable clothes. You've been rolled bro. U mad? Here's what you got to do. Slash the throats of your enemies. Teach them all not to fuck with you and if they do make them pay. Get yours then fucking hold it with a clenched fist. You're all you've got"*

On several occasions I had suicidal thoughts, particularly when crossing the West Side Highway to Chelsea Pier. The cars went so fast, and seemed so seductive. They were just a step away from the crosswalk, and the wind gusts they created felt comforting, like the touch of a friend, like they were inviting me to step forward, whispering to me that the way out was merely a footstep away. Just one step and my life as a homeless forty year old failure could all be over.

I'm ashamed to say that in those moments I never gave a thought to how a suicide would impact family and friends, much less the unfortunate driver. At that low place I couldn't see anything more than what was in front of me, and that was Brawny. I imagined watching from above as he barked and ran around my lifeless body, and not being able to comfort him. I don't know if I was ever close, but it was Brawny that kept me going.

## 207. Writing Woes

One of my original objectives was to make my living from writing, and I applied for a few reporter positions. The pay was abysmal, a third of what I was making in Berkeley, and I'd have to continue living with Joe to make it work, which wasn't part of the plan. He was probably going to need that room for one of his kids because both had tenuous living situations.

The real money was in writing for the pharmaceutical companies, and Adam introduced me to a good friend of his named Jarvis who ran a department at a Madison Avenue agency.

Jarvis was half Black and half Jewish, tall, well built, and perfectly polished with a shaved head. He was a gentleman, but a story was shared about the time he lost it with a guy who'd been pickpocketing at gay bars. The pickpocket had stolen his phone, but tried to convince him he was actually a witness.

"I saw a guy run out of here and go in that corner store a few minutes ago" the pickpocket began. "They sell the phones in there. I know those guys, and I can convince them to let me buy your phone back for twenty dollars."

When he saw that Jarvis wasn't buying his story, the pickpocket's demeanor changed.

"You fags are so stupid. You go in there and get drunk and then leave your phone sitting around and then cry about it getting stolen."

Jarvis went crazy. "What did you say to me?" he began, and then he grabbed a metal trashcan and proceeded to beat the pickpocket with it. I thought Jarvis was attractive, but after hearing this epic tale I found him unbelievably sexy.

Adam had a popular food blog and knew all the big players in the fine dining industry. He took the two of us to one of New York's top rated restaurants where we were treated to a multi-course meal followed by a tour of the kitchen.

Over wine we discussed my credentials and Jarvis was excited.

"Sure, we can make something work" he said.

Adam then began to hammer out the salary. "Do you think we could get him in at a hundred k?"

Adam was so New York, and I was glad to have him on my side.

## 208. Soul Numbing

I met with Jarvis a few days later, and he described writing for the pharmaceutical companies as soul numbing work.

"These drug companies are so awful and they'll sell anything" he began. "For instance, eczema is caused by an overactive immune system, so the drug to treat it suppresses your immune system, making you susceptible to everything else in the world."

He said he thought I was a great writer, and he hated to see me waste my talents on that kind of work. I then decided I'd go back into property management, and work on my book in the evenings.

## 209. "Nobody will hire you in this town"

I looked up at the Empire State Building, where a staffing agency specializing in property management was located. I showed up unannounced. This was New York and it was time to be pushy. The main front desk called to ask if I had permission to go up. They handed me the phone and I convinced the receptionist to speak with me.

The office was old school, with metal desks covered in paper scattered around the large open room, with about a dozen windows overlooking the city. The pleasant, older man who met with me looked to be as much of a fixture as the gray metal office furniture.

"You've got a great resume but everyone here wants New York experience. They think Californians are too soft" he said, shaking his head while he thought for a moment. "I've got one client in Queens who might be interested, though, and I'll put a feeler out to him."

Head hunters began contacting me about jobs in Connecticut and Philadelphia, but absolutely nothing in Manhattan until a few weeks later, when I got a call from a different agency who wanted to interview me.

"When can you get here for an interview?" the man asked.

"I can be there in an hour" I replied.

"Okay. Be here in an hour."

I sat down for an interview with two pacing men in a small office overlooking the Chrysler Building. They were presenting three candidates to the owner of a new high-rise set to open, and I got the feeling they were short one candidate, and I was a qualified filler to show they'd conducted a thorough search.

"Why'd you leave San Francisco?" one of the men asked. When I told him my marriage had ended, he seemed to take pity on me, and cut to the chase.

"Look, nobody in New York is going to hire you. Everyone wants New York experience, and if you're not from here they think these tenants will trample you" he said, while saying he'd do his best to sell me to the owners.

I began applying for positions within a hundred miles of Manhattan, following up with the recruiters about the opportunities in Connecticut and Philadelphia.

## Story Box 17: Fight of the Hermit Crabs

Low tide along the Northern California coast reveals the most exquisite tidal pools that are like the sea's jewel boxes, filled with sea anemones, hermit crabs, starfish, urchins, seaweed and pink coralline algae.

One day I noticed two hermit crabs engaged in a tug-of-war over a 1x ½-inch by half inch piece of seaweed. There was other seaweed around, but for some reason they had their claws set on that piece and weren't letting go.

As an experiment I introduced a new hermit crab into the mix, delicately dropping him into the scene. He hadn't even landed when he extended his claw and began scrapping for the same shred.

In the moment I thought it amusing, but after some time in New York I realized the crab had it right. In this city you needed to dive in with your claw extended and ready to scrap, and the fog I was in was keeping me from effectively scrapping for mine.

## 210. The Monster & Crazy Jay

My cousin Eden worked at the Manhattan Monster Bar, which was my kind of classic gay bar, right across from Stonewall on Christopher Street and filled with colorful people. I went there to visit him and befriended Paul Hagen, editor of *Metrosource Magazine*. I was a fan his work so it meant a lot to me when he once said, "I'm a great admirer of your daring investigation of life, darling."

One evening he pulled me aside the second I arrived and said, "It's a real shitshow in here tonight!" but before he could elaborate he was called over to the piano, where a group was singing which included a drunk, weathered old queen they called Crazy Jay, who for some reason was barefoot and kept rubbing his nipple.

The pianist started playing "It's Raining Men" and Crazy Jay got so into it he poured a full bottle of water over his head and it splattered all over the piano.

Needless to say, Crazy Jay's literal interpretation of rain served to rain on the parade, and he was escorted out.

## 211. No Love

Joe's storage was in Queens, and one day I had a fun outing with him and Lilly. It was a complicated place to get to, requiring two trains and a long walk, but we stopped at the Brooklyn coffee shop where Lilly worked, took in some sights, and enjoyed one another's company. We were going to carry artwork back, and not being employed, it felt good to be useful.

His storage space was filled with art, some furnishings, and a book of drawings by Courtney Love, which I picked up to look at.

"Would you like to have that?" he offered.

"Yeah. What's the story?" I asked.

"A gallery owner was trying to get me to do a show with him, and gave me that book because he'd recently done a show with Courtney Love. Because he did the show with her I turned him down."


## 212. The Soul Speaks

During a very low point in my life when I was 21 and had just left an abusive partner, I found myself sitting at a gay church in Oklahoma City on a cold and dreary winter day.

I hadn't sold anything at the real estate office and had only earned $350 in leasing commissions, which happened to be the amount of my rent. I signed over the paycheck to my landlord, went home and zoned out looking at the flames in the gas wall heater, wondering how much gas I was using and how I'd pay for it.

Back in the pew I sat with my bruised face and empty wallet, too lost in my own thoughts to pay attention to the sermon, but the preacher became increasingly animated and in a booming voice that thundered through the rickety building, he exclaimed, "Life is not easy! Life is a hard rocky road!" and before I knew what happened an "AMEN!" involuntarily erupted from my body, as if while my mind was occupied my soul took its shot to speak.

In New York City, Adam sat across from me in a cramped diner and we discussed life.

"What is it that you really want?" he asked.

I don't know what I said, but think it was a pat answer about making my living from writing. He kept probing.

"Look ahead a few years. Where do you want to be?" he pressed.

"I want to be in St. Louis" I said, and it was the closest thing to that Amen moment I'd ever had.

It wasn't anything I'd planned on saying, and I don't think I fully knew it until I said it, but a sense of peace came over me. It was such a similar moment to that one in the pew.

My mind was preoccupied with a thousand things, but my soul knew what it wanted and snatched the mic.

## 213. And then there's Philly

A recruiter approached me with an incredible opportunity in Philadelphia with a company that reminded me a lot of Dolores Housing in San Francisco. The non-profit developer specialized in housing homeless people, and really liked that I had so much experience in that area.

They were interested in me for a Director level position that paid ten thousand more per year than I'd been earning in Berkeley, with a cost of living comparable to St. Louis. While only ninety miles from Manhattan, I could buy a nice home for a hundred thousand dollars.

I grew intrigued by Philadelphia as I learned more about it. I love underdog cities, and it certainly was one. For example, I was surprised to learn it was the second largest city on the east coast, which I imagined few knew, since it seemed overshadowed by D.C. and Boston.

As much as Damon loved California, he wanted a home. I could get established in Philadelphia, buy a home, and we could start a new life there.

I had a good phone interview, took their online personality and aptitude tests, and waited for them to schedule the face to face meeting.

"It's like herding cats getting everyone to agree on a time. I'll touch base next week" the Human Resources Director told me.

I was excited about the possibility of working again, and getting my own place. At the same time I felt confused about what I was even doing. I called my Luxury Czar Steven Fang with my thoughts.

"My life makes no sense to me anymore. Why is it I'm sitting in Manhattan, considering a job in Philadelphia, that's similar, but likely more stressful, than the one I was so happy to leave in Berkeley?"


## 214. Fantasy Meets Reality

I mentioned earlier how several credit me with inspiring them to make major geographic moves, and no example is more dramatic than that of Fantasy.

We ran around the Habana at the same time, back in the early nineties. After I'd moved away I came back to visit and ran into her. She was in awe of my adventures.

"I wish I could leave Oklahoma City" she said.

"You can, Fantasy. Whatever you're doing for a living here, you can do somewhere else. It's really not as scary as people make it out to be." I drunkenly pontificated, having no idea the impact I made on her.

Well, she went on down to the Greyhound Station, bought a ticket, and with $33.00 remaining in her pocket, headed to New York!

With the late afternoon Midtown Manhattan skyline as our backdrop, I caught up with Fantasy at a trendy rooftop bar a lifetime later and a world away from the dingy 39th & Penn strip where we used to roam.

While heavier than she was twenty years earlier, she looked really good. Back in Oklahoma City she was a tacky drag queen with no front teeth, clad in stilettos, cheap jewelry, and ill-fitting animal prints. Now she was well put together with a sophisticated wardrobe, a gleaming smile, and most importantly, confidence.

"It's so wild having you here in New York" she began. "All of the memories are flooding back."

She lived across the river in Jersey City with her longtime partner, a man she said was basically straight, except for the part about having sex with men. She was working as a stylist at a respected salon in Hell's Kitchen, and several of her coworkers were also at the bar. All were intense people.

One, an attractive woman in her late thirties, broke down crying later in the evening while discussing how lonely she was because there were no good, available men in New York.

A little Australian guy she worked with, built like a jockey, became very agitated as the night wore on, making me wonder if he was on cocaine. Staring into my face he said,

"Everyone's always waiting for the perfect person, and then they just end up alone. Why can't, for instance, you and I just get together and be happy. Just decide right now that's what we're going to do?"

"You know, if it wasn't for you I'd be dead" Fantasy proclaimed. "I was stuck in Oklahoma City with all kinds of destructive forces and I didn't see any way out, then you just show up and tell me I have what it takes to move, and nobody had ever told me that before. I wouldn't be sitting here if it wasn't for you, and now (twirling her wrist at the skyline) I want to help you make your dreams come true in New York".

She said she wanted to introduce me to important people, and offered to give me a free haircut the following week, which I gladly accepted.

A few days later I received an angry, impassioned email from her that caught me off guard. She proclaimed she'd loved me since I was nineteen, "…but you only see me as a jester or as a mother hen, but I am so much more than that!" then closed by saying just being friends was too painful, and not to waste my time writing back to say I don't see her like that. She unfriended me.

I responded that I respected her wishes and would give her space, then I blocked her to avoid any additional drama. She had my email address from when I wrote her bio for the salon's website, and sent me the following:

"Chris! Really there's was no need to block me I'm not going to go two years without speaking to you. So don't try me!! But understand how I feel. I care but I'm torn, I'll always be here for you. Always."

## 215. Wanted in Philly

I did a lot of thinking in Madison Square Park during my four daily visits with Brawny. In addition to my own life, I'd contemplate the changing of the season, how the trees had been bare when I arrived, and the way they looked as they flowered, then leafed out. I'd think about the stories of the skyscrapers around me. The art deco Metropolitan Life North Building was supposed to be the tallest structure in the world, but was cut off at thirty stories due to the Depression. Chelsea Clinton lived in the red brick building to my left, and then there was One Madison, a pencil thin condominium tower that was largely vacant because the developers went bankrupt after half a dozen units were sold, leaving the handful of residents rattling around in the empty skyscraper in the middle of America's most crowded city. I'd think of the movie plots that could take place there as I admired its soaring, spindly profile.

I was watching Brawny play with a Boston Terrier when the call I'd been waiting for, the big job in Philadelphia, finally came. I looked at the Caller ID, and slipped the phone back in my pocket. Why didn't I take the call? I wondered to myself, then it occurred to me I didn't want to go to Philadelphia.

While I did have the epiphany about wanting to be in St. Louis, that wasn't part of the plan, at least for the foreseeable future. I felt I needed to prove myself on the east coast, and had been eager about this opportunity.

What I didn't like about California was being isolated, a long way from people I loved, and Philadelphia wouldn't be much better. I had no close friends there, and started to think the ninety miles to Manhattan was going to feel farther than it sounded. It was going to be a stressful and demanding position requiring long hours, meaning I'd have to leave Brawny alone or in day care, and there would be little, if any time to write. It would push my book back a few years or maybe derail it altogether.

Corporate or material success wasn't going to change things with Damon, after all I had been successful in San Francisco. Benny would spin anything in a negative light, just as he had for seven years. If I pulled a child out of the path of a speeding train, Benny would argue it was my fault the child was on the tracks to begin with, or that I simply saved her to get attention.

Benny had long ago convinced Damon that being with me was a sign he was unhealthy and codependent, and as far as Damon moving to the east coast, Benny already tainted that well when he heard I said I'd like him to join me in New York one day.

"Well he's treating you like quite the afterthought isn't he? What he's saying is 'I'm going to New York, and by the way, you can come if you want.'" Benny mocked. Damon later parroted that line to our friends.

The voicemail confirmed they wanted me to come down for the final interview. I called the recruiter and left him a message thanking him for all of his work, but said I was pursuing another opportunity. After weeks of dragging their feet, the idea I had another offer made Philadelphia shift into high gear, asking the recruiter to call me back and let me know the final interview was basically a formality, and they want me to hear their offer before making a decision.

After being unemployed for the longest stretch in my adult life, it felt great to be pursued. At the same time, I needed to tell them I wasn't interested.

"It's not about the offer. I decided at this point in my life I don't want to be so far away from friends and family" I wrote.

I knew some would see leaving New York as a failure, but I decided to start doing what was good for my soul, and living the life I wanted to live.

My New York family was supportive of the decision.

"I think things are going to be great in St. Louis. That city's always been good to you" Joe said.

That evening I met a friend at a gay sports bar for drinks and everyone was glued to the televisions showing that Michael Sam, the first openly gay NFL player, was going to the St. Louis Rams.

The following day I posted, "I'm pulling a Michael Sam and going to St. Louis."

## 216. Returning to my City

I was driving across the eastern third of the country with the wind at my back. Everything about it felt right, and all kinds of offers began pouring in for everything I could possibly need to set up my new life. Miltonia sent a message offering all of her worldly possessions because she was moving to New Orleans for school. Francis and Edie asked me to visit their basement storage, which was like a Crate & Barrel Outlet, and was full of treasures including a one year old television, and my elegant friend Rae, a beautiful and prominent socialite who also hailed from Oklahoma, offered me free, unlimited use of her two bedroom poolside carriage house in an affluent West County suburb.

Turning down the big job in Philadelphia was difficult, but I had no doubt I'd made the right choice. Like Joe said, St. Louis had always been good to me, and my spirits were sky high as I surveyed the city in the morning light from atop a viewing platform on the Illinois side of the river, then made my way to Villa Ray to unload before returning the rental car to the airport.

When Ray learned I was planning to take the train back from Lambert he called Jimmy Curry to see if he could give me a ride. I'd first laid eyes on Jimmy five years earlier when he was dating Steven Fang, and contemplated how he'd become a really good friend.

The always energetic and animated Jimmy approached me with his arms spread out like an eagle's wings.

"I've got my push up buddy back!" he exclaimed, in reference to our friendly fitness competitions.

In the car he updated me on a drug addict he'd wasted seven months pursuing.

"So I had to call Loser Larry because I was out of seizure meds and remembered I'd left a few pills at his house. I go over there and he's counting change for food because he'd spent all his money on crystal, then he asked if I'd take him to the Food Bank, and I was like 'Dude, here's forty dollars and I'll take you to Vincent's Market or wherever'. There was no way I was taking him to the Food Bank on a Wednesday, because you know who volunteers on Wednesdays? Fang! Imagine that. I take some broke ass drugged out new boyfriend to get free food where my ex is working!"

The topic turns to tricks:

"I was really drunk at JJ's and I'm all into this good looking blond, tan guy and I went home with him. In the middle of sex it started to hit me he was much older and less attractive than I'd thought, and in the middle of fucking him I had to give myself a pep talk, 'You can do this, Jim', but the next morning was the worst! I'd gone to bed with this hot, blond and tan guy and woke up with some old geezer who looked like he'd just wandered out of the VFW hall!"

At this point I was laughing so hard it was painful. "Only you can make me laugh this hard, Jim."

### 217. Freaky Fantasy

I left things with Fantasy by telling her she needed to give herself a few months to process her feelings before we made contact again. When I was pulling out of New York in the rental car, she had to get what I thought were her last words in. In a message she said,

"Every comment from one of your friends saying how excited they are you're going to St. Louis is like a kick in the gut reminding me how I wasn't good enough."

I didn't take the bait.

Back in St. Louis I thought the Fantasy drama was behind me, then I received the following:

"Okay we give a few months and my feelings don't change then what? I don't have a problem with my feelings. What I have a problem with is your withdrawing of this friendship that you hold so dear. If you had told me that this friendship was only good in the city limits. I'd be okay. But like you said. 'You're like family to me', the family I know ask how are you doing? What's new? Are you so afraid that I'm going to go crazy and think it means more than what it is?? If I'm like family then take the time and show it. My feelings are my feelings and if I've been able to manage them of over twenty years I'm sure I can continue to deal. But I'm not going to pretend that I don't have them to make you feel comfortable. So if u need to process my feelings I understand. But at least be a friend.. P.S. I've got MANY MANY men that I have feelings for and who returns the feelings back to me so please stop thinking I'm all about u. There's plenty of dick & ass out there u don't hold the market on it!"

A few minutes after that, she sent the following:

"I'm persistent Chris. Look up and I'll be in St. Louis. Real talk!"

### 218.  A Place of My Own

I parted with my worldly possessions many times
while moving around. Three years earlier I was
depressed to be emptying our home in Tower
Grove to get back on the California roller coaster,
then I wrote to myself,

"Once again I'm trading treasure for adventure, but
the fact I still have something to trade shows that
the treasure always comes back."

Now, I had a rent-free park front apartment I'd
negotiated in exchange for managing a building, and
it was completely furnished by my friends Francis,
Edie, & Miltonia. Several of the items were things
I'd given them over the years, including a wicker
chair, a lamp, and cookware.

With a hand open to both giving and receiving, my
treasures went on an adventure of their own, and
meant more to me for the journey.


# The Twisted Tale of Ryan McCormic


## 219. Unrequited Love & Sudden Tragedy

The stunningly beautiful Ryan McCormic made
many friends over social media after relocating to
St. Louis from Florida. When he'd meet someone
new he'd explain he came to town for three reasons:

1.  To attend med school.
2.  To live with his parents while attending school.
3.  To be close to the unrequited love of his life,
Rustin Winchell.

Yes, that Rustin Winchell. The notorious con man and convicted felon who served time for pretending to be an attorney in St. Louis County. That ruse, coupled with revelations about his countless other scams, shocked the city and spurred headlines like this one from *The St. Louis Post Dispatch*: "St. Louis County lawyer-entrepreneur-candidate was really none of those."

Ryan McCormic, however, thought Winchell hung the moon, and they frequently exchanged flirtatious banter publicly over Facebook. In private messages to friends, he confided that he'd cheated on Winchell in the past, and now they could never be together. He'd have to settle for a mere friendship, and a lucrative business partnership in a multi-level marketing skin care company called Pyramid.

Ryan was really outgoing, chatting up anyone interested, and seemed to always be out and about, checking into various bars, restaurants and parties. Then one Sunday Rustin announced that Ryan had died in a drunk driving accident. Condolences poured in to Winchell as he asked for help planning a local memorial service, since the family's service would be out of state.

### 220. Déjà vu

The donation pleas had some recalling similar requests Winchell made a few years earlier, when despite his purported wealth, he took to the streets to raise burial money for his infant nephew.

"As soon as he pulled my partner aside in our veterinary clinic and showed him a picture of a dead baby in a casket, I knew something was fishy. First thing, it looks like they already afforded the casket for their child. Second, is the little boy who cried wolf so many times, it's hard to differentiate the truth from his lies. They seem to run together. More than likely, a friend of his had a miscarriage and he sees this as a business opportunity rather than a period of mourning. If he's a millionaire entrepreneur, why couldn't he raise the funds himself? He is the absolute worst kind of unscrupulous businessman!" said his former friend Carl.

At the time, Winchell claimed to be an owner of Attitudes Nightclub, and posted the following Facebook update, as later noted in a scathing piece by *St. Louis Magazine*:

"Ok I'm off to bury my nephew. Do not call me between 9:30-3PM.
YES I will be back in time for our HUGE Attitudes Nightclub Jägermeister Birthday Bash...so don't worry."

## 221. Investigation Already In Progress

A few days prior to the fatal accident I'd been alarmed to see several Facebook posts from acquaintances excited about getting great new jobs working for Winchell, even more so when I learned they'd given him money and credit card numbers. I was amazed so many weren't familiar with his scams, but then again he had threatened to sue anyone who so much as whispered a bad word about him for years. Many had never heard of him and those who had weren't talking.

I posted an update and it caught fire as the thread grew to well over six thousand comments from people sharing their stories.

Many had taken a pass on his hard sell offers for Hawaiian vacations for pennies on the dollar, copper bullion, Rolex watches, investment and legal services, but others had fallen prey to his assurances he could help them.

"He told me he was in the code enforcement business and I paid him two thousand dollars to help me bring my bar up to code, and then never heard from him again. I went to the address on his card and it was the Clayton Post Office!" one man complained.

"My brother has a printing business and Winchell was running some stupid magazine for a few months and racked up three thousand dollars in printing he never paid" wrote a friend known as Crazy Peg, who I'd met at the Metrolink Prom.

One deli clerk spoke of how she loved Winchell like a brother. He convinced her she needed to get her career on track, and said for a simple $49 initiation fee he'd mentor her and help establish a profitable business selling Pyramid's beauty products. That $49 quickly escalated to fifteen hundred dollars, which was his pattern.

Among Winchell's biggest Pyramid success stories was the late Ryan McCormic, who boasted about making money hand over fist. When this came up in the thread, a commenter posted a photo of an Israeli model named Eliran Biton, a face known to grieving St. Louisans as that of Ryan McCormic.

It appears McCormic was merely the invention of a very twisted mind. Everyone believed he was real because everyone else believed it, and the virtual world blurred the lines of reality.

## 222. Written Off

In the wake of the revelation, friend Jasmine Gaza, nicknamed "Jasmine GOTCHA" for her investigative skills, began asking questions of Winchell, which prompted a bizarre Facebook fight between "Ryan", Jasmine and Winchell.

"Ryan" was furious about the rumor he wasn't a real person, and in a drunken rage said he was going to the Grove to confront Jasmine. Winchell, concerned about Ryan's mental state, posted,

"If Ryan does anything to hurt himself the blame will fall squarely on YOU, Jasmine."

"Look for Rustin to kill off Ryan tonight" former friend Jordan Jamieson predicted.

And right on cue Ryan was written off Rustin's delusional drama with the dramatic death announcement, much to the delight of the viewers/commenters/investigators in the ever growing thread.

## 223. Penelope Chimes In

*Vital Voice* Gossip Columnist Penelope Wigstock had two memorable quotes about Winchell: "Rustin Winchell is like a less charming version of one of those wife murderers that appears in every Lifetime movie that's ever been made." And, "My momma always said that two of the tackiest things in life are ponchos and pyramid schemes."


## 224. Closing Doors

Winchell frequented Sensation, and sensed owner Tim Beckman wasn't happy with him after some less than sympathetic responses to his posts about the death of his beloved friend. He wrote to ask if Tim had a problem, and Tim replied that yes, he did.

"You really need to quit playing this game of imaginary crap. It is catching up to you so bad. I don't care if I am deleted or not. You are making stuff up as you go along. Friends, profiles, business ventures etc! In two phone calls it was found that you never owned a Little Caesars! [as he claimed, complete with a copyrighted website with store locations] If you took the energy it takes to make all this up, you could do good things." Beckman fumed.
"But instead you choose to make things up, scam people and make them not trust others. Are you're so mental that you believe this stuff? Being a man is owning up to mistakes and moving on. Not telling more lies and made up stuff that can always be found out. It makes you look totally stupid. Why would someone want to be thought of like that?"

Beckman continued, "I don't get you and think it would be best for you to stay away from my business, me and anything connected to me. I defended you for a long time, because everyone makes mistakes, but you make honest living people that actually do work and own businesses look inferior and I want no part of it. Go to a REAL school and get a REAL degree. See what satisfaction you will feel then. Put some of that energy to good use instead of making things up and looking for the next scam."

Winchell responded, still asserting that Ryan was real, despite the fact that nobody met him, there were no fatalities reported by the media or any local or state agencies that evening, and the fact that his images belonged to an Israeli model.

"Good luck in your life Tim. I am not deleting you. You can believe what you want. The truth always comes out. Wait for the obituary."

Then he followed up with a most bizarre question.

"Did you ever meet Ryan and was he in your bar the other night? And you don't want me in Sensation anymore?"

Beckman came back swinging.

"Stop with the lies. Do you realize we are talking to the guy whose real pic you all are using? You have dug a hole so deep that not even you can get out of it. I don't get it. I mean seriously, people are collecting info about you and ready to take it to your probation officer because you continually lie. Pictures with dates and you drinking in bars (prohibited by his probation terms), pics and posts of you and your companies, messages from Pyramid that you are scamming consumers. Stuff like this from America Marketing claiming they have nothing to do with you and that you are using made up emails. Pyramid is checking on the emails. It is a string that you keep making bigger. I want no association with you. You cannot even be honest with yourself. Yes, stay away from my bar. Now I see why no one wants you around. You are a liar, thief and are only out to make money on the backs of everyone else. Stay away from me. I am gonna sit back and watch the town tear apart the person that has no belief in himself, so he invents things. "You are nothing more than an opportunist user with no real training. Go back and read some of your lies and inventions you have in your mind. You NEVER owned shit! This crap is so easy to prove, yet you keep telling lies so much you actually believe them. Good riddance. No more chances for a pathological liar. You are the true meaning of sociopath!"

Winchell did in fact unfriend Beckman.

## 225. You Meddling Kids!

Jasmine really hit a nerve when, over text, she questioned Winchell about whether he was even allowed to be involved in internet sales while on probation.

"YOU BITCH! YOU'RE TRYING TO GET THEM TO TAKE AWAY MY PYRAMID BUSINESS! I'M SO SUING YOU!"

## 226. Life Goes On

Model Eliran Biton was contacted in Israel, very much alive, and thanked me for bringing this to his attention. Many in town viewed the saga with humor, including Gabe Goldstein of suburban O'Fallon, Illinois, who'd been entangled in Winchell's scams twice.

Winchell had made a plea deal for an ex of his and when it came out he wasn't an attorney it caused major issues. Fast forward a couple of years and Goldstein chatted with McCormic regularly and was upset by his passing, but threw a big "Ryan Resurrection Pool Party" at his sprawling home to celebrate, complete with a life-sized cutout of the Israeli model.

Ryan's Facebook page, deleted around the time of his death, was recreated by tricksters bent on tormenting Winchell. On the page Ryan claimed he was locked in the vault of one of Winchell's Fortune 500 companies where every other day Winchell would stop by to bring him a Little Caesars pizza from one of his franchises.

"GOD I'm a pickle!" the parody Ryan would often say.

Many friendships were made and camaraderie shared between the people in that nearly seven thousand comment thread, which grew for many days. Half dozen or so kept in regular contact for the purpose of debunking his outlandish claims, and even spun off to investigate other shady happenings around town.

The biggest thing to come out of all this was the realization that the tiger had no teeth. Few were scared of him any longer, and that sea change took the wind out of his sails for a time.

The con artist who once picked up gubernatorial candidates in a limo and practiced law in the courtroom was relegated to low-level pyramid schemes and reduced to trying to convince people via Twitter that he was close personal friends with celebrities like Cher and Justin Bieber, responding to their general Tweets as if they were to him personally.

His brother, a big country boy from central Missouri, saw the thread and contacted me. He said he enjoyed the stories, but the talk of a "dead baby scam" was upsetting.

"He was a living and breathing baby for a little over an hour after birth. I trusted my brother, knowing better, and he used my son's death as a way to make money. Something I can and never will forgive him for because Rustin doesn't see the fact he needs help."

We exchanged messages on and off for the next four months, until one day I asked about Rustin's time in the psych ward. His response gave me pause, making me wonder if Winchell was more dangerous than I'd given him credit for.

"For the safety of my children I can't talk about Rustin anymore. Sorry."

I never heard from him again.

Later that year Winchell and a transsexual closed down the bar and took a taxi to his North County home, and when his credit cards were declined the driver refused to unlock the doors. Winchell tried to convince him he had money inside his house, but when the driver said he was calling the police Winchell stabbed him, his date, and himself.

He took to social media almost immediately with photos of his stab wounds and a heroic tale of how he shielded the transsexual from the crazed taxi driver's knife attack. He pitched story to local media but nobody was buying.


## 227. Mr. Slave

So now there was a fetish where men acted like puppies, and a group of my buddies including Steven Fang and Taylor Christopher went to Bad Dog bar to witness the puppy convention in town. I chatted up a leather queen, asking what the deal was.

"I find it really irritating, because I know people who live the lifestyle, but so many of these other guys just go out now and then in puppy gear and are like 'Oh look at us, we're puppies!'" he fumed.

"Puppy posers!" I exclaimed.

He then told us about his recent trials and tribulations as a leather slave, getting choked up in the process.

"I moved all the way to Corpus Christi to be with my Daddy, and it turned out he's a *big liar*! He pretends to be a Daddy to win these pageants but he's really the *biggest* pig bottom! I got down there and found he had a Dom of his own!"

Without skipping a beat, Steven Fang shook his head and said, "Oldest story in the book."


## 228. Fassen Your Seatbelts

Brian Fassen was one of the most provocative men in St. Louis with his brazen openness on the topic of sexuality, and his role as an S&M Master. His devilish good looks—shaved head, dark, mysterious eyes, thick black goatee—pulled people in, while his intense personality kept most at bay.

He talked to me about overcoming addiction, and what it was like to be in the hookup scene while using. For my first *Tales from the Emperor* column since returning from New York, I decided to do an interview piece with him, and I might just go to my grave never getting such memorable quotes again.

### Sex, Drugs & Apps: Brian Fassen: After the Party (*Vital Voice*, July 2014)

*Party & Play*

"Do you party?" asked the headless torso over instant message. Brian knew what he meant. "'Party' always refers to meth, AKA 'Crystal', 'Tina' or 'T'," he explains.

In the dark days of his past, Brian Fassen expertly navigated St. Louis's sinister parallel universe – a world for the sleepless, their gaunt faces illuminated by the glow of devices while desperately attempting to quell their insatiable appetites.

"Apps are the perfect medium for drug users," he begins. "It's the perfect deceiving medium, because you can claim whatever you want and present whatever image you want. Most of the pics are from years ago, before the drug use, then you show up to some shithole apartment and the guy's got dark circles around his eyes and looks fifteen years older, and there's some drug dealer on the phone in the corner. But if they've got the right audience, the tricks who show up won't care about any of that."

## The Soft Reality

Although the drug intensifies the want for sex, it also makes sex more difficult.

"Meth will turn the most brutal top into the most insatiable bottom," Fassen explains. "When you smoke it your dick stops working, so you couldn't top if you wanted to. But even if you love to bottom, it's never enough. You're never satisfied. "One guy lived in a basement apartment," he continues. "I walked in and it was pitch black. I couldn't see anything for nearly sixty seconds while my eyes adjusted. He was there with his ass up and head down saying 'Yeah yeah yeah, do it.' We're having sex and my eyes are closed while I'm trying to get into it, then I hear him talking, open my eyes and find he's on his phone trying to line up the next trick! That was the first time I'd seen anything like that, but things like that happened a few other times."

Fassen spoke of the erotic picture guys will paint of sex parties, making it sound like you're going to walk onto the hottest porn set.

"You'll always get these messages about sex parties, someone will say they've got four guys there and they want you to come over and fuck all of 'em. In reality, one bottom was smoking meth and pulled a trick over who then got high, so now you've got two bottoms. They pull over a third who gets high, so now you've got three bottoms sitting around with limp dicks, and it goes from there."

*"Meth heads are weird"*

I asked if it's like The Walking Dead for the top when he arrives, with everyone swarming around. Fassen laughs. "No, no it's not like that at all. Meth heads are weird. You show up, they've all been getting high for the past eighteen hours and one's absorbed in his tablet, one's watching television, one's on the phone and one's into you."

I asked what percent of the time condoms were used during these hook ups. "Are you kidding?" Fassen asks. "Never! I've never had anyone on meth even mention a condom."

Fassen explains that meth makes one fidgety, and guys will often interrupt sex every couple of minutes to look out the window, pick at their skin, etc. Of course, the bizarre behaviors aren't limited to sexual situations.

"When you are high, you have to occupy the mind — whatever it takes. Sometimes someone will spend hours feeling the floor to see if any meth powder sticks to their fingers. I knew a guy who'd break into storage units just to organize what was in there."

I ask if the guy stole from the storage units.

"Maybe, but that's not why he'd break in. He needed something to do." Asked if he'd ever been stolen from personally, Fassen responds, "You don't go into these situations with your wallet! C'mon!"

With all of the unprotected sex, STDs are part of the package, and Fassen was open about having had gonorrhea and syphilis. "I don't care what anyone says: if you've been to a 14-man bareback gangbang, you've had syphilis."

*"I don't want this anymore."*

Brian simply wanted to go to sleep, but there's no rest in that world. "I just laid there and thought 'I don't want this anymore'. The sleeplessness, the awful sex, the STDs. There's no connection and I missed that. It's not fulfilling."

He managed to quit on his own, although he has maintained his sobriety with support from Narcotics Anonymous and Alcoholics Anonymous.

"It's hard, but it has to be something you want to do," Fassen says. "There's an ambivalent phase where you kind of want to stop and kind of don't, but once you get to the point you're ready to quit, the struggle's really over. Sure there's days when it sucks, but it doesn't suck as much as using."

*See You on the Other Side*

Brian often sees people he'd partied with at the NA and AA meetings. "It's always great to see friends on the other side because they look totally different, they act totally different...It feels like I didn't know them at all while they were using."

His bad boy street cred still intact, Fassen continues to lead an adventurous life, only now he can actually enjoy it. For Brian Fassen the "party" is over, but the fun is just beginning.

### 229. Rainbow Steps

Before Brian was the clean and confident man I interviewed, he was a troubled kid hooked on drugs and haunted by a childhood of horrific physical and sexual abuse. He sought help from a twelve step program called Rainbow Steps.

Rainbow Steps was by and for LGBT people, and when the club came up in conversation one day, weeks after Sex, Drugs & Apps was published, Brian mentioned, "When I was at rock bottom with my addiction Benny Babbish offered me a hundred bucks if I'd let him fuck me."

This had me seeing red. Taking advantage of someone seeking help was as low as you could get, and hearing it was Benny *Fucking* Babbish really pushed me over the edge, and I knew it was true, not only because I knew Brian to be an honest guy, but it fit with Benny's reprehensible pattern of exploiting desperate men. I wanted to see if anyone else would come forward, so I posted an update without mentioning the specific club:

"I'm hearing troubling reports of people being mistreated at a local twelve step program, with one person being offered $100 for sex. If you have a similar story, please let me know."

Brian described Rainbow Steps as a rogue program, picking and choosing the tenets they wanted to follow. They achieved this through a maddening assortment of overlapping entities. For instance there were the various groups that met in the building, which were generally referred to as Rainbow Steps, and the Rainbow Steps LLC, which owned the building.

"AA and NA don't kick people out for showing up to a meeting under the influence, but Rainbow Steps does. When called out on this they'd say 'It's the LLC kicking them out, not the program'" he said.

I invited him over to tell me his stories.

"Mark Sampson was one of the 'Chosen Frozen', as we called them, along with Benny and one or two other guys who'd been in the group for years and felt they were above sharing their personal struggles with everyone else. Instead they'd just pontificate. They claimed to be all about brutal honesty, but were much more interested in the brutality than the honesty," Fassen began.

"They were dicks to everyone, and when someone would complain they'd twist it around and say 'You should be willing to pay any price to maintain sobriety'- as if putting up with their abuse was an important part of staying sober, and if they didn't want to put up with it they were a loser and would never succeed. And they loved when people failed. They'd get such a look of smug satisfaction when they'd tell them they would've succeeded had they done things their way."

Fassen recalled an ill-fated romance between Sampson and a member.

"Mark had been single for many years, but fell in love with this guy in the program named Rick, who was about ten or fifteen years younger. Really nice guy, always at the meetings smiling and talking to everyone. They decided to be a couple and both got tested for HIV and came back negative. Maybe six months later Mark was getting routine tests and came up positive and was so livid he called the police and pressed charges against Rick. In an instant he went from love to hate, and wanted to nail him to the wall."

In Missouri you could be prosecuted for knowingly spreading HIV, and might remain locked up until you prove your innocence.

"Missouri has these draconian laws I disagree with where you can be criminally prosecuted for giving someone HIV, but sometimes it's not detectable for months, so the person may not have known they gave it to someone- which was probably what happened with Rick," Fassen speculated.

"I didn't know Rick was sitting in jail all that time because there are many different meetings so I just figured we were missing one another until one day I asked about him and heard all this. I couldn't stop thinking about him just sitting in jail and how fucked up it was and how alone he must feel, I don't think anyone from the group had even gone to see him, and maybe a week later I asked someone which jail he was in because I wanted to visit and was told he'd hung himself. He was dead, and his story will never be told."

Four days after my post asking people to come forward, Mark Sampson sent me a message saying Facebook wasn't the place to discuss any issues concerning Rainbow Steps, he doubted the accusations were true, and that I should bring any concerns to the board. I responded as follows:

412

Mark,

I'm very familiar with the accused and the accuser.
My husband worked with the accused and I've
attended his parties where he openly discussed his
fetish for paying straight married men hard up for
cash to let him anally penetrate them. The fact they
didn't want to do it, and were in fact humiliated by
it, was what got him off.

It's no secret that I've loathed this individual for
years. I've told him as much.

When a young man I know very well told me this
man offered him $100 to be penetrated while this
guy was struggling with addiction, I was sickened,
but not surprised, that he would exploit those
vulnerable people who turned to your group for
help. I've seen his questionable behavior with group
members before, like him inviting a guest from the
group to his party and then telling other guests the
person had genital warts and that's why his
boyfriend dumped him.

I'm certain you know exactly who I'm talking about,
as you two are apparently close, he's active in your
organization and quite cocky about his paid
conquests. If he isn't formally on the board, he
certainly is one of the "frozen chosen" - which I
hear are the upper echelon who operate by a
different set of rules.

If others come forward and it becomes clear your
group is being used as this vile man's playpen there's
no way in Hell I'm keeping quiet about it. If the
board finds inappropriate action and deals with it
on its own I'll make sure the spotlight is on this
individual and not the organization as a whole.

Chris Andoe

413

Brian later agreed to allow me to tell Mark that he was the one propositioned. At first Mark thanked me, but then flippantly said,

"Frankly I'm thinking this is another one of Brian's dramas. If you think the board can do something to help let me know. Perhaps Brian should contact the police or an attorney. Benny is not associated with Rainbow Steps in any way. Slandering an innocent nonprofit seems like the wrong action to take."

I replied: "That mindset is what kept the predatory priests going for so long. There are predators who hide behind righteous organizations. Benny always presented himself as a pillar of your organization, and you insinuating that Brian is the problem here is troubling. Benny is open about using money to sexually degrade desperate people. I gave you Brian's name in good faith, giving you the benefit of the doubt you would take this seriously. There's really nothing else to discuss at this point. The post is days old now and nobody has come forward yet. If they do I'll tell you first, despite your disappointing response."

Someone contacted me about being felt up at a meeting, but initially nobody came forward with any accusations of being offered money for sex, other than reports about the rent boy websites Benny trolled where he told drug addicted hustlers of his desire to dominate. And the statement about Benny not being associated with Rainbow Steps "in any way" was complete and total bullshit. Several members reported that he was just as active as ever. Maybe the duplicitous Sampson meant Benny wasn't active in running the brick and mortar LLC "in any way."

Months later a young man came forward claiming Benny's partner offered him "Tina" (meth) if he'd fuck him and get fucked by Benny. A pillar of the twelve step program offering a stash of drugs for sex. I decided such information would be wasted on his buddy Sampson, and I would save it for the right time.

## 230. A Predator's Paradise

Benny Babbish wasn't the only noteworthy predator Fassen met at Rainbow Steps. One evening his group was letting out at the same time as a sexual compulsives meeting upstairs, and he locked eyes with a handsome blond man in his forties who introduced himself as Ron Brascome.

They soon began dating, and Brascome explained he couldn't have sex with Fassen until their tenth date, due to a rule of the program. Fassen appreciated his dedication to recovery, and after a few weeks Brascome told him there was something he should know.

"I need to tell you that I served time in prison and I'm on parole for something," Brascome began, "But it will end soon."

"Okay. What were you in for?" Fassen asked.

"I'm not ready to talk about it just yet" Brascome replied.

"Can you tell me if it was for something violent? Am I in any danger?" Fassen asked.

Eventually, Ron Brascome revealed he was the man at the center of the biggest and most humiliating scandal to ever hit the city's LGBT community. He was the former Pride President turned convicted sexual predator.

In 2003, during his tenure as Pride President, Brascome was one of many men who, online, chatted with a 6' tall guy and met him for sex. Despite his height and bulk, it turned out the kid was only in his mid-teens.

"He said he didn't know they guy was underage, and it did sound like he got a raw deal" Fassen began. "The prosecutor knew it would hurt their case to tell the jury this kid was victimized by *twenty* men, so they just picked a few to prosecute, and zeroed in on Ron because he was so high profile."

In the following months, though, Fassen began to notice odd behavior. "He'd always get up and peek through the blinds at the teens getting off the school bus" he recalled.

He was also concerned with comments he made about his probation ending.

"He'd talk about the end of his probation and say, 'You know, I think for old times' sake I'm going to do a bunch of crystal and go to the bathhouse and get fucked by a lot of guys.'"

The two stopped seeing one another a few months before his probation ended.

I had lived a few doors down from Brascome in Tower Grove and told Brian about the night I was walking the dogs with Damon and the police were at his apartment. One officer was talking to a young man at the curb, and the other with Ron on the front steps. A friend of ours across the street was sitting on his porch and said it was a domestic situation, something about Ron getting violent.

"Yeah he said that happened a couple of times and acted like he had no idea why. 'Sometimes guys just freak out on me and call the police!' he'd say."

After Fassen broke it off, he saw him one last time.

"A month or so after his probation was over he called for a hook up. I walked in and his place was disgusting. I mean it was so dirty it was like the food left on the plates had decomposed to dirt. He was sitting there watching TV and jacking off, with his cock in one hand and the remote in the other, and he didn't stop jacking when I walked in. He was kind of in a trance, and seemed oblivious to the conditions around him, and completely unaware of how disgusted I was. I then looked at the television and it was some Hannah Montana type show!"

Fassen said he shook his head and left.

### 231. The List

For months I'd been using Damon's old computer bag. It appeared to be empty when he gave it to me, but one day I was looking for a pen when I came across a neatly folded note in one of the pockets.

Sitting at the kitchen table I unfolded the lined notebook paper and saw the handwritten title *Worry List*. There were several categories which included Money, Pets- the plural told me the list wasn't recent, Job, and Relationship. Under that last topic he listed three options: Stay, Go, Work on it.

I sent him a photo of it with the message: "I hope your list is a lot shorter now."

After many hours he replied, "Sort of. I hope finding that didn't upset you."

"I felt many different emotions, but mostly I was grateful to be off such a list."

I came to realize Benny didn't rule Damon's mind as much as he ruled the wound in our relationship, settling in like an opportunistic infection. That was his domain, after all he didn't want Damon to move back to California, but his opinion carried no weight in that decision.

No, the scope of his influence and manipulation was narrow, and with the host relationship dead, the vile parasite was powerless, meaning, I hoped, that Damon was finally freed from him too.

A few months after I left New York Damon flew to St. Louis to visit his family, and to see me and Brawny. On a beautiful fall afternoon we went for a long walk in Tower Grove Park. That was our place, and our walk was poignant.

"We met for the second time right there" he said, pointing to the area where I called out to him during Pride fourteen years earlier.

"Do you remember when the sky was so pink and we sat on that bench and talked?" I asked.

"I do" Damon replied.

"Over the Summer I brought Brawny for a long walk one evening. The sky was golden and there were people everywhere. I must've been lost in my own thoughts, because I looked up and it was dark, and nobody was around. You know back in 2000 people thought this park was dangerous, but you, me and Francis ran all over it every night with no fear. I'd never been afraid here. On that evening though, all the people and the commotion masked that I was alone while the sun was still up, but it was like one minute I was walking with you and Francis, and a few dogs, and then everyone faded into the blackness except for me and Brawny, and I felt truly alone for the first time, and felt vulnerable, exposed, and unsafe," I recalled.

I decided to bring up Benny. Not to start an argument, but because I felt like my understanding of him and his impact on many people, not just Damon, was one dimensional. He was the villain of my story, and I wanted to know what I was missing.

"I know this is a sensitive subject, and we don't have to discuss it if you don't want to, but what I can't understand is Benny's motivation, and why he has such an impact on people."

When it came to Benny's seven year battle, Damon said Benny initially tried to bring me into his orbit, and when he couldn't co-opt me, using me to entertain guests at his parties, and when I didn't follow his recommendations on how I should live my life, he turned against me.

As far as the hold Benny had on others, Damon said, "Professionally, he's very good at what he does. He's successful. And when you have his confidence, and he wants to mentor you, it feels like an honor. If he had hit on me, I would've understood what his interest was about. But he never seemed to want anything in return. I just couldn't see that his motives were nefarious."

"When I met Benny we had just lost everything in Oklahoma City" Damon continued. "I was frustrated about our lack of forward momentum, and he latched on to that theme and never let go."

We were never able to move past the Oklahoma City collapse, in large part, because Benny kept the wound from healing. He picked at it constantly, and once he understood the depths of Damon's financial anxieties and his fear of being poor, he knew exactly what nerve to hit and where to pour the salt.

For seven years Damon had been terribly conflicted. On one hand he described himself as being obsessed with me for a long time, to the level it was unhealthy, but on the other he was embarrassed in front of Benny. This led to an inner conflict, and a cloud over every otherwise joyous moment.

It also created a duplicitousness in Damon. Any happy or beautiful moment we shared was spun in a negative light when relayed to Benny, whose sinister brilliance was framing relationships as a zero-sum game.

"I'm so bitter about what he's done to us and countless others. He tears relationships apart while he enjoys the companionship of a partner. He convinces people he's a pillar of the community while offering drugs for sex to guys who need help. Look at what he's cost us, all the wasted years." I said.

"Ignore Benny. Put him out of your mind. Focus on your generalities: good looking, talented, intelligent, healthy, and extremely well-liked. Don't carry the bitterness from the past into your future" Damon replied.

We sat near a fountain and watched a group setting up speakers and chairs for a wedding. Frank Sinatra's rendition of "Wonderful World" was playing.

We all see life through our own lens, and Damon indicated that there was never much between him and Patrick, and that I'd blown it out of proportion. He also said I had misinterpreted his Worry list. As he spoke I played with a fallen leaf, watching the way the light came through it in a way that reminded me of a stained glass window.

"It's kind of hard to see that you're happy" he began. "The last time I saw you, you basically said I was killing you. That's the only reason I didn't try to get you to stay."

While I disagreed about there not being much between him and Patrick, distinctly remembering the conversation that began with a comparison of the two of us, and how conflicted he was, I let it go. It was no longer about being right. Instead, I agreed that I was having stress related health problems in Oakland, and that I had been healthy as of late.

Despite the heaviness of the discussion, the mood wasn't hostile or adversarial.

"I had internalized Benny's narrative" I said, "But for the first time in seven years I like myself again."

While we loved one another, the situation was intractable. He was starting to see Benny's impact, but they were still friends and Benny still "coached" him on his Facebook wall, which made me want to vomit. Living under Benny's influence was like living near Chernobyl. Even if Damon decided he wanted nothing more to do with him, which wasn't the case, "we" were probably far too damaged to survive.

I wished things were different. I wanted to hold him and know he was mine. I wanted to put all of this behind us.

"So I guess we should talk about a divorce," Damon said.

"Isn't this sad? Sitting here discussing divorce while joyful people are preparing to marry," I remarked.

And it was.

## 232. Brunch with Reggie Edwards

Actor and activist Reggie Edwards, one of the busiest and most entertaining men in the city, met me for brunch on the second floor veranda at Soulard Coffee Garden on a drizzly summer morning when the topic of Rita Revlon came up. Unlike me, Reggie knew her before her transition, back when she was still a gay guy named Rick.

"She, well, he, at the time, was the most machismo guy – except that he'd wear cut off jean shorts that were way too short. And he'd wear them to important community meetings. It was like 'Here's the Mayor's staffer, and here's Daisy Duke!'"

Before going to war with Simone Shasta, it was Reggie in Rita's crosshairs. Reggie and his partner Emanuel had gotten a lot of press for their Marriage Bus trips to Iowa, which stuck in Rita's craw.

"Marriage is an issue gay white men care about, so therefore it's all that's being focused on" she'd say over social media.

"Rita, half of the people on our buses are people of color. These are people who'd go down to City Hall to get married if they could," Reggie replied.

The tension would spill over when they'd see one another out. Drunken Rita would shout, "Damn you Reggie! Don't come anywhere near me!"

She was now a Catholic lady by day, talking about God and baking cookies. Catholicism seemed a strange choice for a headstrong Transgender activist, but some said she'd fallen in love with a straight man who convinced her to convert.

"When she goes in, she goes all in! I mean next week she'll post about having stigmata!" Reggie joked.

She only became the Dark Mistress during occasional but lively evenings when she got up in her cups.

"The Dark Mistress was out last night!" I said. "She posted dozens of tirades, most about Simone but some about the community at large. This one reads, 'Guess it is time to write that chapter why you candy ass faggots, trannies and lezzies no longer sparkle in my mind as social justice advocates. Heave Ho the vodka.'"

Reggie cringed, "My God! Her liver must wanna transition to a pancreas!"

## 233. Real Housewives of West County

An acquaintance forwarded me an invite to a monthly Orgy Club held in a banal West County home, complete with a snapshot of the "dungeon" and its freshly vacuumed carpeting.

The invite instructed guests to bring a friend, all the supplies they would need, and food. At first glance it sounded like a frugal voyeur's crafty way of asking people to come over and have sex in front of him.

I posted an update about it that garnered thousands of comments, as well as a few private messages from those who had attended. I learned the event was all the rage, and also that Ol' Gladys Kravitz peeked through a basement window and called the police, who simply asked the homeowners to cover their windows.

One of the messages was from Ivan Manassas, a wealthy man in his mid-forties who I'd never met in person, although we'd been connected via social media for a few years, and I was aware he'd been a major donor to the LGBT Center and many other charitable causes.

Manassas and his friend Dimitri Summers invited me to a clandestine lunch at Plaza Frontenac, an upscale shopping center anchored by Saks Fifth Avenue and Nieman Marcus, to tell me whatever I wanted to know about the sex parties, and said they had several other topics to discuss.

Initially, as we strolled past the high-end boutiques on our way to the restaurant, Summers was nervous and somewhat hesitant, unsure of how much he wanted to reveal, but said, "I'm at the age where I really just don't give a fuck anymore."

We sat at a busy bar where we ordered martinis, and I took note of Summers's enormous diamond rings, platinum bracelet, and Rolex watch. He made a few comments about being distrustful of "The A-Gays," which he said included myself, Darin Slyman, Jimmy No Show, William Collins, William Lowe, Reggie Edwards, the heads of local advocacy groups, etc.

"You don't consider yourself an A-Gay?" I asked, surprised. "You're always sponsoring tables at charity events, you chair a scholarship foundation, you live on ten acres in Wildwood..."

"I married well but I'm just poor white trash," he began. "And at the most recent gala my table was in the back corner for the second year in a row, because I'm not one of the elites," he complained. "I'm not attending that one again."

He asked where we should begin and I suggested we start with the story about Rustin Winchell contacting him.

"It was a few years back," Summers began. "I'd never heard of him but he said he was the head of an Alzheimer's foundation and that we should consider merging. I asked him to send me financials and he said he would, but then I never heard from or about him again until he was all over the news and I was like, oh my God! This guy's a convict. I later learned he'd convinced a friend of mine to invest five thousand dollars in a magazine venture, which was a scam."

One sip into his second martini and Summers lifted and swirled his glass. "Okay, these are taking now. What do you want to know?"

The orgy was old news, so I asked about the LGBT Center.

Ivan chimed in. "First of all, I wasn't a fan of the Williams Show" he said, in reference to former Board President William Lowe and former Board member William Collins. Turning to Summers he said, "Tell him about what happened at Forest Park."

"When I first got involved there was a big event on the Forest Park tennis courts and I was talking with Lowe, who has the personality of a piece of plywood, when Simone Shasta walked in and I was starstruck. I told Lowe I was a huge fan and wanted to approach her but was too intimidated. Lowe then quipped, 'Oh you don't need to feel that way. She's a big coke head' and I was shocked he would say something like that about his executive director. It just didn't sit well with me. I got to know Shasta and I never once heard her disparage anyone behind their back."

Summers complained that everything the Center did seemed to be for the glorification of "the Williams," and he was particularly irked by Lowe's heterosexual grandfather being honored at a veteran's ceremony at the Pride celebration.

"I know many gay and lesbian veterans, but Lowe decided to put Ol' Gramps on stage and in the parade, all because he was okay with his gay grandson. That was offensive to me. God, I was so sick of the Williams Show."

Manassas continued, "And if it wasn't about the two of them it was about the drag. They're obsessed with drag queens and every single function involved having their pictures taken with drag queens."

The topic turned to West County living, the women they ran around with, their mutual love of Botox, and how they prefer life out there.

"Whenever I'm inside the 270 loop I feel like I'm downtown" Manassas said with a snarl as Summers agreed.

"Really? So you feel like we're Downtown now?" I asked, incredulously.

We were barely inside the 270 loop, twelve miles from Downtown, in a very exclusive, old money suburban neighborhood of palatial estates.

"Yeah," Manassas replied, shaking his head.

"Clayton, Ladue, Town & Country, Frontenac, those are some of the wealthiest municipalities in the nation," I said.

Manassas began to explain when we were interrupted by the handsome Latino bartender, who asked, "Anything else I can do for you right now?"

427

"Not here, there isn't," Manassas shot back with a wink. The two were feeling loose and talkative.

"My partner Rex met me when I was just poor white trash living in a trailer park, then he got with me and bought the trailer park. We still own it," Summers offered.

"So do you go there for any reason?"

"To collect the rent" he replied.

"Are any of the same people still there? And when you pull up in your big ol' Cadillac like Boss Hog are they like, 'Bitch, I remember when you were my neighbor!'"

We all laughed and Summers moved on to his Rita Revlon tale.

In addition to his work with his scholarship foundation, he taught a class at a suburban college and recalled the time he asked Revlon to participate in an LGBT Diversity Day for his students.

"I hadn't been out of the closet for very long, and decided to host a Diversity Day at a local restaurant. I was told Rita Revlon was who I should contact about Trans representation, and she agreed to come. Well, I'd never seen her before and when she lumbered in looking like a seven foot tall Ozzy Osborne in an Easter hat my stomach sank, and things just went downhill from there," he recalled.

The event was intended as a light, feel good introduction to the LGBT Community, but Rita had other ideas.

"The whole point was to show these suburban kids that we're just like everyone else, but Rita was so militant, so confrontational. She was up in everyone's cringing faces saying, 'Trans are being *killed!* We're being *murdered* and shoved under beds!' Oh, it was terrible. I had to step into the restroom and cry, and later I had to sit in not one but two meetings about it. It was humiliating."

The drinks kept coming, and so did the stories. Manassas, who like Summers was in a long-term relationship, told me about his 50-something boyfriend on the side, and the secret house he owned in St. Charles where the two would rendezvous.

"I like 'em older. Always have. Problem is he has trouble..." Manassas shook his limp finger to symbolize a flaccid penis. "So I drug him and he doesn't know. He's like, 'Why am I seeing blue rings?' and I'm like 'Oh hon, that's just the lighting in here.'"

The bill for our two-hour martini lunch was steep. Summers picked up the check, and on top of the gratuity on the credit card receipt he slipped the handsome bartender a fifty-dollar bill.

"You guys don't care for drag, so how do you square that with your love of Simone Shasta?" I asked.

Summers replied, "I don't see Simone as a drag queen. I just see her as Simone. And there were times when she's really lifted me up when I was down. I know what she did, but I love her anyway. A lot of people stopped supporting the Center because of the stolen money, but I stopped because of the Williams Show. I'm disappointed in Simone but will always love her."

He thought for another moment, and continued, "I don't like when she's Sammy, her boy self. It's weird. She was at an event once as Sammy, in a tie, looking like a man. I was like, 'I don't know this person.' It was disturbing to me," he said with a furrowed brow, then Manassas looked at his watch and raised his eyebrows, seemingly startled by the time.

"Oh hon, I gotta get to my secret house!" he said with a flourish of the wrist.

## 234.  Crosshairs of the Conflicted Catholics

I broke a story about two women fired from Cor Jesu Academy, a Catholic all-girls school in South St. Louis County, for being lesbians. There was a cloak of silence and it took a lot of legwork to get anyone to even confirm the firings occurred.

My break came after I solicited the help of friend Ryan Reeve, who attended Catholic schools in St. Louis and was well connected in that community. He knew a teacher who, like the rest of the staff, was forbidden from speaking, but on the condition of anonymity confirmed that a teacher and a coach applied for a mortgage together, and the employment verification request tipped off administrators.

The teacher I quoted was glad the story was going to get attention, and lamented that there wasn't much of a response, other than a vague and secretive alumnae movement about withholding funds from the annual fund drive. I'd soon learn the leader of the vague movement, Kathy Lager, was pretty kooky.

Kathy had worked with Darin Slyman on a local morning show years back, then moved to Los Angeles with her girlfriend, whom she married, and worked as a production assistant on some *Access Hollywood* type program. The relationship ended and she had a rough landing back in St. Louis, where she applied for a job with *Vital Voice*, got drunk during the interview, and afterwards posted, "I'm the new Entertainment Director for *Vital Voice*! Yay!" on her Facebook page, when no such offer had been made.

Lager formed a Facebook group which aimed to "support" the women fired with affirming messages, and to gently suggest alumnae consider withholding or reducing their annual contribution to the fund drive – only if they were comfortable with that. The secret society had another mission, as well, which was to keep this out of the press and protect the school.

My story, which went national, enraged Kooky Kathy on several levels. First, that I broke it in the first place, but it made matters worse that I was with *Vital Voice*. More than anything, though, she was angered by the teacher's statement that there wasn't much of a response from alumnae, which she felt disrespected her group and their efforts.

"We've got a Facebook group with two thousand members!" she posted to *Vital Voice*'s Facebook wall, along with numerous indignant rants about the story being "factually incorrect," which was odd because she wasn't denying the fact that the women were fired for being lesbians, or the fact that some were withholding donations in response – which were the only reported facts I mentioned. What she disagreed with was the *tone* of the quoted opinion implying her group's response wasn't that noteworthy.

431

Somehow she was able to get other supposedly educated women to echo her assertion. Angry letters poured in to Vital Voice demanding I be fired and the "factually incorrect" piece retracted. I hadn't received such hate mail since Bush was in office, so I was pretty excited.

A few days later *The St. Louis Post-Dispatch* picked up the story, and having seen the blowback Vital Voice received, made their article all about the "outcry" of alumnae. I'm not sure how you can call a secretive Facebook group telling members to maybe consider withholding or reducing contributions— if they're comfortable with that, an "outcry", but anyway Kathy was happy with the piece. "This is how to write a fair and balanced story!" she posted.

The following day *The Washington Post* and *The Huffington Post* picked it up.

People were puzzled by her outraged comments on the threads, which went on for days. In a different thread on a friend's wall someone asked me what her issue was.

"Days ago Kooky Kathy was livid that I broke the story, but now that the P-D made it all about the supposed outcry of her group, she seems pacified. I think the drama's behind us" I wrote.

Apparently she'd been trolling and saw that comment, took a screen shot, and got her group to send a new wave of letters demanding my termination. Most went straight to the magazine, but a few came to me. I replied as follows:

*Cor Jesu staff members forbidden from speaking deserved to have their voices heard, and it was my honor to help them.*

*It's unfortunate that a portion of your group has been co-opted by one disgruntled member and the pursuit of her sundry vendettas, setting aside the fact that two lovely, talented women are still unemployed.*

*Demanding an additional LGBT person is fired doesn't seem to fit within the group's original objective.*

*Best of luck to you,*
*Chris Andoe*
*The Emperor of Saint Louis*

One former member contacted me lamenting what had become of the group.

"I was added to this group that was about supporting the fired women, but it's devolved into trying to get you fired," she wrote.

She wasn't the only one uneasy. Christina, one of the women fired, didn't agree with the attacks, and attempted to calm the waters by issuing a statement defending Vital Voice:

*I just want to say that we appreciate greatly the fact that this article did not state our names until after I commented on the story. Although it was never our intent to go public, we do not have an issue with the way we were portrayed in the story. Vital Voice has been the only media outlet that has even attempted to give us some privacy while trying to get the story to the public. We thank them for remembering that we are people, not just a story.*

By this point, however, the group wasn't really about "supporting" the fired women anymore. And when Reggie Edwards organized a demonstration outside of the school he was contacted by a member who said the group *might* participate in his protest, but only if he first disavowed and unfriended Chris Andoe.

When learning her statement didn't slow them down, Christina, the terminated staff member, shook her head.

"I can't even believe they're doing that. Just another example of people using someone else's business to push their own agenda. Dumb."

In the end I had a lot more respect for the conservative alumnae than the moderate to liberals. The conservatives owned it. "Yeah, we fired them. It was against our teachings." None of the letters came from the conservatives.

The conflicted liberals and moderates, led by Kooky Kathy, were the cranky and illogical ones. They'd straddled the fence so long they had thighs full of splinters.

## 235. Andoe Show at the Bamboo

I drove down to Tulsa for my brother Bill's wedding reception. It had been awhile since I lived within a reasonable driving distance, and it was nice to be able to just load up Brawny and go.

Like me, Bill had in many ways come full circle. He married a woman he'd taken to his high school prom, and they bought a great rambling ranch with an enormous yard only three miles from where we'd grown up.

The reception was at their home, and I was honored to be asked to give the toast. The family enjoyed sitting in the yard, in the same metal chairs that once belonged to Grandma Andoe, and telling stories around the fire.

When the party was winding down my nephew Alex and his girlfriend asked if I'd take them and my two youngest nephews to the Bamboo Lounge, my favorite gay dive bar, which had become a tradition when I was in town. Joey and Tate had never been, having just recently come of age.

I'd already moved away when they were born, so I hadn't gotten to know them as well as the older kids, and was pleasantly surprised they were interested in accompanying old Uncle Chris to a gay bar.

It was karaoke night, and as usual the bar was mostly empty aside from a few clusters of odd characters sitting around, and a morbidly obese man holed up in a corner booth like it was his personal office.

For each karaoke performance the participant received several raffle tickets entering them in drawings for Jell-O shots, which bar staff conceded weren't very good. The solitary obese man, a prolific performer, easily had hundreds of tickets spread out across the table.

There was a costume box containing wigs, hats, and other apparel, which each of us took advantage of for our performances. The climax of the night was the show Alex and his girlfriend put on, which will go down in Bamboo history. She massacred the 80's ballad Take My Breath Away, while Alex, a strapping guy in his late twenties, danced slowly and seductively while stripping down to nothing but his boxer briefs.

As if this duet wasn't memorable enough, the obese man, with his red shirt that didn't even begin to cover his pasty white belly, stood before them showering his fortune of raffle tickets like confetti until he had no more.

It was quite a sight, and for me it felt like time slowed down as I watched the bizarre scene, including Joey and Tate laughing and cheering, and I felt like everything was going to be alright. All the generations of my family not only loved me, but they got me, and that sense of belonging was easily worth all I'd gone through in order to find it.

## 236. In Response to the Riverfront Times' Takedown of St. Louis

St. Louis became a hub of police brutality protests after Mike Brown, an unarmed teenager in Ferguson, was shot and killed by police. The demonstrations roiled for weeks, with participants coming from all over the nation.

In the midst of this, the *Riverfront Times*, the city's weekly tabloid, ran a piece calling the region "a boil on the butt of Missouri."

I wrote the following rebuttal, which was published by *Delux Magazine*:

A city's weekly alternative paper is where one turns to find writers who really get the culture of a place, so it was nauseating to see *The Riverfront Times* run a story about what a worthless burg St. Louis is, or as they described it "a boil on the butt of Missouri."

When it comes to our image we already have an uphill battle, but if the publications our local businesses advertise in opt to kick us when we're down, and we just take it, we're in big trouble.

The piece in question, "The Nine Distinct States of Missouri," includes a woefully distorted and one-dimensional take on our region. Nobody at the RFT would even put their name on it, making me wonder if perhaps it was written by an intern at the corporate headquarters in Phoenix.

I find this city so interesting I moved here from California to write a book about it. Some have asked if I'm embarrassed to champion the city in the wake of Ferguson, and I tell them Ferguson only enforces my premise. A 2013 report by the Malcom X Grassroots Movement One showed that a Black man is killed every 28 hours by the police or security officers in the United States. Sadly, the situation in Ferguson was not rare, but the response from St. Louisans was.

Whether you're supportive of the protest actions or not, international media wouldn't have come here to cover the events if they weren't interesting. If the Malcom X report is correct, several Michael Browns have fallen in the weeks since, but just happened to fall in municipalities where people were less passionate, and instead of taking to the streets they may have simply mourned the victim over potato salad.

When New York police officers choked a Black man to death for selling cigarettes there wasn't nearly the same outcry there, and the people who did complain aimed their rhetorical fire at the NYPD, not New York as a whole. When a Black man was dragged to death in Texas, Texans of all races did a whole lot of nothing, and nobody down there dared talk smack about their area.

I'm normally coming to the defense of St. Louis with detractors outside the region. As up and coming middle-American cities jockey for relevance, it seems their boosters often feel compelled to take swipes at St. Louis, finding the mighty but PR challenged old queen an easy target.

In 2009 a mayoral candidate in Austin, Texas made his campaign about equating St. Louis's zenith of 1904, when the city hosted the World's Fair, to Austin's recent boom, warning voters that without good stewardship their city could become another (shudder) St. Louis. My response, published in the Riverfront Times, was as follows:

*"Brewster McCracken is correct in noting St. Louis was one of the most regal and important cities in the nation in 1904, but he's presumptuous to imply Austin enjoys even a fraction of that kind of international attention and relevance today.*

*I'm familiar with 1904 St. Louis. I've studied 1904 St. Louis. And, Austin, you're no 1904 St. Louis!"*

Many cities feel they've arrived when they land a sports franchise or a fad restaurant or retailer. Their civic boosters, chests puffed out with pride, inevitably take pot shots at St. Louis- a city that felt she arrived when Native American mound builders constructed the largest metropolis north of present day Mexico, larger than London in 1250 A.D., at the confluence of two mighty rivers. A city that felt she arrived in 1894 when she opened the largest and busiest train station in the world. A city that felt she arrived when, as the fourth-largest city in America, she hosted the first Olympic Games in the United States. A city that felt she arrived when launching the first transatlantic flight, which bore her name.

They argue she's past her prime. Maybe so, but before she peaked she built the West, and the shimmering crown she received from a grateful nation forever cements her place in the American psyche and gives her one of the most recognizable skylines in the world.

Some are afraid of this city, which is one of the things I like about it. I've lived in New York and have spoken with many New Yorkers who felt their city was much cooler when Times Square was the domain of drug dealers and porn theatres, as opposed to chain restaurants, tchotchke shops and tourists. I've also lived in San Francisco where longtime residents are being purged from the city by the thousands as lawyers and investors work to circumvent rent control laws. These longtime residents were the soul of that city, and are replaced by the soulless who work to sanitize and lobotomize it while still claiming the street cred.

Our coastal capitals have fallen to corporate interests. Many of the places deemed "interesting" are little more than parodies of their former selves, dumbed down and commoditized. Much of America is suburban and dull. Give me classic Gotham. This real city that inspires passion and fear, where people gather, where helicopters hover, where characters clash, where artists create.

The *RFT* article should be a humiliating wake up call to everyone in this region, from the protesters in the streets to biotech researchers to the historic preservationists to the Cardinals fans, to the advertisers in their very paper. A city is the people who inhabit it. If you live within the *RFT* distribution area, you are St. Louis, and they just called you a boil.
Screw them.

## 237. Fading Flowers

I woke up on a Wednesday and checked social media. The first status I saw was from my friend Clint announcing Clementine's was closing after the coming weekend. I was floored, and hoped it was just a rumor. The historic bar was one of my favorite things about St. Louis, and symbolized permanence.

All morning I tried to get confirmation as I began working on the article. Bars were always rumored to be closing, and there'd been embarrassing retractions in the past. The *Vital Voice* team had to balance our desire to break the story with our need to get it right, and Jimmy No Show decided we weren't running the piece until we made contact with one of the owners.

I wrote the piece like a eulogy, recalling the storied past of the place, how it was a cornerstone of the community, was the oldest LGBT bar in St. Louis, and how there was no more prestigious spot to be during Mardi Gras than on the grand balcony above the entrance.

The piece was essentially written when I arrived at the bar and spoke to the bartender, who'd just learned himself and had a letter from Gary. It was then I got word that William Collins just broke the story with a brief announcement and a single quote from the same bartender. We ran our piece twenty minutes after #blast. I then began working on my next piece.

I embedded myself at the bar and for days interviewed dozens of people, most of them ranging in age from 50 to 70, with some as young as 30 and as old as 80.

"It's like Cheers, when I'm down and out there's always someone here to lift me up. That's the one thing that scares me to death: Where am I going to meet my friends? Where will us fading flowers go?" said Josie, a heavyset man of 52.

That first night the news was so fresh and most everyone was in disbelief, while some were angry. A festive man named Johnnie was excited about my interviews, and told me who I should speak with.

"See the guy with the hot pink goblet? That's Miss Davey. He's been coming here every single day for years and they keep that goblet just for him. One day I asked Jan, 'How do I get my own goblet?' and she said, 'Well, you've gotta come here every day!' You need to talk to him!" Jimmy said, then returned a moment later, "He's too upset and is afraid of what he might say. Give him a little time."

I spoke to a big, gruff, bearded man named Dennis who, in his booming voice, told me Clems was his first gay bar, then a frail, petite man walked through the door and Dennis yelled, "HEY HOWARD!" and pulled him in. "This is Howard, he was here for the grand opening!"

I greeted Howard, who told me he was seventy-nine, and I suggested he grab a drink and then come back to talk.

"You're giving him too much time, he might die in the next five minutes! He's about a hundred and forty!" Dennis joked.

Later, at the tables on the front sidewalk, Dennis and his buddies agreed to tell me more stories if I'd smoke a joint with them. A group of six shared tales about Clems, and some were about Midnight Annie, who was entombed in the wall.

"Oh I remember Midnight Annie," one man began. "She was a trust fund baby and when she'd get an installment she'd blow it in no time. Once she sauntered into a Cadillac dealership and bought two Cadillacs. One for her and one for her trick! That's just how she was. God, I still remember her sitting at that bar drunk as Hell with her lipstick going up her wrinkled face and her wig on crooked. She had this trademark high-pitched sound she'd make, and when she'd do it everyone around the bar would mimic it. Like a bird call."

Stories were shared about gay bars that were long gone, many of which were in East. St. Louis, because they were less likely to get raided in that lawless, mafia-run town. Some of the bars sounded a lot like speakeasies.

"Those early days were revolutionary," began a silver-haired gentleman named Beaux. "There were bars that were straight by day and gay by night, and Helen Schrader's started out that way. Helen had been a notorious madam with fifty women working for her during her heyday. When one of her first girls, Alice, got old she worked the front door at the bar. You'd knock and Miss Alice would slide a little slot open and look at you. If she knew you, she'd let you in. If she didn't, she'd tell you to go away."

During those final days, stories also came in online, and were posted to my Facebook updates. One post from my friend Dan struck me because it was about a passing generation.

"One really busy night many years ago I had sex right there on the counter of the bar, maybe 400 in the bar at the time. Surprised? It brought back memories of the first owner, Wally Thomas. He sold it in '85 but it stayed a gay bar. People don't want to let go, but the past HAS to go. The past, the bars, the buildings, the people all have had their time and now need to go. And they will – no matter what is said. That place leaves far greater a legacy than I ever will. As one person said: The old heart of Gay St. Louis will cease to beat. I see the passages. The old gay ghettos, the book stores, the peep shows, the gay bars, their time has passed. My tribe, my people, my places, become part of yesterday's mist. Museum pieces that fade and collect dust. And so does yours truly."

While Monday would be the last day, Sunday afternoon was when the community at large came to say their goodbyes and it looked like Mardi Gras as the overflow crowd spilled into the intersection, where a BMW blasted music for the hundreds of people outside.

I was so thankful to be in St. Louis during these final days, and for all the people who shared their stories which were now on the Vital Voice website and would be archived by Steven Brawley of the Saint Louis LGBT History Project.

Steve Potter, a local NPR personality, was so moved and inspired by the tributes in my piece he came out on the air, discussing his first visit to the bar decades earlier.

On that last Sunday, one day before they closed their doors forever, I brought a pizza-sized Gooey Butter Cake, a local specialty, to share with everyone.

It would have killed me to miss those final days.

443

As the world opened up, gay bars nationwide were going the way of the dinosaur, especially those serving an older clientele. But this haunted town had such a memory, and rather than disappear, Clems would simply take its place in the local folklore.

I once worked for a company where an accountant passed away, and in the same way a team retires a jersey, they retired his office. People and places are never really replaced in St. Louis, they're just integrated into the present in a different form.

## 238. Delusions of Grandeur

The timing of Clems' closing was especially poignant for me, coinciding with the conclusion of this multi-year project of writing about my characters and experiences. Coming out in my teens in the pre-internet Bible Belt, I was fascinated with all the colorful, older queens I met who didn't have a pot to piss in, yet had the most fascinating delusions of grandeur.

Until recently LGBT people weren't allowed to be themselves publicly, so they created tiny fantasy worlds where they could be whatever they wanted, be that a pageant winner, a macho biker, a celebrity, one of the popular kids in their own high school reenactment, or royalty. Even their relationships were pretend, not being recognized outside the walls of gay establishments or private homes.

Like a porcupine's quills, a sharp wit evolved out of necessity, used for defense and as a deterrent in a hostile world.

The new environment of acceptance and integration was healthier and preferable, but the flip side of that was a culture built on imagination, cleverness and camaraderie was quickly vanishing with the rise of the millennials, who were largely integrated into mainstream culture. They didn't have the same need for alternate realities or exclusively gay venues. Many didn't even know how to cruise in person. They didn't go to bars to search for sex, and if they happened to see an attractive person at the bar, they'd search their apps to make contact.

I'm certain I'll see the passing of other legendary institutions as well, including the Habana Inn, which was much like a brick and mortar Facebook and sex app rolled into one.

Since a woman is born with all of the eggs she'll ever have, I was born from an old egg. I've always felt a connection with those twenty years older, and understood at the time of this writing, their era was drawing to a close.

I straddle the generational fence in my own family, a decade younger than my closest brother and a decade older than my closest nephew, and at the time of this writing I seem to straddle the generational fence within my community. I'm reverent about the past while interested in the present and future.

I see myself as a link, and will continue telling stories of my family, my city, and of this vanishing culture, while at the same time riding the waves of change.

I'll carry forward my piece of old school delusions, and I'll do so wearing my crown and embracing the thoroughly delusional moniker of Emperor of St. Louis.

## 239. Midnight Annie's Final Performance

I almost didn't go to closing night at Clementine's, and Ray didn't plan on going either. It was a Monday night, I'd spent all of my time there since Wednesday, and I thought it would be too sad. Around eight, however, I decided I would always regret not going, and since I was going Ray came out as well. I walked in, and on the glowing dry erase marquee near the pool table I wrote, "Going down with the ship."

The bar was crowded but not overly so, and the characters there were the ones who really loved the place. The spirits were higher than expected and the camaraderie was simply incredible as old friends hugged, laughed, and made toasts. Miss Davey, the daily regular who had his own hot pink goblet and had been too upset to be interviewed, came up and gave me a hug.

"I'm really sad, but I'm going to be ok" he said, smiling.

When owner Gary and his late partner Jim bought the bar in 1985, they held their first drag show with their friend Midnight Annie as the headliner. Unbeknownst to her they billed it as "Midnight Annie's Final Performance" to make it more of a draw.

"Would you quit telling people this is my final performance?" an exasperated Midnight Annie kept admonishing.

She carried on there for many more years, and even after she passed she was still a draw, remaining among us in the wall.

I was less than a foot from Gary when, in the final hours, he took the mic, and the quiet, introverted man who'd hardly said anything over years gave a rousing farewell speech, and the whole place stopped to listen and applaud. He spoke about how much times had changed since the bar opened in 1978, and changed for the better. He spoke of the historic old brick building which was erected in the 1860's. He said all drinks were on the house until the last bottle was dry, and then he then brought up Midnight Annie.

"I always say my only child was a seventy-five year old drag queen," he began, "and she's leaving with me. Ladies and Gentleman, next to Jan is Midnight Annie!" and I'll be God damned if he didn't have Midnight Annie's dusty urn, complete with the yellowed and water stained label, sitting on the bar with a cocktail!

The crowd went mad with uproarious cheers and applause.

On that final evening there were people in attendance who'd come to see Midnight Annie's final performance back in 1985. After a thirty year wait, she and Gary Reed finally delivered with a closing number the city will never forget.

## 240. Airing the Laundry

The Gayborhood was an LGBT radio show hosted by Show Me Charlotte, a popular burlesque performer, and Tim Beckman, owner of Sensation nightclub. I was a guest shortly after returning from New York and William Collins of all people called in to sing my praises on air. I thanked him, and like I always did when his name came up, spoke about how he and Darin Slyman gave me my start.

My relationship with Collins had been both strained and strange for some time, beginning with him not returning my calls or email after I'd booked Sensation Nightclub for my Hot Mess event, which made it unavailable for his beloved William Lowe's birthday party. I had assumed everything blew over, but when my relationship collapsed I wrote him a lengthy, heartfelt letter about it, and got the cold shoulder.

I didn't see him in person until he and William Lowe showed up at a leather event wearing matching red leotards, which would be a difficult look for most anyone to pull off. I was with Penelope Wigstock when Collins approached.

"You shouldn't write for Darin. He's sleazy!" he snarled.

"Well it's not like you asked us to write for #blast, or even returned my calls" I quipped, but my words seemed to fly right past him, and the four of us wound up having a pleasant ten-minute conversation unrelated to media.

On the Gayborhood, I was simultaneously honored and suspicious by his on-air call, and it wasn't until I was on the show a second time that I heard from him again.

The program booked the controversial Rita Revlon, and while she initially jumped at the offer, she couldn't get past her anger at Beckman for hiring Simone Shasta to cook at Sensation after her fall from grace. Shasta was famous for her fried chicken, and drew huge crowds each Sunday.

"I won't be coming on your show because you people are fascinated with an embezzling whore!" the Dark Mistress wrote in a statement.

In response, Beckman gave her slot to Simone Shasta herself, a bold move considering Shasta had been low-profile since leaving the LGBT Center in disgrace eighteen months earlier, and she never wanted to discuss what had transpired. To make things even more interesting, Show Me Charlotte invited *me* to co-host and read a few of my stories about the Revlon & Shasta feud.

While Simone and I liked one another personally, our styles were like oil and water. In traditional St. Louis fashion, she liked to keep a lid on backstory, while I stirred the pot with my tales. This caused her to keep me at arm's length and she'd sometimes express irritation about my inquisitiveness.

"See, it's this kind of shit that pisses me off. People are always trying to keep this stuff going" she'd say.

In his opening monologue, Beckman decided to fill listeners in on the backstory of Rita's cancellation, and the gloves came off.

"Crotchety old Rita Revlon decided to cancel because I hired Simone Shasta despite her having a past," Beckman began. "Yes, I called you crotchety. Everyone's sick of your mean-spirited rants, so why don't you just take your cane and go home."

You could feel the ground shake from the jaws dropping all over the city.

"I've never understood why she hated me" Shasta began. "When her husband died I carried that man to his grave!"

"Well, you did steal Trans Central from her for seven dollars," I interjected to uproarious laughter from everyone in the studio, including a blushing Shasta.

"That was only after weeks of harassment and threats," Shasta replied, still laughing.

I read an excerpt about that maneuver, as well as one about Rustin Winchell. Shasta was amused, seeming to relax and soften her stance towards me and my work. Beckman then went in for the big question.

"So, Simone, about the LGBT Center, do you care to talk about what happened?"

"Yes I did it. I took $5,578.14. I can tell you to the penny. It was wrong. It left the Center in a bad position and I'm sorry."

Show Me Charlotte had many great shows, but that one had everybody talking.

When we went off air, Shasta seemed ten pounds lighter. "It actually feels good to get this out in the open" she said.

Many messages poured in to the show and to each person on it, including myself. William Collins wrote me to say he loved the stories and was really proud of Shasta. He ended his note with, "If I'm in you book, give me a heads up, ok?"

I called and left a message asking that he call me that evening, which he didn't.

Walking out of the studio with Charlotte, the two of us spoke about how many fascinating stories the city held, but how it was part of the culture to not talk about them. For example, Kansas City played up its mob history as part of its branding, while St. Louis downplayed hers, which dates back to the 1890s. We've got a mobster who built a massive moat around his house, and the city had a well-known rash of car bombings in the 1980s, one which curiously targeted the Mayor's uncle.

But those tales won't be in any tourist brochure alongside plugs for the zoo, the Cardinals or frozen yogurt. St. Louis has long been a city that preferred to keep her secrets.

Months later, out of the blue, Collins invited me to lunch. I assumed he wanted to ask about the book, and I was right.

Sitting across from one another at a deserted Mexican restaurant on Cherokee Street was awkward for both of us, but we engaged in friendly conversation before he nervously cut to the chase.

"Am I in the book?" he asked, making darting eye contact.

"Wouldn't it be an insult if you weren't?" I replied.

I discussed a few of the main tales he was in and to my surprise he didn't seem to dispute my version of events, other than a few details. Initially, he denied saying anything bad about me or the Hot Mess event, but after some friendly prodding he admitted to calling it a vanity project.

I really wanted to get his side of the story regarding his split with Darin Slyman, but there wasn't much there other than his irritation with Jimmy No Show's ascendancy, and it was clear there was still bad blood.

"I don't know how someone can go from being an intern in a squirrel costume one minute to being on the masthead the next! It's crazy, and frankly I've never seen anything like it," he fumed.

Regarding Simone Shasta and the Center, he said he only went public because Darin Slyman leaked the information around town, including to the Dark Mistress herself, forcing his hand.

Just before we got up to leave, he said, "I do wish you would have at least contacted me about my side."

"I did! And you never called me back, which has been your pattern for years." I replied incredulously.

"Oh you did?" he asked, seemingly confused as he scrolled though his phone log.

We left on a relatively high note, with him even offering to run a story on the book.

"I think your book will be a big success locally. Not sure about outside St. Louis though," he said as we hugged.

Days later one of his young writers, who was also Lowe's on again, off again boyfriend, came after me with full force over social media, saying I should be shot, calling me "scum" and posting, "I wish someone would get rid of that idiot emperor."

When the same man falsely claimed I'd been making fun of people for being HIV-positive on my blog, the blowback from his own readers forced him to remove the accusation in less than ten minutes.

When Collins was my editor he pushed me hard, sending back stories two and three times, and it made me better. Despite all that had happened, I had respected him, and was disappointed he was allowing such sloppy and dishonest behavior on his team. I figured it was because he'd never stand up to Lowe, and I wanted to believe the smear campaign was Lowe's design, not my former mentor's.

I wrote the entire #blast team and told them if they were just making shit up now, professional courtesy was out the window going forward.

Of course they didn't reply.

## 241. Passionate City

Over a hundred days passed since unarmed teen Michael Brown was shot and killed by Ferguson police officer Darren Wilson, and as the region braced for the grand jury's decision on whether to indict Wilson, it became popular to speculate about the coming storm. The public was whipped into a frenzy by the media, particularly the false reports from local right wing blowhards like "The Arch City Pundit," who circulated a fake list claiming the protesters planned to shut down the region's hospitals.

I'm not scared of much. I've walked from San Francisco's gritty Tenderloin to the pre-gentrified Mission drunk, many times. I've wandered alone all over NYC at fifteen, back before Manhattan turned into Disneyland. I've strolled past ruins in Detroit. I've climbed through the pitch black basements of abandoned buildings and have been to the East St. Louis projects at two in the morning.

When something is perceived to be scary I often make a beeline to check it out. That's also how I've made some great friends.

I wasn't going to hide from protests. This was my city, and I wanted to see what was happening and talk to the people. My cosmopolitan friend Karen, a professor who divided her time between her hometown of St. Louis and her husband's hometown of Milan, Italy, had been reading and offering feedback on this book. I invited her to join me in going up to meet the Ferguson demonstrators who'd been camped out along New Florissant Road around the clock for months.

It was a drizzly night, and we first went to dinner at the Ferguson Brewing Company, a microbrewery a few blocks from the encampment, and then drove up to find a group of about a dozen holding down the corner. Florence, a heavy Black woman in her sixties, sat on a cooler wearing a disposable poncho while commiserating with Dan, a white man also in his sixties, about eyesight problems, particularly when driving at night. Behind the cooler was a bottle of Orange Crush and a bucket of soup.

"Would you like some soup?" a young man offered.

We'd just pissed away a chunk of money on dinner and drinks, and it was humbling that this scrappy group of people, who were feared and vilified in the media, were offering to feed us.

"How does it feel to be the most feared group of people in the country right now?" I asked Florence and Ed, while a diverse cluster of twenty-somethings stood behind them.

"The media needs a villain," Florence replied.

We then drove to Canfield Green, where Mike Brown was shot and a memorial was set up in the middle of the road. We passed boarded up businesses where artist Damon Davis plastered posters of raised hands, images that were being shown in galleries as far away as Boston.

The creativity coming out of the region was getting national and international attention. London's *Daily Mail* marveled at the elegant protest of song that interrupted the St. Louis Symphony, with protesters singing "Which side are you on?" as banners demanding justice for Mike Brown unfurled from the balcony. Chalk outlines symbolizing unarmed Black men shot by police, a concept created by St. Louis artist Mallory Nezam, had spread around the world. The cutting edge .Mic proclaimed, "Ferguson Now Has the Most Powerful Street Art in America" and the Ferguson Protesters were in the running for Time's Person of the Year.

There was no bigger critic of the city than my estranged husband Damon, who was raised within a mile of Ferguson, and even he gave a nod. "There's a lot of good work happening in St. Louis right now."

On a Monday afternoon it was announced that the Grand Jury reached their verdict, and the announcement would be delivered at eight that evening.

455

Businesses around the region that hadn't done so already boarded up their windows, especially in Ferguson and in Clayton, the county seat. Local governments and businesses closed early. My dog groomer and several others I knew fled for the countryside.

I knew I had to be in Ferguson.

I called John Aravosis to let him know I would cover the events for *AMERICAblog*, and then asked Karen, who was preparing to return to Milan, if she'd like to join me.

Hundreds of protesters shut down New Florissant Road through the heart of Ferguson while reporters from around the world mingled. Chants included, "We've got nothing to lose but our chains," and, "Stop killing our kids."

I sent photos to Aravosis, but he asked for video. My phone didn't have enough memory, so I had to decide right then whether to delete hundreds of photos from the past year or two. Photos from the California coast, from my cross country trip, from my time in New York. All pictures symbolizing past lives and what I'd traded to be where I was standing.

I was near a beat up, graffiti covered car in the middle of the street that was serving as a stage for several protest leaders who stood in anticipation of the verdict. Quiet fell over the crowd as Brown's mother, Lesley McSpadden, climbed atop the car to stand with half a dozen others as the Prosecuting Attorney read his long, meandering statement, which was broadcast over loudspeakers. Before most of us heard it, she shook her head as tears rolled down her face.

"Defend himself from what? From what? Tell me that!" she yelled in response to the assertion that the officer acted in self-defense.

"That's right, sista" said a soulful woman standing next to me. "We with you, baby. It's ain't over. It ain't over."

"Everyone wants me to be calm. Do you know how those bullets ripped through my son's body? What they did to his body?" McSpadden continued as cameras clicked and flashed in the frigid night air.

"Ain't no peace!. Ain't no calm!" a woman in the crowd yelled in support. "He didn't die in peace, there ain't gone be no peace!"

"They wrong, they wrong!" McSpadden sobbed as she doubled over in grief.

"They don't care about us! Fuck them!" someone yelled.

Brown's stepfather, Louis Head, then shouted, "Burn this bitch down!"

The video I took was on its way to 180,000 hits, and my social media was blowing up, mostly with people telling me to get out of there.

From Arizona, Rita Revlon's ex, Miss Crystal, posted: "Head up, eyes open, keep feeding us what's what. There ain't too many white boys I'd feel okay about being in the heart of it all—but you've always had the street smarts of an old whore, so I figure you'll be fine. And you can consider that high praise from an old whore."

Even Rustin Winchell got in on the action, tweeting:

"If I were still practicing law in St. Louis County none of this would be happening. Share that #ChrisAndoe. I need the publicity." (A week later he reconsidered that stance and sent me a Cease & Desist letter after one of my investigators found the photo he was using for his supposed Arizona senate campaign was actually a photo shopped picture of *Birdcage* star Nathan Lane).

The crowd was restless and tense, bottles and other objects were thrown at the police, who were lined up in riot gear behind barricades. I reported to John Aravosis over the phone and when the crowd began to move, I told him I was leaving. I knew chaos would break out any minute.

From Karen's elegant St. Louis Hills apartment we monitored the situation on television and on our computers. Several buildings in the Ferguson area were burning, looting had begun, and the FAA diverted flights from Lambert St. Louis International Airport due to machine gun fire.

In the Shaw section of South City, protesters shut down Interstate 44, and a mile away on South Grand protests turned violent as numerous windows were smashed. Hours after the violence ended police heavily tear gassed the intersection of Grand and Arsenal, where many peaceful demonstrators and brand new 15th Ward Alderwoman Megan-Ellyia Green were taking sanctuary at MoKaBe's Coffeehouse. With nowhere to go as the tear gas seeped in, patrons and demonstrators sought refuge in a sealed basement.

The issue of police brutality was front and center on the national conscious, with tragic cases in New York, Cleveland, and other places around the country, spurring massive demonstrations, and the epicenter of it all was the great awakening in St. Louis.

The night of the verdict, as I logged off, I made one final post, making sure the pearl clutchers didn't misunderstand where I was coming from with my coverage of the fiery mayhem. Many were looking on in horror at the images on their screens, but while I'd prefer there to have been no arson and looting, I saw it as a mere forest fire. There are pinecones that only release their seeds in fire, and I knew there would be much sprouting from the charred and storied ground.

The moment was so powerful, there was no place on Earth more relevant that evening. The change happening here would transform the dysfunctional structure of St. Louis County and the ninety municipalities/ fiefdoms that stifled regional progress, but would also impact people around the world, as we'd see from subsequent protests.

I wrote: *For the record: There's no place I'd rather be right now. I don't want a gentrified or suburban life. I'd rather live in a passionate city in flames.*

## 242. Simone Shasta's Comeback

When the cavernous leather and fetish bar at the edge of the Grove announced they were closing, Tim Beckman and his business partner Rose Principal swooped in to take it over.

The building also featured a long underutilized commercial kitchen, and an announcement was made to great fanfare that Miss Shasta's Fried Chicken would launch in the space.

After about two years of keeping a relatively low profile, Simone was back on top, winning awards, appearing on the news, and she even attended the splashy *Vital Voice* holiday party in a shimmery royal blue gown. As you could probably imagine this infuriated Rita Revlon, who made numerous posts about how vile the community was for continuing to support a "thieving whore."

"Rita, I heard a beautiful story about a time when you and Simone worked together for six hours to find shelter for a Trans girl," I commented.

"Shasta didn't do shit! She wanted to get the girl off her greasy hands so she could lock up! I sheltered her in my home office and then put her on a bus to Dallas the next morning. FUCK THAT ASSHOLE!"

"I also heard she was a pallbearer at your husband's funeral," I continued stirring.

"She wasn't there. And I'm going to file a restraining order to keep her the hell away from my funeral. And I'm going to have someone wire several car batteries in the casket, and if she's there, someone will tell her to touch the casket first!" the drunken Rita plotted.

Both Miss Crystal and Darin Slyman confirmed Shasta was indeed a pallbearer at the funeral. I'm fond of Rita and don't believe her to be a dishonest person, so I wondered if her obviously insane hatred for Shasta somehow erased the few positive memories she had of her.

Nearly a dozen more Dark Mistress updates were posted that night, mostly asking the community what Shasta's ass tastes like.

I replied that I detected just a hint of oregano.

## 243. Fall of the False Profit

Life is full of unexpected turns, and after years of being under the influence of Benny Babbish, Damon decided to cut him out of his life.

It happened a day after he sent a grumpy message about how all of *our* friends were really *my* friends, and that he was going to unfriend many of them, including Francis & Edie. I once again made my anti-Benny argument, but this time, for some reason, it stuck.

"We were happy when we operated as a team, and we were in torment after Benny framed everything we did as a competition. Benny's corrosive advice led you to this place of hurt and frustration. He's an evil deceiver who argues dark is light and light is dark, convincing you that good friends who love and care about you are bad, and only he is good. You've been under his influence for seven long years, and where are the fruits of his advice? Where's the self-actualization he promised? If you want to be bitter, be bitter at him. If you want to cut someone out of your life, cut that vile snake out of it."

Initially he responded in the same knee-jerk way he had anytime I mentioned Benny, but after a day of contemplation, he couldn't think of a single example of Benny doing anything for anyone other than pontificating and manipulating.

For so long Benny defined me in the ugliest possible way and made him feel ashamed, but he said the kindness I'd shown to him since we split up made him reconsider everything. He now wanted to move forward with his life without Benny's influence. I believed him, and felt as relieved as Dorothy when Toto escaped the Wicked Witch's Castle.

With Benny's curse broken, the old barriers between us fell away and we were able to communicate in ways that were impossible before. There were times when I was hit with setbacks on the book and was almost ready to scrap the entire project. During the Babbish era I would've never shared feelings of doubt or vulnerability with Damon, knowing they'd only serve to feed Benny's narrative. But now I found the supportive ear of a friend in Damon, who during my down days helped me see the big picture.

"If what you were doing was easy everyone would do it," he said. "Remember: optimism is your super power."

### 244. Dinner & Double Cross

There were times Rustin Winchell became furious with me, sending angry tirades and the Cease & Desist, but he'd quickly return to his charming and collected baseline.

Aside from a lawsuit and countersuit involving a pyramid scheme, he'd kept a low profile for several months until reclaiming the spotlight with a dramatic hostage standoff at his longtime North County home. A call was placed to 911 claiming one man had been stabbed and another was tied up. The news anchor reported:

"The suspect is well known to police and faces a variety of charges, and police say he stabbed a cab driver last year…"

"Anyone aware of the whereabouts of the suspect is asked to call…"

As I watched footage from the hovering news helicopters above I emailed Winchell, delicately asking if he was aware of the situation. He said he wasn't, and that he now lived in a loft downtown. Later it was confirmed the call was a hoax. I emailed him the latest news clip.

"I'm talking to the police right now. I told them I wasn't aware of this until you brought it to my attention. They want to speak with you." he wrote.

Since I was the first to message him, it seemed I was an alibi of sorts.

After spilling so much ink over Winchell I regretted never having a face to face meeting, and thought it might be now or never if he was getting ready to go down. He jumped on my invitation and suggested a restaurant near his Washington Avenue loft in forty minutes.

Cage, a musician I was dating, was on the sofa and as I hurriedly got myself ready I gave him instructions.

"Message the War Room," I began, in reference to my team of investigators, all veterans of the infamous Winchell thread. "Tell them I'm meeting him at Rosalita's in forty. Ask them to notify police and the media."

"What if something goes really wrong?" he asked, thinking about the man's unpredictable nature.

"If something happens see to it that Brawny gets to Francis & Edie."

Winchell met me at the entrance, and while I knew he was tall he was still taller than I expected. He carried himself confidently, as if we were business associates meeting for happy hour, and his open collar revealed his Star of David pendant.

We exchanged pleasantries and ordered drinks. He discussed the defamation lawsuit against him by the multi-level marketing company where, according to him, he'd served as Senior Executive Vice President. During his tenure he claimed the Boca Raton based CEO stole thousands of dollars from him and made threats of violence. From St. Louis Winchell filed for an order of protection against the Floridian, which somehow was granted.

The CEO said he'd never met Winchell, Winchell had never been a member of his corporate staff, nor had he even paid the simple fee to become a member of the organization.

Winchell responded by saying the CEO's statement was just a ploy to get leverage.

"They're after me for fifteen million" he lamented, as if he had fifteen million to lose.

He then moved on to my coverage of him.

"So my friends tell me I haven't been mentioned in a while," he said.

"I've been bogged down covering some unsavory characters. It's actually refreshing to focus on you again," I began, which he found amusing.

I had realistic expectations from the start. I knew he wasn't going to admit anything and he didn't. According to him there's a logical explanation for his entire history, which makes for boring conversation.

"You know of all the people who say I've scammed them, none have proof, right?" he confidently asked.

"They have civil judgments to prove it," I replied. "You owe a lot of people a lot of money. The limo driver you used to usher politicians around Jefferson City, the thousands in printing for your magazine..."

"Well, I was talking about the gay people who made claims," he dismissed, before rattling off his excuses for the bad debts and claiming he was settled up now.

He said he moved out of the home where the hostage standoff took place some time ago, but needed to maintain the address for probation reasons. As far as the hoax, he claimed he was set up.
About half a dozen officers arrived and huddled inside the doorway of the restaurant. He glanced their way but never broke a sweat or lost his train of thought. A manager walked over to ask what they needed and I could hear fragments that included "earlier today" and "hostage." Two officers walked right past our table and still he was completely at ease, almost amused. Then they all just left.
When the check arrived he grabbed it and placed two crisp fifties on the table, which surprised me.

"I've asked all the questions," I said. "Do you have anything you'd like to ask me?"

"No," he replied. "Just let me know if you learn anything about who was behind the hoax."

There was a good reason he was so relaxed. The police weren't there to see him. They were there to see me.

Shortly before dinner he met with detectives and told them I was a jilted ex-lover, and should be considered the prime suspect. The following day I was questioned.

"He said you've got an obsession with him," the detective said.

"As far as being obsessed, I guess that's fair. I've told him he's my muse," I confessed, regaling the detective with my "Best of Rustin Winchell Highlight Reel," excitedly going over the laundry list of scams and hardly letting him get a word in.

The detective asked that I not post about this on social media because he didn't want Winchell to feel cornered, as that's when he was at his most dangerous.

"That's what happened when he was with the cross dresser in the cab" the detective said.

Despite Winchell's well publicized history he seemed to have done a masterful job at throwing investigators off his trail and getting them to zero in on me. After I was questioned they contacted others in the media, including Farrah Fazal of Channel 5 News and Darin Slyman to ask about my potential involvement.

I have no regrets about meeting Winchell for dinner. The conversation was relatively dull in the moment, but the fact each of us was prepared to see the other arrested before our eyes, in retrospect, makes the evening all the more interesting.

## 245. Fortieth at the Lemp Mansion

Edie and Ray planned my fortieth Birthday party at the world famous Lemp Mansion, known as one of the most haunted houses in America due to the multiple suicides by members of the Lemp brewing dynasty.

The morning of the event, Rustin Winchell randomly emailed asking that I meet him at the Police Station so he could serve me with some sort of legal document. I suggested he instead serve it during dinner at the mansion. He politely declined, citing other plans, but thanked me for the invitation.

I laughed about it with a friend and fellow writer named Karla, who had recently asked a local rabbi about Winchell's involvement in the synagogue.

"Look, we all know Winchell's not Jewish" the rabbi said.

"Well shouldn't you do something for him? Maybe even a prayer circle?" Karla asked.

The rabbi deadpanned, "Karla, there's not enough prayer in the world."

Forty loomed large in my mind for several years. Dad died of a heart attack at 41, and at 39 I had been faced with bizarre ailments and severe depression from the stress of not being on sure footing in my personal or professional life.

In my darkest moments, on the curb of the West Side Highway thinking about stepping into traffic, I was obsessed with thoughts of wasted time and the investments I'd made in the wrong people, consumed with bitterness over lost opportunities, being Benny Babbish's lab animal for so long, and being betrayed by people I had helped.

The day of my birthday celebration I couldn't have seen the world more differently than I had just months earlier.

I checked in to the Lemp in the late afternoon and sat in the two room William Lemp Suite, which Francis & Edie rented for me, and looked out over the neighboring mansion and gardens where they were married eight years earlier. I savored the sense of love, history, and belonging. The guests had yet to arrive, but I didn't feel the least bit alone.

What had felt like a period of flailing and failure now seemed triumphant. In my 39th year I'd realized a drastic change was needed, and demolished life as I knew it to begin anew. I threw myself on a mosh pit of family, friends, and professional connections, and everyone carried me.

Kathy Looper offered me a room in San Francisco if I decided to come back. Joe made space for me in New York City, Ray David let me live with him for a few months in St. Louis. A longtime professional connection offered a rent-free park front apartment in exchange for managing a building, Francis, Edie and Miltonia filled that apartment with everything I needed. Darin Slyman, who gave me my start years earlier, stood by me amid the never ending barrage of letters demanding my termination, as well as the threats of lawsuits.

In my 39th year the weak links in my chain were removed, and my lifeline was stronger than ever.

In the private dining room, under the dimly lit chandelier and in the glow of the fire, people I loved raised glasses and made toasts. Old friends from as far away as New Orleans and San Francisco were in attendance, as well as a few incredible new friends from the past year. People who stood by my side during controversy, and in the streets of Ferguson as the city burned.

The investments I'd made in the wrong people, which plagued me months before, were now meaningless compared to the faces before me.

I was moved by a speech Edie read about how she wouldn't have the life she had now if I hadn't encouraged Francis to move to St. Louis.

In the forties my Grandma Wadley put her friend Mert through beauty school, and in return Mert styled Grandma's wigs for the rest of her life. I found myself in a similar situation with Francis. He was always there to hang artwork or help me move, and the little help I lent him many years ago had been paid back a thousand times over.

Francis and Edie always looked after me, and even had me over for weekly dinners. I lived next door to Francis as a child, and now, four hundred miles and thirty years away from where we started, we were still in walking distance from one another.

I was careful to not drink too much because I wanted to be present in that moment, surrounded by my tribe. At forty, the footing I was on was as strong as the limestone bluffs under my city, and was as enduring as the old masonry mansion where I was holding court.

When it was time to retire for the evening I slept like a stone, paying no mind to the reported ghosts haunting the mansion.

The spirits might have been restless, but I was at peace.

# ACKNOWLEDGEMENTS

While storytelling was always in my blood, my brother Joe encouraged my writing, and over the past seven years he was always ready to listen, laugh, and offer advice.

Many friends read this work, some repeatedly, and helped me shape it into the finished product. My team of readers included Marie Blackard, Heather Crovo, Jason Dercola, Patrick Dilley, Paul Emery, Karen Irwin, Ben & Norah Shambaugh, and Gina Sheridan.

Paul Emery was my most aggressive and enthusiastic promoter, twisting arms and calling in favors to get big East Coast players to read my work.

Author Robert Julian gave me the toughest feedback of all, which led me to cut a third from the original book, creating a far superior finished product. Much of what was cut will go into another book about my early years coming out in the pre-internet Bible Belt.

Attorney Joseph Paul Smith offered insight and generously vetted the book for legal issues.

Indie publishing guru Meghan Pinson taught me the nuts and bolts of publishing a book.

Prolific author and former Boston Herald editor Crystal Hubbard offered her editing services and provided valuable advice.

Steven L. Brawley of the Saint Louis LGBT History Project reviewed the work.

I was concerned about dying before the book was done, and sent each new draft to Donald Cole for safekeeping with the instruction to see that the book was posthumously published.

Darin Slyman & Jimmy No Show of Vital Voice were interested in this project from the moment I presented it, and were unwavering despite the deafening howls from detractors and the barrage of letters demanding they cut ties.

I want to thank Damon for supporting me and this book, even though it's intensely personal, and his version of events don't line up perfectly with mine. There were times I was tired, frustrated and defeated, but he encouraged me to push forward.

Finally, I want to thank the People of St. Louis for always taking care of me.

Made in the USA
Monee, IL
25 September 2023

43411582R00288